# ENGLISH HISTORY

## FROM

# ESSEX SOURCES

## 1750—1900

Prepared for the Records Committee

by

A. F. J. BROWN, B.A.

*Colchester Royal Grammar School,*
*formerly Organising Tutor for Essex,*
*Workers' Educational Association*

*Published by*

THE COUNTY COUNCIL OF ESSEX, CHELMSFORD

ESSEX RECORD OFFICE PUBLICATIONS, NO. 18

*Printed by*

J. H. CLARKE & CO., LTD., CHELMSFORD

1952

# FOREWORD

IT is the hope of the Records Committee that this series of source books, while designed to provide readily accessible illustrative material, will incidentally draw attention to the rich and varied nature of the material in their custody. No printed source book, however skilfully compiled, can ever be an adequate substitute for personal examination of the original documents.

The Essex Record Office is open daily, 9.15 a.m. to 5.15 p.m. (8.45 p.m. on Mondays, and 12.15 p.m. on Saturdays); students are advised to make an appointment. Its resources have been described in the *Guide to the Essex Record Office* (1946-48), *Catalogue of Maps* (1947) and its *Supplement* (1952), and *Essex Parish Records* (1950); and an attempt has been made to ease the initial difficulties of reading such documents by the publication of *Some* (and *More*) *Examples of English Handwriting* (1949-50). The reproductions of different types of document (with transcripts) in all these publications are therefore supplementary to the printed extracts in the source books, as are also the illustrations in the small picture books *Eight Centuries of History in Essex Records* and *Essex in Pictures* (1951-52), which could well be used in class in conjunction with the source books.

In addition to these printed students' aids, in the Office itself are comprehensive indexes which largely eliminate the need to search catalogues. Besides parish and personal names indexes, there is a widely cross-referenced subject index both for approach to general subjects, such as Agriculture, Prices, Education, Poor Law, and to more specialised subjects—the H section opens with Haberdashery, Hairdressing, Hairpowder duty, Halls, Handwriting, Hanging,

Harbours, Hats and Hatters, Headboroughs, Health (Boards of), and Hearth Tax. Details of special facilities available for long-term researchers may be obtained on application.

The Office is, moreover, constantly enlarging its resources. Just before going to press, it acquired a large number of 19th century Essex newspapers, a source usefully exploited by Mr. Brown from the collection in the Colchester Borough Library, and now also available at Chelmsford.

While the compilation of a similar volume covering the medieval period would present peculiar difficulties of its own, the Committee are considering the best means of completing the series by the preparation of such a volume.

F. G. EMMISON,
*County Archivist.*

*Chelmsford*
*July, 1952*

# CONTENTS


PAGE

Foreword by the County Archivist ... iii

Introduction ... vii

Industry ... 1

The Cloth Trade in Decline ... 2

The Silk Industry ... 9

Other Essex Industries ... 12

The Movement of Population ... 19

Agriculture ... 24

Essex Farming, 1750-1850 ... 25

Essex Enclosures ... 29

Recovery and Depression, 1850-1914 ... 31

The Farm Labourer ... 37

The Standard of Living ... 37

Nineteenth Century Changes ... 42

Farm Labourers' Movements ... 47

Transport ... 52

The Parish as Highway Authority ... 52

Attempts to improve the Roads ... 55

Coaching, Canals and Railways ... 61

Local Government ... 66

The Government of the County ... 68

The Municipal Corporation ... 73

The Scope of Parish Government ... 76

The Parish Officers ... 86

The Supersession of the Parish Police ... 89

Further Curtailment of Parish Authority ... 93

Public Health and Local Government ... 95

Later Developments in Local Government ... 99

The Old Poor Law and its Passing ... 102

The Constitutional Pattern ... 103

The Scope of the Poor Law ... 108

The Village Health Service ... 111

The Parish Workhouse ... 113

The 'Speenhamland' System ... 115

Attempts to Economise ... 117

The New Poor Law and its Opponents ... 119

| | PAGE |
|---|---|
| EDUCATION ... | 128 |
| Early Secondary Schools ... | 129 |
| The Education of the Poor ... | 133 |
| Later Progress in Education ... | 141 |
| PROGRESS IN MEDICINE ... | 145 |
| THE USE OF LEISURE ... | 151 |
| The Social Life of the Wealthy in the 18th Century ... | 152 |
| Farmers' Relaxations in the 18th Century ... | 158 |
| Town Life in the 18th Century ... | 161 |
| 18th Century Amusements, Genteel and Vulgar ... | 163 |
| 18th Century Sports and Spectacles ... | 169 |
| The Movement for the Suppression of Vice ... | 173 |
| Civilising Influences in the 19th Century ... | 176 |
| Sports and Holidays in the 19th Century ... | 179 |
| ESSEX AND NATIONAL POLITICS ... | 183 |
| Parliamentary Politics before 1832 ... | 184 |
| Reform Movements ... | 188 |
| Politics, 1832-67 ... | 195 |
| The Emergence of the Political Parties ... | 199 |
| Women's Suffrage Movements ... | 203 |
| Working-Class Movements ... | 204 |
| INDEX ... | 211 |

*The great majority of extracts in this book are from documents in the Essex Record Office and their appropriate catalogue marks are noted at the beginning of each extract. Where the extracts are from documents in Colchester Borough Library their source is indicated by 'C.B.L.'. The spelling, punctuation and syntax of the extracts have been modernised except those taken from printed sources or where otherwise noted. Repetitive and superfluous phrases, such as 'before mentioned' or 'in the county of Essex', have generally been omitted without indication. Three full points indicate other omissions.*

A companion volume, prepared by A. C. Edwards, is entitled *English History from Essex Sources, 1550—1750* (1952).

# INTRODUCTION

The purpose of this book is to illustrate certain aspects of English history from 1750 to 1900 from the records of a single county. It is not itself a history of Essex nor is it intended to provide the material for such a history. Planned in the first place to meet the needs of W.E.A. classes, its scope has been widened to assist all types of students wishing to supplement their reading by a study of original documents. The material has therefore been arranged for use in the class-room or in private study by those who already possess a working knowledge of the general history of the period. The extracts have been left to explain themselves with such editorial comment only as is necessary to establish their context or avoid obscurities. For the same reason the introduction to each section has been made as short as possible.

The sections of the book correspond with some of the chief aspects of British history. Inevitably certain aspects have been omitted : some through lack of space ; some because they cannot adequately be illustrated from local sources ; others again because, although prominent in the early years of the period 1750-1900, they belong more properly to the subject-matter of the source-book for 1550-1750, shortly to be issued as a companion volume in this series. On the other hand certain outstanding developments in Essex history, such as the decline of the cloth trade and the agricultural depression after 1874, have received detailed treatment because of their importance in national as well as local economic history.

It is not possible in this introduction adequately to describe the full range of the historical sources open to the student in Essex. The extracts reproduced in the following pages are representative of a great mass of Essex records and documents. The Essex Record Office, among other material, holds comprehensive series of county, borough and parish records, important estate and family archives, a varied collection of maps and a growing number of local newspapers. It has also published several books designed to assist the inexperienced and the mature student alike to make best use of its facilities. Colchester Borough Library has an extensive collection of local newspapers and some valuable pamphlets. Among the few books which throw light upon Essex history between 1750 and 1900, those of most value to the student include the annual volumes of the *Essex Review*, Volume II of the *Victoria County History of Essex*, the works of Arthur Young, and the contemporary trade directories. They are available in most Essex reference libraries as well as in the Essex Record Office.


### *ACKNOWLEDGMENTS*

In conclusion I record my grateful appreciation of the wise and informed guidance which the County Archivist, Mr. F. G. Emmison, F.S.A., F.R.Hist.S., has consistently afforded me in the preparation of this book. The Record Office staff as a whole has generously given me information, advice and help of many kinds. I am very much in the debt of the Colchester Borough Librarian, Mr. A. T. Austing, and his staff, for their courtesy and competence in facilitating my access to the resources in their charge. I acknowledge with thanks my use of material in the possession of the British Museum, Essex County Library, the Chelmsford and Ipswich Borough Libraries, the proprietors of the *Essex Chronicle* and the *Essex County Standard*, the Halstead R.D.C., and H.M. Customs and Excise Library. I am indebted to a number of individual friends and to members of my family; in particular to Miss Hilda Grieve for her encouragement, advice and practical help, and to Mrs. D. L. Woodward and Mr. John Holmes for their valuable suggestions and other acts of assistance. Finally, I thank many friends in W.E.A. classes, whose preference for first-hand historical evidence suggested the need for such a book as this, and my recent employers, the Eastern District of the W.E.A., for giving me the opportunity and encouragement to write it.

A. F. J. BROWN.

July, 1952

# INDUSTRY

In 1750 the Essex cloth trade made bays and says, chiefly for export to Spain and Portugal. At Colchester, Braintree and Bocking, Halstead, Coggeshall and other North Essex towns substantial 'clothiers' organised the production. They sent wool to be spun in neighbouring villages, gave the yarn to urban weavers and had the cloth fulled and finished for despatch to London exporters. Spinners and weavers generally worked at home. Throughout the eighteenth century the industry was declining, and during the Napoleonic Wars it came to an end. The causes of failure are not yet completely clear.

Manufacture of silk partly replaced that of cloth. From about 1800 firms from Spitalfields and elsewhere set up businesses in the former cloth centres of North Essex, bringing wool-spinners into their throwing mills and employing cloth weavers on silk looms. Numerous firms operated at different times in about a dozen North Essex towns but one after another ceased production as protective tariffs were lowered and in 1860 abolished. Two firms in the Braintree district survived through technical efficiency and a high quality of workmanship. Other trades replacing the cloth industry were straw-plaiting, tambour lace making and domestic tailoring.

Between 1750 and 1850 most Essex townsmen worked, not in textiles, but in handicrafts, transport and other non-industrial occupations. Artisans either managed their own small businesses or worked with a few other journeymen for a small master. Towns and villages on main roads drew considerable income from travellers and transport. A few thousand fishermen earned a poor living, supplemented very often until about 1830 from smuggling. Mills, breweries, brickworks and shipyards were mostly small, local establishments, and other industries were few.

After 1850 the population of the county became more urban and its economy more industrial. Many left North Essex villages for London, Canada and elsewhere, but most towns continued to grow, especially in South Essex where London's rapid expansion exerted a powerful influence on economic development. Handicraft trades like shoe-making and tailoring became more mechanised. Local mills, breweries and brickyards were closed and their place taken by fewer and larger establishments. Agricultural machinery firms expanded and new engineering and allied industries were founded in several centres.

## *THE CLOTH TRADE IN DECLINE*

### 1. *The Dutch Bay Hall at Colchester*

Defoe describes the Dutch Bay Hall shortly before the dissolution of the Dutch community in 1728.
Defoe, *Tour through Great Britain,* Vol. I.

Bay-Hall, an ancient Society kept up for ascertaining the Manufactures of Bays ; which are, or ought to be, all brought to this Hall, to be viewed and Sealed according to their Goodness, by the Masters ; and to this Practice has been owing the great Reputation of the Colchester Bays in Foreign Markets ; where to open the side of a Bale and shew the Seal has been enough to give the Buyer a Character of the Value of the Goods without any farther Search ; and so far as they abate the Integrity and Exactness of their Method, which, I am told, is of late much omitted ; I say, so far, that Reputation will certainly abate in the markets they go to, which are principally in Portugal and Italy.

### 2. *Overseas Markets for Essex Cloth*

Essex clothiers sold much cloth to Portugal and therefore favoured the closest possible trade relations with that country.
*Chelmsford Chronicle,* Feb. 2, 1787 (E.R.O.).

This day the principal manufacturers of the towns of Colchester, Bocking, Braintree, Coggeshall, Dedham, Hedingham, Halstead, etc., will meet at the Angel Inn, in Kelvedon, in order to take into consideration that part of the commercial treaty which more particularly affects the woollen trade of this country. They seem unanimously of the opinion that the admission of French wines into this kingdom on lower duties than those of Portugal will prove prejudicial to their interests ; and that should the French vessels in addition to this be enabled clandestinely to make more extensive importations of our long wool, the whole trade must fall a sacrifice ; and the landed property of the several towns and parishes will be unable to support so large a body as 60,000 starving manufacturers.

### 3. *Decline of the Cloth Industry, a Contemporary View*

**Morant, *History of Colchester,* 1748, pp. 75-6.**

This Trade was first most sensibly hurt by our Wars with Spain, especially by Q. Anne's Wars, more glorious than profitable to England, by which means and other disagreeable concurrent causes the Dutch Congregation, not being able to carry it on, dissolved themselves in 1728. But 'tis undeniable that it was Queen Anne's Wars which gave it the fatal blow. Since which, (besides what the French have stolen from us) it is removed in a great measure into the West and Northern parts of this Kingdom, where Provisions are cheaper, the poor more easily satisfied and Coals are very plentiful. However, we have not been all along without some tolerable share of it, though a Spanish War always hurts us extremely. But, upon the Prospect of Peace, we hope it will revive and flourish again, though it is in very few hands and in a manner monopolized.

Some wrong-headed people have indeed been wishing that it were entirely out of the place, but herein they neither show their Judgement nor Affection to this Town. For, in that case, the Workmen would remove from it and not stay here and starve. And then what would become of our Houses ? Must they not be taken down, as too many have been since the decline of Trade ; and what an inestimable loss would that be both to the public and to private persons ? To the latter, whose only subsistence, in many instances, depends upon the Rents of those Houses, and to the Public and our Royal Master, which would be very great losers in the Taxes.

Moreover what would become of the great Quantities of Provisions, which through God's goodness plentifully grow all around and, by proper encouragement and a quick consumption, are industriously cultivated and brought to our markets ? There would be an end of them. The Rents of our lands would fall, universal Poverty would ensue and this flourishing Town would be reduced to a despicable village.

And not only this Town, but also the greatest part of this noble and populous County, of which the poorer sort are almost universally employed in Spinning the Wool, would be reduced to inexpressible streights and misery. For what Employment could be immediately substituted in its room ?

Supposing the generality of our numerous Poor were to stay here and inhabit our Houses ; yet how would they be employed or live till some other business was established among us, and how long might it not be before they could learn it or before it could turn to a tolerable account.

The Riches of a Kingdom, and of every part of the same, consist in the Number of People. And there they will always throng where there is Business and Wages. Therefore, the way to bring Riches and Plenty in this place, is, Not to take all base methods imaginable to banish Trade from hence, as too many have done, but to use all honest and proper means, nay to strive to the utmost, to call it in again; which may be done by Sobriety, Contentment and due Diligence on one hand and by Justice, Humanity, and not an immoderate Greediness of Gain on the other.

### 4. *Opposition to Dilution of Labour, 1700*

Essex Quarter Sessions uphold apprenticeship regulations in the cloth trade.
Quarter Sessions Bundle, Easter 1700 (Q/SBb 17).

Whereas several complaints have been made to this Court by the whole Company of the occupation of Fullers and Tuckers inhabiting in the town of Bocking that diverse and sundry of the inhabitants and others, who having not heretofore been bound out as apprentices into the trade . . . , as well husbandmen as others, have not only set up the trade of fuller and tucker, but also have kept and set such on work in the same trade as have not thereunto been lawfully bound, contrary to the statute laws of this Realm and against diverse good orders made and consented unto by the whole Company . . . of Fullers and Tuckers within the said town; whereupon this Court, regarding the cause of the said complaints, have at length considered of the premises and by daily experiences finding them to be much wronged by such as have intruded themselves into the art of fulling and tucking; and forasmuch as the orders in their ancient book of record registered are not altogether grounded upon the penal laws of this land and also have been disorderly and confusedly kept; it is therefore ordered by this Court that this new book be made now authentical and agreeable to the several branches of every statute in that behalf made and provided, promising, so far as in this Court lieth, to ratify the said orders hereafter in this book of record registered.

### 5. *Opposition to Machinery*

The rowing mill referred to in the following passage was probably a water-driven wheel for raising the nap of cloth.
*Ipswich Journal,* April 10, 1762 (C.B.L.).

March 31, 1762.

Whereas there was found under my Door this Morning the following threatning Letter: Whoever will discover the Person or Persons concerned in writing the same, so that he or they may be convicted thereof, shall receive of me Fifty Pounds Reward. Isaac Boggis.

'Colster, Fy. 25, 1762

Boggis this is to Lett you know that I Will be damn'd If I don't Blow youn and youn sons Brains out if ever you Consent to have a rowing mill I have a great family and before I will see them want I will be damn'd If I dont blow you and youn house and youn family to HEL so no more nor no more than truth. I remain your Executor. Now find it out and I'll Suffer but it shall not be for nothing.'

### 6. *Colchester Weavers' Complaint, 1749*

Colchester weavers ask Essex Quarter Sessions to lay down a rate of wages for their trade.
Quarter Sessions Bundle, Easter 1749 (QSBb 184).

And your petitioners further shew unto your Worships that from the reign of Queen Elizabeth the woollen manufacture hath been largely carried on in the town of Colchester and many thousands of families creditably maintained thereby, and from that motive your petitioners have been induced to bring, teach and instruct their wives [and] children to employ their lifetime in weaving, spinning, combing, carding, beating and the several other branches necessary to that manufacture, so that at present there are by computation more than 3000 hands employed therein who are not able, on account of their habitual sedentary way of life, to maintain themselves or get their bread in any other way of business. That within these 20 years last past, by the death of several eminent baymakers and their policy in not taking of apprentices, the trade of baymaking is come into [the] hands of a few who, by taking uncommon advantage from our labour and under the specious pretences of bad trade and the difficulties they met with in vending their goods for want of proper convoys and other arguments unanswerable by us, have by degrees so reduced our wages that we are not able to support ourselves and families with the wages they give us. And they have in that interval acquired to themselves large fortunes.

That your petitioners humbly conceive that the aforesaid pretences and suggestions for lowering our wages ought to carry no weight, the same, or rather more, labour being required now than when they paid 15s . 6d per bay. Besides whatever the maker pays his workmen, he makes the Spaniard, the consumer, repay him double, and the lowering our wages is an additional profit to him only. For the Spaniard must have the sort of bay and no place but Colchester can furnish them with merchandise so good of the sort.

And your petitioners further show that as the wages we received before the War, which was 15s . 6d for the best sort of bays and 10s. for the worst sort, would not pay your petitioners for the neat labour of a master weaver for six days' weaving more than 7s. 6d, so what we receive now will not pay us more than per man for a week 6s. 3d. or thereabouts.

That when we remonstrate to our masters the hardships we undergo in working at such wages, that we cannot support ourselves and families under it, instead of receiving a kind, humane answer, we are called idle rascals, factious fellows, and threatened with punishment for unlawful combinations and that instead of relieving us they would lower us 1s. a bay and that, if we refused to accept, would starve us into a compliance.

That ever since the making [of] the recited Acts your petitioners and their predecessors could have no opportunity of getting their wages settled (the Law empowering the Dutch manufacturers to settle them whilst they subsisted, and after them the Mayor and his associates by the said Acts had the power of putting the said Law into execution), and whenever your petitioners made application for that purpose, the interest of the baymakers there was too great for them to obtain redress of their grievances. The Dutch manufacturers' company being long since broken up and the Corporation being now an inactive body and no Mayor to put the said Acts into execution and fresh grievances arising to your petitioners from their hard taskmasters, your petitioners most humbly beseech your Worships that you will (in regard your petitioners have no other persons to hear our complaints or [to] flee to for Justice) rate, assess and limit the wages ; that the baymakers of Colchester (who have notice of this our intended application) ought to pay the poor artificers, their weavers, for weaving every bay in the great or by the week, month or otherwise as you in your discretion shall think meet, and to give us all that equitable relief the said laws empower you to give and the nature of our case upon proof shall reasonably require.

### 7. *Condition of Braintree Weavers, 1767*

Young, *Six Weeks' Tour,* 1768, p. 65.

From Gosfield I proceeded to Bocking and Braintree, places adjoining and exceedingly full of manufacturers, who work up says in general and some druggets. By all the accounts I could gain of the weavers, I found that they earned on an average about 9s. a week ; woolcombers about 12s., stout girls, 15 or 16 years old, four-pence or five-pence a day at spinning; and girls of seven or eight 1s. a week for rolling the weavers quills; all these prices are lower than the Sudbury ones. They further informed me that in summer they did whatever husbandry work they were able, being better paid for it, such as hoeing turnips and wheat, making hay and harvesting; That the prices of necessaries are as follows: bread 2d per lb., mutton 5d, beef 3½d, and veal 4d. One man, who had a wife and four children, informed me that they eat half a bushel of wheat-flour every week.

### 8. *Furniture in a Colchester Weaver's House*

*Original spelling retained.*
Colchester, St. Nicholas, Overseers' Accounts (D/P 176/12/1).

1774. An Invatory of Eliz. Finch's Goods Remov'd into the Workhouse Two Bedsteads 2 Beds 1 pair of Curtains 7 Sheets 3 Blanketts 2 Coverlids 4 pillows 4 pair of Cases 2 Bolsters 1 Pair of Drawers 3 Tables 1 Copper Saucepan and Cover 1 small Boyler 1 Iron pot 1 Iron Kettle 2 Box Irons and heaters 2 Iron Candlesticks 1 Looking Glass 3 Jugs 1 pair Bellows 12 pictures 3 glass Ditto 1 pair Tongs Sifter poker and Fender 1 Frying pan 2 Chamber pots 1 Iron Tramell 3 Basketts 2 Earthern pots 1 Wash tub 1 pail 2 Bowl dishes 9 Glass Bottles 3 Dishes 16 plates 9 Basons 4 Tea pots 16 Cups and Saucers 2 Silver Spoons 3 Quart pots 1 Trunk 1 Sweeping Brush 3 pewter Measures half pint Quar$^{r}$ D$^{o}$ and ½ quar$^{r}$ Ditto 1 Bird Cage 1 4 Gallon Cask 1 Bay Loom Quill wheel pedon Block and Blades

### 9. *From a Baymaker's Account Book, 1785*

Josias Nottidge, a Bocking baymaker, sold yarn and flocks to firms all over North Essex, had his bays and 'Bocking whites' fulled at a local mill and then sent them to London by carrier.
Nottidge Accounts (D/DO B1).

| | | |
|---|---|---|
| Sent by Challis 12 bays | | 18 . 0 |
| Sold Mr R. Daniell 2 packets warpy yarn | | 25 . 0 . 0 |
| Sent by Challis 30 whites | | 1 . 2 . 6 |
| | 6 bays | 9 . 0 |
| Sold B. Blower 10 packets woof yarn | | 110 . 0 . 0 |
| Sold Stephen Unwin 6 packets woof yarn | | 69 . 0 . 0 |
| Sold Mr Is. Hitchen 4 packets white flocks | | 16 . 0 . 0 |
| Do., | 3 packets greasy and coloured flocks | 9 . 0 . 0 |
| Thos. Chipperfield, milling 18 bays | | 10 . 6 |
| Do., | milling 77 pair whites | 2 . 3 . 2 |

### *10. Weavers' Procession, 1787*

*Chelmsford Chronicle,* April 20, 1787 (E.R.O.).

Order of the Procession,
Which is to be exhibited by the Weavers of Coggeshall,
On Thursday, the Tenth of May, 1787.

Two Leaders ; Two Ensign Bearers ; Flemings Two and Two ; The Union Flag ; Two Garlands ; Drums and Fifes ; Guards Two and Two ; King Henry the Second with his attending Lord on Horse Back ; Guards Two and Two ; Lieutenant of the Guards ; Guards Two ; The Weavers' Arms ; Guards, two ; Band of Music ; Lads, two and two ; The Shepherd and Shepherdess ; A Slay Maker ; A Shuttle Maker and Loom Maker ; Two Ensigns of the Trade ; Jack of Newbury ; Two Pappers

---

Platform, with the several Branches at Work, viz. Spinning, Winding, Warping and Weaving.

---

Two Pendants of the Manufacture ; Maids, two ; Attending, two with Garlands ; Maids, two and two ; Attending, two with Banners ; two Orators ; Followed by the Cavalcade, two and two.
The Procession will set out precisely at Seven O'Clock from the Fleece. The Procession will not go out of Coggeshall.

Same evening will be a grand Concert of Vocal and Instrumental Music and a Ball, adjoining the Chapel, under the direction of Mr Moore. Admittance 2s. 6d. each

### *11. A Relic of the Cloth Trade*

Cobden visited Colchester in 1843.
Hurnard, *The Setting Sun,* Book 3, p. 122.

Another piece of household furniture
We value much—a lady's spinning wheel ;
A little heirloom of the family,
Handsomely wrought in good mahogany
It stood an ornament of our old hall,
A puzzle and a mystery to many.
Our modern spinsters, who no longer spin,
Could throw no light upon the way to use it.
When Cobden came it caught his searching eye ;
He placed his foot upon the little treadle
And set the tiny wheel in harmless motion,
Comparing doubtless in his musing mind
This relic of departed slow-coach times,

With the transcendent power and enginery
Of manufacturing Lancashire and Yorkshire
With all their world of noisy spinning jennies.
We named our heirloom Cobden's spinning-wheel.

## *THE SILK INDUSTRY*

### *1. Prosperity in the Silk Industry, 1823*

*Chelmsford Gazette*, Sept. 12, 1823 (E.R.O.).

The poor-rates have already been reduced at this place from 8s. to 3s. 6d. in the pound ; but a future moral evil threatens, which will we fear be more than commensurate with the present good. Means are afforded by this lucrative employment for the young women to dress in the greatest extravagance, so much so that on a Sunday those who formerly moved in the most humble social sphere and appeared in woollens and stuffs have lately been so disguised as to be mistaken for persons of distinction. A ludicrous deception of this kind, we are informed, occurred a few Sundays since at a parish Church in the vicinity of Saffron Walden, where two young women entered, dressed most elegantly in silks of their own production, to which were added fashionable bonnets, plumed with nodding feathers ; the clergyman politely directed the strangers to be shewn into a pew suitable to their appearance, and at the conclusion of the service inquired of the clerk whether he knew those elegantly dressed ladies, when behold, it was discovered, that they were two girls from the Walden silk manufactory.

### *2. Attempt to Recruit Juvenile Labour, 1823*

Chelmsford Vestry Minutes (D/P 94/8/4).

June 16, 1823 . . . The Vestry Clerk was desired to acquaint Messrs Sawer and Hall that, having considered those gentlemen's proposal of taking some of the poor children of the parish into their silk manufactory at Coggeshall, they beg leave to decline it, having other views of employment for their poor at home.

### *3. Depression in the Silk Industry, 1832*

A Coggeshall silk manufacturer is questioned about his business by a Parliamentary Committee.
*Select Committee on Silk Trade*, 1832.

11925. Where do you carry on your business ? In Spital-square and Coggeshall in Essex.

11926. How long have you been engaged in the silk trade ? About 23 years, with the exception of four years, when I was engaged as a silk warehouseman.

11927. What has been the greatest number of looms you have employed ? About 250.

11928. In what branch of business have you employed your looms ? In nearly all the branches of the broad silk trade, but principally in an article of serge for coat linings and in fancy waistcoatings and velvets . . .

11945. You do not continue to manufacture fancy velvets ? I have given that trade up altogether.

11946. On what are your looms employed now ? They are principally employed on the lowest description of works, the three singles, serges, and other works by which the weavers can earn 7s., 8s., or 10s. a week, with so many reductions they grumble dreadfully. I used to give them £2 a week ; then they were well clothed, comfortable and happy.

11947. In what branch was that ? In weaving rich fancy silks and velvets. I was driven by the high rate of labour from Spitalfields and I established a factory in Essex. I used to pay 2s. 6d. for an article in Spitalfields, which I now make and sell at 2s. 4d. per yard ; I give 7d. or 8d. for weaving it now. I stopped all my looms about a month or two ago and offered a reduction of wages of 25 to 30 per cent, which necessity has compelled them to accede to, but I have only been able to supply a small portion of my looms at that price. About two years ago I made a similar reduction of wages and received a letter signed " Swing ", stating that, if I did not advance my labour in two days, my factory should be burnt down. As I was not then insured, I paid men to watch and, as a proof the threat was not sham, two houses were destroyed at that time. I was refused by two offices an insurance. I now have my factory insured at some difficulty at 11s. per cent., and the weavers could not do me a greater favour than to burn it down.

11954. Is your market principally American ? No ; I send to the Colonies, North and South America, New York, Rio, Cape of Good Hope, Lisbon, Valparaiso, Cadiz, Demarara, Palermo, Vera Cruz . . .

11976. How are your weavers now employed at Coggeshall ? Very badly indeed, many of them upon low works, such as three singles, serges, and a few upon figures ; the remainder, I believe, are out of work and have been for the last three or four weeks. I am fearful to speculate upon fancy silks in the autumn lest I may be served the same trick as I was last year when I did so ; Messrs Leaf and Company imported a great quantity from France for this market and caused mine to be sold at 15 per cent loss.

### 4. *Courtaulds use Steam, 1836*

*Essex Independent,* Nov. 12, 1836 (C.B.L.).

Halstead. A great outcry is made against Messrs Courtauld and Taylor for having introduced into their manufactories additional machinery, which may throw out of employment some of the weavers. We sympathise with those who may thus lose employment, but it must be recollected that it is by the perfection of our machinery alone that England can expect to maintain the proud position which she occupies. In order to enable the manufacturer to employ the poor, he must have a market for his goods, for no man will be so insane as to incur all the responsibility and risk of trade without a remunerating profit. It is to the excellent nature of the machinery of these gentlemen that their employment of so many hands is owing, and if their only means of continuing this employment is in their adoption of more extensive means of production, surely the poor, much less the farmers, ought not to murmur against a mere temporary interruption of work which may take place.

### 5. *The Effect of Free Trade, 1860*

*Braintree Advertiser,* May 16, 1860.

*TOTAL REPEAL OF THE SILK DUTIES*
*H. W. MORLEY*
Family Draper, Silk Mercer, Hosier, Haberdasher, etc, etc.
Invites special attention to an extensive assortment of
*FRENCH AND ENGLISH SILKS*
Which, owing to the recent depression of trade, he has secured at LOWER PRICES
*THAN HAS EVER BEFORE BEEN HEARD OF.*
*COMMENCING AT 15½d PER YARD.*
He has also some *DECIDED BARGAINS IN*
Flounced Dresses, Mohairs, Balzarines, Prints, Etc, Etc,
*AN ENDLESS VARIETY OF*
*BONNETS* (trimmed or untrimmed), *FLOWERS, SHAWLS, MANTLES, RIBBONS, ETC., WHOLESALE AND RETAIL.*
(Bank Street, Braintree.)

### 6. *Opposition to Free Trade*

In 1860 the Cobden Treaty with France left English silk unprotected by tariffs.
*Essex Standard,* Feb. 29, 1860 (C.B.L.).

A petition to Parliament is in course of signature among the silk weavers of Sudbury, Coggeshall, Braintree, Halstead, and other neighbouring places, praying the House to modify the terms of the proposed treaty with France, considering that it will materially injure the trade and interests of the country.

### 7. *Decline of the Silk Industry, 1879*

*Colchester Mercury,* Aug. 30, 1879 (C.B.L.).

CLOSING OF THE SILK FACTORY. Our readers will regret to hear that that important source of industry in Colchester, Messrs Durrant and Co.'s Silk Factory, is now closed. It is now a considerable time since that place was in full swing, and instead of furnishing work for from 270 to 300 hands, as it formerly did, it has latterly only found employment for some 150 women and children . . . The languishing condition of the silk market has necessitated this step, and until some decided revival, which at present looks far distant, takes place, there is little prospect of the looms and spindles at Colchester being brought into requisition. Fortunately the manufacture of clothing, for which Colchester is an important centre, is very brisk, and many of those who are thus thrown out of work will be able to gain a livelihood in that direction; but there are many others—children known at the factory as half-timers, from half of their time being spent at School and half at work—who cannot be employed in this new industry.

## *OTHER ESSEX INDUSTRIES*

### 1. *A Start in Life, 1762*

*Ipswich Journal,* June 19, 1762 (C.B.L.).

To be put Apprentice to the Sea, in a Merchant-Ship, till twenty-one Years old.

A Boy in the Parish of Fingringhoe, near Wivenhoe, about ten Years old, lately had the Small-Pox, and of honest Parentage.

Enquire of Thomas Cooper of Fingringhoe aforesaid.

### 2. *Harwich Fisheries, 1763*

*Ipswich Journal,* Oct. 22, 1763 (C.B.L.).

We hear from Harwich that the Scheme of sending Fish by Land from thence to London answers so well, that eight Cod-Smacks are engaged to supply the Store-Boat in that Harbour. There were only four Cod-Smacks employed last Year in this Undertaking.

### 3. *Smuggling through Official Eyes, 1767-79*

The following are extracts from reports by the Harwich Collector of Customs.

H.M. Customs Records, Harwich (accessible to authenticated researchers on application to Commissioners of Customs and Excise, London, E.C.—selected transcripts in E.R.O., T/A 124).

21 May, 1767. I received the petition of Thomas Cross in the

Fleet Prison for smuggling in which he sets forth his great poverty and inability to pay the penalties incurred. It is talked of by the neighbourhood, and I am inclinable to think it is true, that he is now worth £700 or £800. My reason for this belief is that he smuggled in consort with Salmon and Hallumoss Thorp for several years without any considerable loss. By their weekly contracts with Sextro and others for large cargoes of spirituous liquors, teas, etc., their profits must be very large.

6 Oct., 1777. Having been informed by undoubted authority that there are upwards of thirty sail of small cutters constantly employed in smuggling between the Naze Point and the mouth of the Thames, which vessels easily elude the pursuit of the 'Argus' and the 'Bee' cutters stationed at this port by running over the sands where on account of their great draft of water those cutters dare not follow, by which means they escape and carry on with impunity a great trade in the rivers and creeks which abound in these parts.

29 June, 1778. The account of the seizures made by the 'Argus' cutter for 4 years to 5 Jan., 1778.

| | | |
|---|---|---|
| 1774 | Liquors, teas, etc. | 2647 . 8 . 2 |
| 1775 | ,, ,, ,, | 5107 . 15 . 8¾ |
| 1776 | ,, ,, ,, | 1979 . 16 . 2 |
| 1777 | ,, ,, ,, | 3623 . 16 . 4¾ |
| | | 13358 . 16 . 5½ |

4 Aug., 1778. We humbly beg leave to send your Honours a list of smuggling cutters who constantly run their goods upon the coasts of Essex, Suffolk and Norfolk. Your Honours will observe at one view the impossibility of Capt. Bridges ever being able, with the present weak complement of the Argus, to bring in any one of them.

| Master's Name | Tons | Guns | Men |
|---|---|---|---|
| Reynolds | 134 | 12 | 45 |
| Stephen Cann | 75 | 6 | 24 |
| Stephen Marsh | 140 | uncertain | 34 |
| John Cock | 113 | ,, | 28 |
| Wm. Marsh | 120 | ,, | 30 |
| James Cree | 114 | 10 | 32 |
| — Baker | 112 | 10 | 28 |
| John Girland | 110 | 4 | 24 |

8 March, 1779. We take this occasion of informing your Honours that a large cutter of near 200 tons, mounting 14 four-pounders and 47 men, belonging to one Wenham but commanded by a man nicknamed 'Swipes', well known as a notorious smuggler upon this coast, has lately made it a practice to bring a very large cargo of contraband goods which she lands in Colne and Burnham rivers as fast as she can perform the voyages between Flushing and this coast. Neither of the cutters stationed at this port are in any way a match for her, but we had a plan to endeavour to take her if we could have the assistance of about 40 soldiers of the 25th Regiment quartered at this place, but, on applying to the commanding officer for that purpose, he informed us that he had particular orders not to furnish any men to assist any officers of the Revenue.

## 4. *The Economic Life of Epping, 1792*

The following extracts from a list of Epping trades show an economic pattern common to most Essex market towns.

*Universal British Directory*, 1792, pp. 43-4 (C.B.L., E.R.O.).

| | |
|---|---|
| Archer, John | Wheelwright |
| Baker, John | Victualler (Sun) |
| Burrell, John | Tanner |
| Chaplin, Henry | Miller |
| Coell, George | Maltster |
| Dorrington, Joseph | Appraiser and Auctioneer |
| Doubleday, Joseph | Soap-boiler |
| Giffin, John | Boot and Shoe Maker |
| Godsafe, T. | Victualler (Thatched House) |
| Green, John | Brandy Merchant |
| Haslam, James | Shopkeeper and Woolcomber |
| Martin, Samuel | Sadler |
| Miller, Thomas | Blacksmith |
| Palmer, Richard | Brickmaker |
| Parker, Thomas | Maltster |
| Pettit, John | Clock Maker |
| Pink, Joseph | Common Carrier |
| Presland, John | Basket-maker |
| Redgrave, William | Cock Inn and Excise-office Keeper |
| Rogers, James | Silkweaver |
| Surridge, Thomas | Cooper |
| Tanner, John | Baker |
| Welch, William | Currier |

## 5. *Essex Occupations, 1831*

The following table illustrates the economic composition of different types of Essex communities. Great Clacton, East Mersea, High Roding and Ugley were agricultural villages; Chelmsford, Colchester, Romford and Saffron Walden, market towns. Braintree was both a market town and a manufacturing centre. Prittlewell parish included Southend. Chingford and Dagenham, still partly rural, were being affected by the growth of London.

*Census*, 1831 (Q/CR 2/8/1).

| Parish | Great Clacton | East Mersea | High Roothing | Ugley | Chelms-ford | Col-chester |
|---|---|---|---|---|---|---|
| Area in acres | 4170 | 1810 | 1450 | 2720 | 1750 | 11770 |
| *Houses* | | | | | | |
| Inhabited | 223 | 36 | 79 | 67 | 987 | 3216 |
| Families | 223 | 60 | 93 | 67 | 1085 | 3488 |
| Building | — | — | 1 | 1 | 3 | 25 |
| Uninhabited | 10 | — | 1 | — | 32 | 119 |
| *Occupations* | | | | | | |
| Families chiefly employed in Agriculture | 161 | 60 | 66 | 53 | 93 | 490 |
| Families chiefly employed in Trade, Manufactures and Handicraft | 46 | — | 23 | 9 | 651 | 2079 |
| All other Families not comprised in the two preceding classes | 16 | — | 4 | 5 | 341 | 919 |
| *Persons* | | | | | | |
| Males | 579 | 152 | 206 | 146 | 2550 | 7471 |
| Females | 570 | 148 | 199 | 172 | 2885 | 8696 |
| Total of persons | 1149 | 300 | 405 | 318 | 5435 | 16167 |
| Males Twenty Years of Age | 285 | 84 | 106 | 84 | 1300 | 3745 |
| *Agriculture* | | | | | | |
| Occupiers employing labourers | 20 | 8 | 11 | 7 | 11 | 69 |
| Occupiers not employing labourers | 5 | 3 | 2 | 1 | 6 | 34 |
| Labourers employed in Agriculture | 173 | 72 | 65 | 60 | 96 | 530 |
| Employed in Manufactures or in making Manufacturing machinery | — | — | — | — | 31 | 73 |
| Employed in Retail Trade, or in Handicraft as Masters or Workmen | 46 | — | 24 | 10 | 610 | 1738 |
| Capitalists, Bankers, Professional and other Educated Men | 2 | 1 | — | 1 | 144 | 250 |
| Labourers employed in Labour not Agricultural | 16 | — | — | 2 | 251 | 745 |
| Other males 20 Years of Age (except Servants) | 23 | — | 4 | 2 | 105 | 225 |
| Male Servants 20 Years of Age | — | — | — | 1 | 46 | 81 |
| Under 20 Years | — | — | — | 1 | 20 | 65 |
| Female Servants | 51 | 8 | 8 | 7 | 354 | 798 |

| Parish | Romford | Saffron Walden | Brain-tree | Prittle-well | Ching-ford | Dagen-ham |
|---|---|---|---|---|---|---|
| Area in acres | 3340 | 7380 | 2500 | 2490 | 3000 | 4550 |
| *Houses* | | | | | | |
| Inhabited | 766 | 941 | 708 | 379 | 194 | 413 |
| Families | 850 | 1000 | 722 | 418 | 196 | 431 |
| Building | 4 | 33 | 5 | 12 | — | 1 |
| Uninhabited | 44 | 18 | 26 | 35 | 19 | 25 |
| *Occupations* | | | | | | |
| Families chiefly employed in Agriculture | 254 | 271 | 116 | 236 | 115 | 288 |
| Families chiefly employed in Trade, Manufactures and Handicraft | 339 | 534 | 371 | 145 | 65 | 112 |
| All other Families not comprised in the two preceding classes | 257 | 195 | 235 | 37 | 16 | 31 |
| *Persons* | | | | | | |
| Males | 2100 | 2317 | 1611 | 1084 | 490 | 1074 |
| Females | 2194 | 2445 | 1811 | 1182 | 473 | 1044 |
| Total of persons | 4294 | 4762 | 3422 | 2266 | 963 | 2118 |
| Males Twenty Years of Age | 1132 | 1116 | 786 | 528 | 275 | 541 |
| *Agriculture* | | | | | | |
| Occupiers employing labourers | 32 | 23 | 6 | 20 | 14 | 30 |
| Occupiers not employing labourers | 2 | 10 | 6 | — | 9 | 6 |
| Labourers employed in Agriculture | 316 | 251 | 144 | 247 | 168 | 316 |
| Employed in Manufactures or in making Manufacturing machinery | 2 | 1 | 155 | — | — | — |
| Employed in Retail Trade, or in Handicraft as Masters or Workmen | 419 | 406 | 307 | 182 | 66 | 107 |
| Capitalists, Bankers, Professional and other Educated Men | 61 | 68 | 21 | 12 | 3 | 15 |
| Labourers employed in Labour not Agricultural | 112 | 283 | 87 | 45 | 4 | 53 |
| Other males 20 Years of Age (except Servants) | 168 | 53 | 44 | 14 | 6 | 7 |
| Male Servants 20 Years of Age | 20 | 21 | 16 | 8 | 5 | 7 |
| Under 20 Years | 7 | 4 | 10 | 6 | 5 | — |
| Female Servants | 203 | 192 | 130 | 110 | 35 | 40 |

## 6. *Roman Cement made at Harwich, 1851*

Lindsey, *A Season at Harwich,* London, 1851, pp. 49-51.

Henry and Charles, who had approached the drawing-room window, whence the broad North Sea and the entrance into Harwich Harbour were plainly discernible, exhibited much delight at a fleet of several hundred boats, all cutter-rigged, that was approaching . . . each striving to reach the appointed haven before his fellows . . .

An exclamation, equally of delight, burst simultaneously from the whole party, whose attention was drawn to the animating spectacle. The Doctor was pleased by their expressions of admiration, and, upon being appealed to, observed—" These are the craft employed in dredging for the stones from which is made the celebrated Roman Cement; and to this material our great metropolis is indebted for many of its embellishments and experiments in architecture; indeed, every great town in the United Kingdom, and many on the Continent, are alike adorned with the produce of these rocks; the exportation of it forming a very important item in the trade of the place. Indeed, it is calculated that from three to four hundred vessels are employed in obtaining this useful article from the West Rocks, and these are some of them, straining, as you see, every stitch of canvas, in the eager endeavour to get into harbour before the rest . . . The barges you see yonder by the jetty, and those again further up the harbour, are now waiting to take cargoes to London and other parts of the kingdom; the boats that get in first have the benefit of an early discharge at once into the vessels lying ready for loading. The next prize . . . is to be enabled to deliver their cargoes on shore for home manufacture . . The stone is first burned in kilns constructed for that purpose and afterwards ground in a mill to an impalpable powder. It is then fit for use and the sooner it is worked up after this latter process, the more durable it proves. When ground . . . it is packed in casks containing about four hundred weight and sold in London at about 7s. 6d. each cask. The price of the stone is now about 5s. a ton".

## 7. *Straw Plaiting at Earls Colne, 1860*

When the cloth industry ended, many spinners in the Braintree—Halstead region took up straw plaiting.

*Halstead Times*, Jan. 31, 1903.

An interesting industry in the village at this time [about 1860] was straw-plaiting. Farmers would cut the ears from the wheat, and tie the straw into sheaves, being careful not to bruise or bend the straws. This straw was sold to the plaiters. I have seen a whole family engaged in their only living room with sheaves of this straw, selecting and rejecting individual straws, cutting off the leaf, outer sheath, and joints from each, and tying approved straws into large bunches. The floor of the room was like a disordered stackyard. The rubbish being cleared, the straws were assorted into sizes, small, medium and thick. They were also bleached by the fumes of burning brimstone, or "stoved" as the plaiters termed it. Each straw was then split into equal segments, by means of a little instrument called an "engine". This was a small bone tool, ribbed at its sides, and having a spiked end. It was fitted into a handle three or four inches long, and might be said to resemble a tiny hammer, with ribs for cutting, with a sharp point to insert into the ends of the straws. After the straws, etc, had been split, the segments were well rolled by means of a short, stumpy, rolling pin to flatten them. They were at length tied into small bunches ready for use, and finally were woven into plait, the fingers of the workers moving with almost incredible swiftness. The work was sold at so much per "score"—20 yards. I think the price was 6$^{d}$ to 8$^{d}$ a score, according to fineness.

*8. The Rise of Industrial Chelmsford, 1887*

County Police, Miscellaneous Papers (Q/APp 13).

Estimate of Cost of establishing telephonic communication between Shire hall and Springfield headquarters, Essex Constabulary.

From R. E. Crompton & Co.
Electric Light Engineers
London E.C.

December 14th 1887

. . . erecting poles . . . running line wires (all necessary wayleaves being free) . . .

2 Patent telephones, of latest type, each a complete station in itself, comprising two receivers, one transmitter, one bell and one switch box, in handsome polished case and suitable for long distance line.

2 Extension bells, and 3 way switch (one to ring in Major Poyntz clerk's office, and one in Mr Somerset's bedroom).

2 Sets of Leclanche cells, (porous pot type) in wood battery boxes—Bronze line wire, insulated ditto for inside buildings, insulators (shackle and Z pattern), earth connections, intermediate poles of good sound wood . . . all . . . labour (skilled and unskilled) & superintendence . . .

£31 . 0 . 0

R. E. Crompton & Co.

*9. Domestic Tailoring, 1893*

*Essex Telegraph,* Aug. 12, 1893 (C.B.L.).

The village of Ardleigh, where I stayed at yesterday, may be taken as a fair type of many in the locality I have mentioned. Turning out of one of the lanes into a by-way you pass half-a-dozen cottages, the front doors of most of them being wide open, and in one you will find three women, in another two, in another one, stitching, stitching, stitching. One woman told me she was often so employed from four a.m. to ten p.m. and as a result of so much work had earned 2s a day.

## THE MOVEMENT OF POPULATION

### 1. *Essex Population, 1801-1901*

From about 1850 West Ham became part of Greatei London. Chelmsford, the county town, was becoming an industrial centre at the end of the century. Rayleigh was a country town. Quendon and Maplestead were undisturbed rural parishes. Frinton was becoming popular as a seaside resort. Stanway was a suburb of Colchester.

*Victoria County History of Essex*, Vol. II, pp. 344-354.

| | ENGLAND AND WALES | ESSEX | WEST HAM | CHELMSFORD |
|---|---|---|---|---|
| 1801 | 8,900,000 | 227,682 | 6,485 | 3,755 |
| 1811 | 10,200,000 | 248,920 | 8,136 | 4,649 |
| 1821 | 12,000,000 | 289,424 | 9,753 | 4,994 |
| 1831 | 13,900,000 | 317,507 | 11,580 | 5,435 |
| 1841 | 15,900,000 | 344,979 | 12,738 | 6,789 |
| 1851 | 17,900,000 | 369,298 | 18,817 | 7,796 |
| 1861 | 20,000,000 | 404,851 | 38,331 | 8,407 |
| 1871 | 22,700,000 | 466,487 | 62,919 | 9,318 |
| 1881 | 26,000,000 | 576,483 | 128,953 | 9,885 |
| 1891 | 29,000,000 | 785,438 | 204,893 | 11,111 |
| 1901 | 32,500,000 | 1,085,790 | 267,181 | 12,627 |

| | RAYLEIGH | QUENDON | LT. MAPLESTEAD | FRINTON | STANWAY |
|---|---|---|---|---|---|
| 1801 | 897 | 123 | 298 | 31 | 422 |
| 1811 | 1,131 | 115 | 290 | 32 | 431 |
| 1821 | 1,203 | 156 | 313 | 45 | 479 |
| 1831 | 1,339 | 211 | 373 | 35 | 665 |
| 1841 | 1,651 | 213 | 407 | 44 | 807 |
| 1851 | 1,463 | 199 | 367 | 30 | 951 |
| 1861 | 1,433 | 165 | 325 | 29 | 964 |
| 1871 | 1,404 | 170 | 302 | 54 | 945 |
| 1881 | 1,327 | 192 | 261 | 55 | 1,004 |
| 1891 | 1,301 | 171 | 217 | 87 | 1,104 |
| 1901 | 1,773 | 126 | 193 | 644 | 1,107 |

### 2. *Subsidised Emigration, 1832*

Steeple Bumpstead Overseers' Papers (D/P 21/18/5).

Memorandum of an Agreement between the Parishioners of Steeple Bumpstead and the undernamed paupers who wish to emigrate to America.

Parishioners to provide for every man, woman, and child, a clear passage and victualling, and to give every man, woman, and child £2 each above 1 year old, and for every infant £1 in money, to be paid to them when the ship sails from London. Also to give such clothing as the Parishioners may think proper.

In default of the paupers causing the passage and other expenses to be engaged for them, they do hereby severally agree to allow the Parishioners to stop from their weekly wages or allowance 1s per week until such expenses be repaid to the Parish.

April 26th 1832 Signed by us paupers as under [one man with his wife and three children, and three other men].

### 3. *Emigration under the New Poor Law*

The New Poor Law encouraged greater mobility of labour.
Widdington Overseers' Accounts (D/P 12/12).

At a Vestry meeting held this 7th day of April, 1835, for the purpose of raising a sum of money to defray the expences of sending fifteen persons belonging to the said parish to Upper Canada in America, we direct and authorise the Overseers to borrow £50 of Mr John Hayden, agreeably to the 62nd clause of the New Poor Law Amendment Act, upon interest of five per cent per annum. [Signed by two parishioners, churchwarden and overseers.]

### 4. *Experiences of a Coggeshall Emigrant, 1853*

*Essex Gazette,* April 1, 1853 (C.B.L.).

We got sight of Australia the evening of Monday, 11th of October, and saw the lighthouse off Cape Otway soon after dark, many of us stayed on deck all night, at daybreak we found ourselves going up the bay with the land on our left, half mad with joy. When we got to the head of the harbour, we found two vessels waiting for pilots ; had been there for three or four days, but our captain kept on without waiting ; we passed seven wrecks, right and left of us ; at one time we were in less than four fathoms of water, we drew three ; the man was heaving the lead all the time, it was a great risk to run, especially as he had not been in before. There are upwards of a hundred large vessels lying here, many of them without a man on board. Our men all deserted the first night, even the second mate, carpenter and two of the boys. We were obliged to get our boxes and luggage out of the hold ourselves, and get them to Melbourne as we could. It cost us £8 to get our things there, had to load them on to a small schooner that came alongside, and unload them ourselves at the wharf.

The vessels anchor close to William's Town, and exactly opposite Melbourne, but we have to go about six miles up the Yarra River to land goods at the wharf. This is the finest harbour I should think in the world. I did not go ashore for two or three days, as they charge 5/- by the steamer to shore and 5/- back. The men in the barges get £16 a month and their board and don't half work.

Melbourne is full of emigrants, not one twentieth part of whom can get house-room. Lodgings are 2/6 per night to sleep on the floor, with fifteen or sixteen others; they charge 30/- a week for a small room unfurnished. Bread is 2/6 the 4 lb. loaf; butter 3/- per lb; meat 4½d and 6d per lb; potatoes from 6d to 2/- per lb; beer and porter 1/- per pint, indoors; gin and rum, 4/- per pint; port and sherry 10/- per bottle . . . tobacco 6/- to 7/- per lb; oats are 20/- per bushel . . . cabbages 2/- each; apples 6d. each, such as you get in England 2d per dozen. Carpenters are getting from 25/- to 30/- a day; bricklayers the same; one of our fellow-passengers, a currier, has got work at £2 per day. There is a great demand for mechanics of all kinds. Labourers can have 10/- to 12/- per day. They are giving 30/- a hundred for sheep-shearing. I could have had a situation to attend a store at the diggings, £3 a week and board, but I hope to do better than that. Directly we came ashore, we pitched our tent outside the town and have been living in it ever since, in regular gipsy style. We found when we came ashore we could not get a house under £80 or £100; they charge at the rate of £120 per ton to take goods to the diggings . . .

I am going up with a Mr Cooke, a Norfolk man, who has been a farmer, and a Mr Fitzherbert, who has been in the army in India, both fellow passengers; we hope to start on Monday morning for some new diggings called the Ovens, about 280 miles from here, on the Murray river towards Sydney. I saw a man yesterday just come down from there, he got 27 lbs weight for his share in 9 days; we shall have to walk it . . . at night lie in the bush. We calculate it will take us a fortnight to get there; we have bought a nice little tent for £4, which we send up by a dray at the rate of 1/- per lb . . .

I shall be better able to give you an idea of the country in about two or three months time, my opinion is now that anybody getting a comfortable living in England would be foolish and bitterly repent it, if they left to come out here to live . . . I have to sit on the ground to write this.

### 5. *Migration to London, 1853*

*Essex Standard,* May 20, 1853 (C.B.L.).

Already many of our best workmen have joined others in the metropolis, as the wages there are at the present time, in most cases . . . double the weekly amount paid to our workmen here, and situated now but little more than an hour's ride from us . . . A journeyman, who recently left this town, writing from London to a friend, says very nearly as follows :— ' My last week's wages in Colchester were eighteen shillings. I last week received one pound, seventeen shillings and sixpence as my week's wages here ; my rent and coals are higher in price than I have been accustomed to pay, but food is generally cheaper '.

### 6. *The Encroachment of London, 1861*

Coller, *People's History of Essex,* 1861, pp. 454-5.

West Ham, from its traffic, trade, and importance, the capital of the Hundred, is the most thickly peopled parish in Essex, more than doubling the whole population of some of the smaller Hundreds in the county. It has, in fact, become a busy suburb of the metropolis, which has rubbed off its once rural character. Its little hamlets have grown into large towns. Fields over which the plough passed a quarter of a century ago are covered with workshops and teeming factories. On its river bank have risen up the largest ship-building works in the world. Its quiet creek and marsh land have been converted into mighty docks, furnishing a haven and a home for commerce for all countries of the earth. Its pleasant spots, on the edge of business, but just beyond the reach of the sound of the hammer and wheel and the wearying hum of the London hive, are studded over with handsome residences. Its population, it is estimated, has risen, since the last census, from nineteen thousand to thirty or forty thousand. Thus, teeming with numbers and alive with industry and growing wealth, this district, the mustering ground . . . of the discontented in old times and in which the serfs of the county wrung a grant of freedom from Richard II, bears great weight—an almost preponderating influence—in the parliamentary and political struggles of the southern division.

### 7. *A Rural Backwater, 1861*

Coller, *People's History of Essex,* 1861, pp. 486-7.

Loughton is a large and delightful parish, with a very picturesque village, and ground of a remarkably undulating character . . . The walks in and near the forest are of such a character as to invite large parties of Londoners to fill numerous excursion trains to Loughton during the summer . . . The health of the place is generally above the average, and the condition of the poor is much ameliorated by local charities, as well as by the general attention to their education, sanitary condition, and improvement. There seems, however, to be a want of energy, and an unwillingness to move from their native place, which greatly characterise the inhabitants, not only of this village, but of this part of the county generally, and which certainly impedes their advancement in the social scale. The proximity of the forest, and the pretext of procuring firewood by means of the loppings of the trees, which the inhabitants claim a right to cut during the winter months, encourage habits of idleness and dislike of settled labour, and in some cases give occasion for poaching, all of which are injurious to the morals of the poor. Enclosures, however, seem to be commencing in the neighbourhood, which will probably check these irregular and, to a certain extent, demoralising tendencies.

# AGRICULTURE

Essex agriculture in the eighteenth century was progressive and prosperous. Most of the land had long been enclosed and farmers were free to produce as much food as possible for the rapidly growing London market. Following the great agricultural pioneers, landowners and substantial farmers in Essex were experimenting freely and reporting their findings to the Board of Agriculture. Farmers with capital improved their technique, increased their output and prospered. They profited particularly from the high food prices of the Napoleonic War period.

Agricultural prosperity diminished the area of the county that remained unenclosed. The total acreages enclosed by parliamentary awards between 1770 and 1893 were approximately 30,000 acres of open-field arable and 10,000 acres of common, heaths and greens. The open-field parishes were chiefly in the north-west and along the western borders (as far south as Walthamstow). Commons and heaths are well shown on Chapman and André's Atlas of Essex, 1777. During 1750-1850 nearly all this land was enclosed either by private agreement between lords of manors and their tenants, or by Act of Parliament (Private, Local or General).

From 1815 to 1850 there were few years of prosperity. Farmers were also troubled by high poor rates, outbreaks of incendiarism and the prospect of Corn Law repeal. After 1850 prosperity returned and agricultural technique rapidly improved, but in 1875 began the long depression, caused by the import of cheap American wheat. Essex, with its reliance on wheat, suffered particularly. Established farming families failed by the hundreds. Farms were left on the landlords' hands, much land became rough pasture, rents fell sharply. By 1900 signs of recovery were few. Thrifty Scotsmen had taken farms on advantageous terms and were making a bare living. Some farmers were paying less attention to wheat and more to stock, milk-production and poultry. Others were specialising in growing seeds or fruit. In general, however, rural Essex remained in poor condition.

## *ESSEX FARMING, 1750—1850*

### 1. *Defoe on Essex Landowners, 1724*

Defoe, *Tour through Great Britain,* Vol. I.

I made it my Road to pass thro' Witham, a pleasant well situated Market-Town, in which, and in its Neighbourhood, there are as many Gentlemen of good Fortunes, and Families, as I believe can be met with in so narrow a Compass in any of the three Counties, of which I make this Circuit . . . It is observable, that in this part of the Country, there are several very considerable Estates purchas'd, and now enjoy'd by Citizens of London, Merchants, and Tradesmen, as Mr Western, an Iron Merchant, near Kelvedon; Mr Cresnor, a Wholesale Grocer, who was a little before he died, nam'd for Sheriff, at Earls Colne; Mr Olemus, a Merchant at Braintree; Mr Westcomb near Malden; Sir Thomas Webster at Copthall, near Waltham, and several others.

I mention this, to observe how the present encrease of Wealth in the City of London, spreads itself into the Country, and plants Families and Fortunes, who in another age will equal the Families of the antient Gentry, who perhaps were bought out.

### 2. *Praise for Essex Farming, 1771*

The following extract is from an article by Arthur Young.
Young, *Tour through East of England,* 1771, Vol. II, pp. 220-221.

From Manningtree to Colchester and thence to Witham, the farmers are perfectly enlightened; throughout this tract as well as the last, all the pease and beans are kept as clean by hand-hoeing, as turnips in other places, but at a much greater expence; wheat also receives the same operation, which I think is a certain mark of the farmers having extreme just ideas of husbandry; for without such, they would never arrive at so unusual a practice. Marle, called chalk here, they use, I believe at a much greater expence than any people in the kingdom; for many of them go from six to ten miles, and give from 8s. to 10s. a waggon load for it: this acting with a spirit that cannot be exceeded. Town manures at Colchester sell at 5s. a load; soot, etc, etc, are used in large quantities; and these noble exertions are not the effect of low rents, as some fondly imagine they must everywhere be; on the contrary, this whole country is let at good rents; that is, from 12s. to 25s. an acre: and various places, in which all these circumstances unite, pay 16s. or 18s. an acre round; and some 20s. Such a rent by no means frightens these sensible men; they spend great sums of money in the purchase of manures, and spare no expence in hoeing, notwithstanding that of rent. What is the consequence of this? Their rich soils so thoroughly manured, produce vast crops without damage from weeds, for their perpetual hoeing totally destroys them. The effect is answerable—from 4 to 5 quarters an acre of wheat; from 5 to 10 of barley; from 6 to 10 of oats; 5 or 6 of beans; and all other crops proportioned—with farmers worth from ten to forty thousand pounds. These shew sufficiently that the above spirited practices form what might emphatically be called *TRUE HUSBANDRY*. Those who exalt the agriculture of Flanders so high in comparison with that of Britain, have not, I imagine, viewed with attention the country in question. It is difficult to imagine common crops cultivated in greater perfection.

### 3. *Essex Farmers and Farming, 1807*

The following extracts are from Arthur Young's final survey of Essex farming. In the first extract he is quoting the Rev. J. Howlett of Dunmow. In the second he gives his own views.

Young, *General View of Agriculture in Essex,* 1807; Vol. I, pp. 65-66; Vol. II, p. 267.

The small farmer is forced to be laborious to an extreme degree; he works harder and fares harder than the common labourer; and yet with all his labour and with all his fatiguing incessant exertions, seldom can he at all improve his condition or even with any degree of regularity pay his rent and preserve his present situation. He is confined to perpetual drudgery, which is the source of profound ignorance, the parent of obstinacy and blind perseverance in old modes and old practices, however absurd and pernicious. He is in a manner shut out from that intercourse with the world, which enlarges the mind and improves and increases knowledge. His understanding and his conversation are not at all superior to those of the common labourers, if even equal to them, as the latter, by sometimes changing masters and working in different situations, extend the sphere of their observation and experience and make some little accession to their narrow stock of ideas.

With regard to the large farmers, the case is extremely different. They not merely superintend their business with the utmost care and vigilance, but, visiting the markets far and near, they mix with persons from every part of the country; the various modes and practices of agriculture in every quarter are frequently discussed and fully examined with a minuteness and liberality that would not disgrace higher assemblies. The reasons for and against any scheme are maturely weighed and if, after a due consideration of every difference of soil, situation, and circumstances, it is likely to be advantageous, no prejudice or prepossession obstructs its adoption. Nay, the more wealthy and opulent do not confine their information to their own country, but not infrequently, during the summer months, form parties and visit the neighbouring counties with the express purpose of nicely examining the various methods of cultivating their land, as well as of rearing and improving the several kinds of live stock, and resolving to bring back and reduce to practice in their own immediate business, whatever may appear to deserve it. Hence a more general diffusion of knowledge and improvement, and all that is gradually increasing from the increasing size of farms and the increasing opulence of the farmers. Hence, too, an improved education in their children and a greater taste for reading, especially of new publications on practical husbandry. All these causes contribute to heighten the character of the higher orders of our Essex farmers and render them persons of as enlarged and liberal minds as any men whatever of similar rank and property and of not superior education.

---

I made inquiry into the improvement which Agriculture in general had experienced in the country, and especially in the last twenty or thirty years.

The country about the Belchamps, Borely, Gestingthorp, Bulmer, etc. very much improved in 20 years—in hollow-draining, in the use of chalk, in converting to tillage all waste scraps of land, and in throwing many little enclosures, crowded with pollards, together in open airy fields . . .

Mr Bawtree, who remembers Southminster almost a wilderness, says that improvements in 40 years are very great and that in 20 they have been considerable.

Mr Strutt, at Terling, has paid attention to the state of Agriculture for above 50 years and is clear that it has been upon the whole gradually improving; and more still in the last five-and-twenty years . . .

Mr Majendie has some doubts whether the improvement of the husbandry of Essex, and particularly about Hedingham, has been great in 20 years. The management has always been good and, upon the whole, so much better than in many counties, that there was not an equal field for it . . .

Mr Hardy, at Bradfield, who has farmed there near forty years, is clearly of opinion that the husbandry of that neighbourhood for many miles is greatly improved ; but chiefly in the last twenty years ; broad hedge-rows are reduced, others removed ; more draining done ; tares introduced, and in general a more careful and attentive cultivation.

### 4. *Depression in Agriculture, 1825*

Rents fell in the depression after the Napoleonic Wars.
Parker Archives (D/DOp B76).

Particulars of Freehold Farms in Essex.

Buller's Farm, in the parish of Little Burstead, within 2 miles of Billericay . . . with a good brick farm house and suitable buildings and 154 acres of rich arable, meadow and pasture land, under a lease for 14 years granted in 1812, which will expire at Michaelmas, 1826, at a net rent of £300 per annum, but which owing to the times has been from time to time reduced to the rate of £200 per annum.

Lancey's Farm, in the parishes of Vange and Basildon within 30 miles from London and half a mile from a chalk wharf where corn may be shipped for London and manure procured. Farm house and suitable buildings and 155 acres of excellent corn and pasture land, under lease which will not expire until Michaelmas, 1839, at a net rent of £170 per annum, but which has been in like manner gratuitously reduced to the rent of sometimes £120 and sometimes £140.

### 5. *Hop Cultivation in Decline, 1825*

Castle Hedingham Vestry Minutes (D/P 48/8/1).

23rd of September, 1825. The Committee, to whom it was referred by the Vestry to consider the rating of the hop grounds do report :—

That the rates on hop grounds do appear to them excessive. The culture of hops in this parish is attended with expenses often amounting to £40 per acre on an article attended by great and certain expenses and most uncertain profits. Under the late valuation, when prices had reached £20 per cwt, the rent of hop grounds were stated at from £2 to £10, since which the depression has been such (even to £3 per cwt) that they have not paid their expenses. The Committee find on enquiry that such high ratings are not put on hop grounds in other parishes in the Hundred nor in Kent where the produce is in higher demand than that of Essex.

Considering that the culture of hops affords more employment during the whole year to the labourers, their wives and children than any other farming occupation, the Committee recommend that the rating of hop grounds be reduced one half.

Lewis Majendie [and 8 other signatories]

## *ESSEX ENCLOSURES*

### *1. Enclosure of Commons and Greens by Private Agreement, 1773*

The copyhold tenants of the Manors of Little Baddow Hall and Middle Mead agree with the lord of the manors.
Strutt Archives (D/DRa M74).

At a General Court Baron . . . it was agreed between Viscount Barrington Lord of the said Manors and the greater part of the tenants : that the commons and waste grounds belonging to the Manors shall be inclosed and apportioned . . .; that a part of High Common about 80 acres shall be allotted to the Lord and that other part of High Common shall be allotted for the use of the poor of Little Baddow and that the residue of High Common about 57 acres and the lower common called Wickey Green about 20 acres and all other pieces of waste ground belonging to the Manors shall be allotted unto each of the tenants in equal proportions . . . and shall be inclosed by each of them at their own expense . . . Further agreed that the Bailiff of the Manors and Richard Sorrell farmer shall be appointed to allot the commons and waste, and the tenants covenant to take up and be admitted to their several proportions at the next court by the yearly rent of 3 pence per acre and pay a fine of 1 shilling an acre on every death or alienation.

[Sixteen signatures, 4 by mark, and signature of the lord of the manors.]

### *2. Enclosure of Commons and Greens by Parliamentary Authority*

The following is the preamble from a Private Act of 1821.
Stapleford Abbots Enclosure Act, 2 Geo. IV, c.48 (E.R.O.).

Whereas there are within the Manor and Parish of Stapleford Abbots a common and waste lands containing 290 acres : and whereas the King is Lord of the Manor and as such entitled to the soil of the common and waste lands and the trees standing thereon and is also entitled to several lands and hereditaments within the parish and holden with the Manor : and whereas His Majesty and also John Rutherforth Abdy, Sir Charles Joshua Smith,

Baronet, the Reverend John Bramston Stane, Edward Russell Howe and divers other persons as owners and proprietors of the demesne lands and of estates within the Manor are respectively entitled to right of common : and whereas the common and waste lands in their present state yield very little profit and are incapable of any considerable improvement and it would be greatly to the advantage of the several persons interested therein if the same were to be divided and inclosed and specific parts thereof allotted to the several persons interested, in proportion to their several rights.

May It Therefore Please Your Majesty . . .

### 3. *A Public Road*

Hornchurch and Romford Enclosure Award, 1815 (T/M 86A).

And we the Commissioners set out and appoint the several public carriage roads and drift ways and the several private roads . . . No. 1 a public carriage road of the breadth of 40 feet (except where it passes between old enclosures) called Harrolds Wood Road beginning at the turnpike road near the gibbet on Harrolds Wood Common and continuing on a northward direction over the said common nearly in its present track to the end of the lane called Clay Pit lane leading to the village of Havering.

### 4. *Provision for Fencing*

The disproportionate cost of fencing forced many allottees to sell their plots.

Felsted Enclosure Award, 1822 (Q/RDc 21).

The several new fences hereby directed to be made by the several proprietors in their respective allotments shall consist of ditches 4½ feet wide at the top and 3 feet deep and of banks adjoining such ditches and formed of earth taken from the same; and that the banks of such fences shall be planted with white thorn layer in a proper manner and that half-hurdles or thorns shall be set on the summit of such banks and shall there remain, or if taken away or spoiled, shall be from time to time renewed during the space of 7 years next ensuing.

### 5. *Provision for Recreation*

The main 'allotment' mentioned below is Writtle Green.

Writtle and Roxwell Enclosure Award, 1871 (Q/RDc 68A).

I allot unto the parish of Writtle all those 3 pieces of land . . . containing 2a. 3r. 2p., 18p. and 3r. to be held in trust as a place for exercise and recreation for the inhabitants of the parish and neighbourhood.

## *RECOVERY AND DEPRESSION, 1850—1914*

### *1. Recovery, 1850-75*

Lord Petre's agent, F. J. Coverdale, reports on the estate.
Petre Archives (D/DP E17).

Tillingham Hall Farm. In 1847 it was let to Mr Joseph Campbell who had been a servant at Thorndon Hall. The then Lord Petre supplemented his savings by a loan to enable him to take the farm, which then comprised 336 acres and was let at a rental of £300 per annum, the tenant paying the tithe on about 100 acres (the residue being tithe free), paying also the land tax and insurance. In 1864 the rent was increased and in 1874 Mr Campbell died, having paid off all the borrowed money and leaving behind him a fortune of £12,000.

### *2. Farmers in the 1860's*

Hurnard, *The Setting Sun,* London, 1878, VI, pp. 268-9.

The farmers at an Agricultural Show
Come forth in all their territorial greatness ;
Their Cheeks are ruddy as a rosy apple ;
Their persons jolly, braced by country air,
Favoured no doubt as well by country living.
Their dress is in the very tip of fashion.
Ah ! how unlike their plodding ancestors !
Their chief ambition is to ride good horses,
Adapted doubtless for the hunting-field,
And show their tastes in various breeds of dogs.
They have the confidence and self-possession
Of gentlemen of independent fortune,
Without the easy air and the politeness
Of well-bred men who mix with well-bred men,
Their features seldom are symmetrical,
Although their persons may be well-proportioned ;
They are men of shrewdness rather than of reading,
Fond of a joke, as are true Englishmen,
And view the engines, and the implements,
The cattle, and the various animals,
With sober, thoughtful earnestness of purpose,
And a keen eye to monetary profit.
How different from their stolid forefathers
Ignorant, obstinate, and intractable,
Fond of hot potions and of long clay pipes,
With minds as narrow as their tastes were low.

### 3. *Greater Use of Machinery*

Hurnard, *The Setting Sun,* VI, pp. 265-6.

Machinery has at length fairly invaded
The last redoubt of stubborn old-worldism,
The once poetic realm of Agriculture.
The farmers formerly supinely trusted
For their advancement and prosperity
To specious laws to put down foreign corn—
Delusive laws that could not bear the strain
Of treacherous weather and deficient harvests.
Cobden and Bright at length dispelled that nonsense
By dint of argument and eloquence ;
They now with better reason trust to science,
And seek the aid of skilful enginery.
Each county has its Agricultural Show,
One of the striking features of the age,
Where implements for every farming purpose
Are brilliantly displayed to wondering eyes ;
Machines to reap and mow by stout horse-power,
And do the work of half a score of men,
Without the toil and back-ache of past ages,
Thus expediting harvest operations,
And making hay in fact while the sun shines,
Here engines worked by steam astound old men,
The stolid, bent day-labourers on the soil,
In antique coats and modern wide-awakes,
Who stand and fumble in their breeches pockets
To find the sense not found within their brains ;
Who never dreampt of any implement
Beyond the two-horse plough and ancient sickle.
In short we see a peaceful revolution
Wrought out by science and necessity . . .

### 4. *The Agricultural Depression, 1881*

The Richmond Commission received the following report from its Essex investigator.

*R.C. on Agriculture,* 1882, III, p. 435.

In June, 1880, I reported at some length on the existence of agricultural depression in this county, and I have now to add that I visited the county again in the autumn of 1881, and found that the depression was in no way mitigated, but, on the contrary, that the state of the county was worse. There is a very large number of farms in the landlords' hands, some of which are practically, though not actually, uncultivated, and others cultivated by the landlords. As seen in several parts of the county, for example between Rochford and Chelmsford, between Chelmsford and Maldon, and in the Roothings, the state of agriculture was deplorable. Some land was altogether derelict, and more was full of weeds and natural rough grasses, upon which a few cattle were picking up a bare living; farm-houses were empty or only occupied by overlookers or caretakers, who not infrequently were the very men who had failed on the farms of which they were the caretakers.

### 5. *The Depression continues, 1893*

F. J. Coverdale, Lord Petre's agent, describes the effects of the depression on an estate in South Essex.
Petre Archives (D/DP E17).

The Petre family have always been liberal landlords, and the Estate at the best of times was lowly rented. I may safely say that at my father's death the list of arrears of rent did not annually amount to £25 and that a similar state of things went on for many years afterwards, in fact pretty much up to the seventies, whereas at the present time the arrears of rent for the half year ending 25th March last amounted to nearly £1600, to say nothing of the heavy sums which have from time to time been allowed or written off as bad debts, and to percentage allowances on rentals, ranging annually for some years past from 5 to 20 per cent . . .

On the accession of William Joseph Lord Petre in 1884 the Agency was placed entirely in my hands. I at once took up the question of the lands in hand and, by sending to Scotland and advertising freely in the Scotch papers, I succeeded in letting the farms which were in hand and have altogether let farms to fourteen Scotchmen, covering an acreage of about 3840 acres, and to three Devonshire and two Northumberland men a further acreage of about 1600 acres . . .

. . . The adjoining farm, Cowbridge Grange Magna, shows even a worse state of things. It comprises 267 acres and was let from Michaelmas 1879 to Mr B. H. Perry at a rental of £306, in addition to which he paid tithe, land tax and insurance. From Michaelmas 1885 the rent was reduced to £217, and a further reduction was made from 1887, rather than let Mr Perry leave, but he became bankrupt in 1893. The landlord had to take possession from the Official Receiver in May of that year which he retained to Michaelmas last, farming it of course at a loss. It has been let from Michaelmas last to Mr Robert Hodge, a

Scotch tenant, at a rental of £210 per annum, from which the landlord has to pay tithe and land tax amounting to £20, reducing the net amount to £190. Since 1880 the amount expended by the landlord in drainage, additions to the house, new covered homestead, 4 new cottages, new cowhouse and cooling house and water supply is no less than £3750, so that the farm may be fairly said to be a dead yearly loss . . .

I will now pass to the Southern portion of the estate at East Horndon, all of which is very strong heavy land, and I am afraid, notwithstanding all the efforts of the landlord and tenant and the advantages of a Railway, which during the last few years has cut through this portion of the property, it will go absolutely out of cultivation unless some very strong measures are taken to relieve the present depression.

The tenant of East Horndon Hall, a Devonshire man and a good farmer, gave notice to quit his farm at Michaelmas next. He died recently and his death was no doubt accelerated by the anxiety of his position.

### 6. *Landlords' Incomes fall, 1894*

*R.C. on Agriculture,* 1894, Essex, pp. 51-2 (E.R.O., C.B.L.).

My estate is 21 miles from London, and the soil is of good average quality . . . I bought it in 1862 for £84,500. It has since doubled in size. The total cost comes to at least £200,000. It would now possibly bring £50,000. Before 1879 the gross rental was between £6000 and £7000, it is now £4000, with every probability of going £1000 lower unless matters soon mend . . . Before 1879, £500 per annum kept the estate up, now it requires £1500. Although the tenants undertake to keep up their premises, the landlord finding rough materials, they simply refuse to do anything. The land does not produce nearly as much as it did, through the impoverishment of the tenants. Few bullocks or sheep are seen, nothing but cows. I get no rent at all for my land, I merely get about 4% on the cost of the building, drainage and fences. From the gross rental (£4000) must be deducted between £1200 and £1500 for repairs, leaving £2500 to £2800 for net rent as against £1800 for taxes and tithe.

### 7. *Prejudice against Stockbreeding*

*R.C. on Agriculture,* 1894, Essex, p. 58 (E.R.O., C.B.L.).

Throughout a large portion of the county, stock appears to be regarded as something like a necessary evil, and corn growing the chief end of farming. Men whose opinions are so moulded are not very particular in the matter of cattle accommodation, and when visiting their farms and inspecting their buildings, I frequently noticed that the roofs and floors of the barns and granaries had been repaired and kept in fair order, when the cattle-sheds and stock-houses were much neglected.

### 8. *Combating the Depression*

*R.C. on Agriculture,* 1894, Essex, pp. 60-63 (E.R.O., C.B.L.).

From the occupier of a mixed soil farm in Braintree district . . . 'if we did not use our brains in getting catch crops, we should soon be swamped entirely . . .' Another reply from Braintree states . . . 'anything to make a little money to help the other crops in value' . . .

In the Ongar, Chelmsford, Maldon and Braintree districts cows in milk or in calf were more numerous in 1892 than in 1882 by 52 per cent. This of course is because of the extension of dairy farming for London . . .

Since 1880 the extent to which poultry farming has increased was described as being well worthy of notice. The evidence I received showed that not only were poultry kept in larger numbers, but more attention is paid to breeding and crossing the best strains. Fattening for London market is now conducted on improved principles, and a large quantity of second-rate corn is consumed in this way.

### 9. *The Scottish Settlers*

*R.C. on Agriculture,* 1894, Essex, p. 43 (E.R.O., C.B.L.).

The oldest Scottish settler that I met in Essex told me he came from Scotland in 1882, but he was not the first Scotchman to take land so far south. So far as his knowledge and recollection went, the Scotch settlement in Essex was founded in the autumn of 1880 by a Wigtownshire farmer who died recently. The incident of his hiring land so far from home was purely accidental. He happened to be visiting Essex, and liking the country and thinking well of the prospects, he left Scotland. By several English gentlemen the highest possible character was given to the few Scotch farmers who between 1880 and 1883 took up their abode on Essex soil. They appear to have been men of energy, intelligence, and, what is equally to the point, substance . . .

The satisfactory results which followed the letting of Essex farms to Scotchmen being generally admitted, and the difficulty of finding local tenants for farms, either surrendered by Essex men or in the hands of the proprietor, being keenly felt, estate agents about the year 1883 began to advertise Essex farms in the leading Scotch papers. Their advertisements attracted the attention of one particular class of Scotch farmer—the dairymen in Renfrew, Ayrshire, and Wigtown. At the time I am writing about, so keen had competition for Ayrshire land become that rents had assumed almost prohibitive dimensions. Moreover, the restrictive clauses in Scottish leases, clauses which forbade tenants to sell hay and straw, but compelled them to farm on certain hard-and-fast rotations, had begun to stink in the nostrils of Ayrshire farmers. Taking all these things into account, the advertisements of "Essex farms within 25 miles of London, at low rents and with freedom of cultivation", came at an opportune moment, and from the western counties a migration to Essex at once commenced.

### *10. Partial Recovery, 1913*

Hall, *A Pilgrimage of British Farming,* London, 1913, pp. 68-69.

It is, indeed, through their high proportion of saleable crops that the Essex farmers are in a thriving condition again; their farming has lost some of its old-time polish, the land is cheaply worked and is not so clean as formerly, but the rents in the district have not dropped much below the 20/- an acre level and are tending to rise with the competition which now exists for vacant farms . . . Essex has many varied forms of agriculture to show, as for example the intensive dairying that prevails in the south-east; but wherever we went we saw no longer the derelict Essex which was once the type example of ruined English agriculture; instead, the countryside seemed to smile with a quiet unexcited prosperity—it was providing bread and butter, at all events, for its occupiers.

# THE FARM LABOURER

Essex agricultural workers received about six or seven shillings a week in 1750. Their wives and children harvested, gleaned and spun wool. In normal years when prices were low, a family could buy enough food. Housing and clothing were poor. After 1750 prices rose, while earnings from spinning declined and finally ceased altogether. During the Napoleonic Wars prices so far outstripped wages that Essex Vestries were obliged to pay 'Speenhamland' allowances to labourers with large families.

The depression of 1815 brought unemployment and low wages. The new Poor Law of 1834 ended 'Speenhamland' allowances. Labourers were alienated by the widening social cleavage between the farmers and themselves. Unable to find alternative work or to improve wages by legitimate methods, they resorted to machine-breaking and incendiarism. After 1850 they benefited a little from agricultural recovery and the increase in charitable provision, but in 1872 they gave strong support to Joseph Arch's Labourers' Union and with its help increased their wages considerably. During the depression after 1875 so many of them migrated from Essex farms that those who remained were able to retain their wage increases even amid falling prices. From the Reform Act of 1884 and the institution of Parish Councils in 1894 the labourers derived some advantage, though less than they had hoped. In general, by 1900 they enjoyed more comfort and greater independence than their grandfathers had done.

## *THE STANDARD OF LIVING*

### *1. Cost of Living in Essex, 1751*

The following extracts from Chelmsford workhouse accounts indicate the contemporary cost of living for the poorer classes.

Chelmsford Overseers' Accounts (D/P 94/12/7).

| | £ s. d. |
|---|---|
| 5 lbs. of soap, 2s. 6d. Starch and blue, 4½d. | 0. 2. 10½ |
| Peck of oatmeal, 1s. 2d. 2 sacks of flour, £2 | 2. 1. 2 |
| 9 stone 3 lbs. of beef at 22d. per stone | 0. 17. 2 |

| | £ | s. | d. |
|---|---|---|---|
| An ox head, 1s. 6d. 1 bushel of peas, 4s. | 0 | 5 | 6 |
| 4 lbs. suet, 1s. 2 lbs. butter, 1s. ¼ thread, 8d. | 0 | 2 | 8 |
| 3 pints of yeast, 6d. 10 bushels malt, £1. 10s. 0d. | 1 | 10 | 6 |
| 1 lb. of ginger, 1s. 4 lbs. of hops, 4s. | 0 | 5 | 0 |
| 2 lbs. of butter, 1s. 2 lbs. of sugar, 8d. | 0 | 1 | 8 |
| A leg of pork at 3d. a lb. | 0 | 2 | 3 |
| A pair of leather breeches for Henry Saval | 0 | 4 | 6 |
| Charles Parr, a pr. shoes, 4s. Alice Jeffery, Do., 2s. 10d. | 0 | 6 | 10 |
| 205 gallons of small beer at 1½d. per gallon | 1 | 5 | 7½ |
| Dentry's child, a pr. of shoes, 11d. Oatmeal, 1s. 2d. | 0 | 2 | 1 |
| 2 lbs. butter, 1s. 2 lbs. sugar, 8d. ¼ lb. pepper, 5d. | 0 | 2 | 1 |
| 1 dozen chamber pots, 2s. Six plates, 6d. | 0 | 2 | 6 |
| 1 lb. of tobacco, 1s. 3 lbs. of candles, 1s. 5d. | 0 | 2 | 5 |
| Dames Herbert, Jeffery, Bale, a shift each at 3s. a shift | 0 | 9 | 0 |
| Wood, a shirt | 0 | 3 | 0 |
| 4 boys' shirts and 5 girls' shifts at 2s. each | 0 | 18 | 0 |
| 2 pair of sheets and making, 10s. 6d. Binding, 1s. 2d. | 0 | 11 | 8 |
| 1½ dozen knives | 0 | 4 | 6 |
| Mary Reynolds, a pair of pattens | 0 | 1 | 0 |
| Bale, a mob | 0 | 0 | 10 |
| Buttock of beef, 4 stone at 22d. per stone | 0 | 7 | 4 |
| 1 peck of salt, 1s. 4d. A quart of vinegar, 3d. | 0 | 1 | 7 |
| 54 mackerel at 1d. per piece | 0 | 4 | 6 |
| A frock, waistcoat and breeches to Thos. Chiswick, put to service | 0 | 9 | 0 |
| 25 lbs. of cheese | 0 | 5 | 0 |
| Pair of breeches for Church | 0 | 6 | 0 |
| 1¾ chaldron of coals and carriage | 2 | 14 | 3 |
| 5 lbs. of mutton for the sick | 0 | 1 | 3 |
| 8 pans, 4d. each, 2s. 8d. 12 mugs at 1d. each, 1s. | 0 | 3 | 8 |
| 35½ lbs. of bacon at 3d. per lb. | 0 | 8 | 10 |
| Making 2 wash tubs, 2s. One hoop, 3d. | 0 | 2 | 3 |
| 5 bushels of beans at 8d. per bushel | 0 | 3 | 4 |
| 6 yards of drugget and 6 yards of body lining | 0 | 7 | 0 |
| 2 mops, 1s. 4d. A brush, 4d. | 0 | 1 | 8 |
| 2 stocks, 8d. 3 pr. stockings, 3s. 6d. | 0 | 4 | 2 |
| 3 handkerchiefs, 2s. 6d. 3 caps, 1s. 4d. | 0 | 3 | 10 |
| Stokes, a petticoat | 0 | 3 | 4 |
| 12 earthen dishes | 0 | 1 | 0 |
| Jug, 8d. Six wooden dishes, 1s. 24 spoons, 1s. | 0 | 2 | 8 |
| 1 lb. of yarn, 2s. 4d. 1 lb. of rushlights, 6d. | 0 | 2 | 10 |
| 2 pints of beer for Dame Fitch | 0 | 0 | 3 |
| A drugget gown for Sarah Wyles | 0 | 7 | 0 |

## 2. *Wages in the Hedinghams, 1767*

Young, *Six Weeks' Tour*, 1767, p. 62.

Labour

In winter, 1s. a day and small beer.
In haytime, 1s. and beer and a dinner.
In harvest, 2s. and beer.
Reaping, 4s. an acre.
Mowing corn, 1s. 3d. and 1s. 4d.; mowing grass, 1s. 6d.

## 3. *Farm Wages, 1796-7*

During the years to which the following extracts from a Latchingdon farmer's accounts refer, wages were slowly rising.

Parker Archives (D/DOp E15).

| | | | £ s. d. |
|---|---|---|---|
| 1796 | | | |
| Oct. | 10 | One day's work, man to Burnham | 2.0 |
| Nov. | 5 | Beer for Mr Trussell's men | 2.8 |
| | 12 | John Pearman, 2 days | 3.0 |
| | | James and Harry [one week's wages] | 1. 4.0 |
| | 26 | Carters from Woodham, 15 days' beer and eating | 7.6 |
| Dec. | 31 | Dedman, 1 quarter's wages | 9. 5.0 |
| 1797 | | | |
| Jan. | 21 | Samson, hedging and ditching 36 rod | 1.18.6 |
| Feb. | 18 | Wright, stubbing bank, 47½ rod at 1s. 2d. | 2.15.5 |
| | | Threshing 56 qrs., 6 bushels of oats at 1s. 3d. | 3.11.0 |
| | 25 | Boy driving plough | 5.0 |
| Mar. | 21 | Samson, waterfurrowing in 29 acres | 8.9 |
| | | Robert, 1 day sawing tops pollards | 1.9 |
| May | 20 | Strangers, hoeing 5 acres of wheat at 3s. 6d. | 17.6 |
| | 29 | Beer for washing sheep | 2.0 |
| | | Bottle of gin | 2.0 |
| July | 1 | Pavely and Burton, 5 days at hay | 1. 0.0 |
| | | Burton's boy, 6 days [at hay] | 5.0 |
| | 13 | Bottle of gin | 2.2 |
| | 22 | 4 gallons of beer from Lion | 5.4 |
| | 29 | Wright, mowing 7 acres of clover | 14.0 |
| | | Richardson and Pavely, cleaning farmyard pond | 2.12.6 |
| Aug. | 5 | Side of mutton for raising dinner | 12.0 |
| | 8 | 14 acres of wheat, 6 men 1 week at 10s. per acre | 7.0.0 |
| | | Money for gloves | 6.0 |
| Sep. | 29 | Supper for harvestmen | 8.0 |

### 4. *A Harvest Agreement, 1847*

Paglesham Harvest Contract (D/DU 49/1).

July 27th 1847. Poole's company of nine men, to cut, gather and cart, stack and stow in barn as herewith stated.

| Acres | |
|---|---|
| 17 | Wheat, Ankles Hill, to reap, bind in small sheaves, trave and cart. |
| 12 | Wheat, to reap, bind, trave and cart. |
| 3 | Parsonage, to reap, bind, trave and cart. |
| 7 | Wheat, Lunt's, to reap, bind, trave and cart. |
| 10 | Barley, Wool Packs, to mow, gather, cart and due rake. |
| 5 | Grove Field, beans, to cut with hooks, tie, trave and cart. |
| 2 | Wheat, Cobler's Pightle, to reap, bind, trave and cart. |
| 2 | Weld's, wheat, to reap, bind, trave and cart. |
| 8 | Acres, granary, barley, to gather, cart, and due rake. |
| 10 | Oats . . . to gather, clean and cart. |
| 9 | Weld's, wheat, to cart. |
| 12 | Lunt's, wheat 8 and 4 to cart. |
| 11 | Beans, Ballards Gore, to cart. |
| 108 | |

And to have three days' work, each man at 5/- per day, to do anything I please, from 4 o'clock the morning till 9 o'clock at night.

For the sum of fifty four pounds, and to have 5 quarts of beer each man per day, when fine weather and at work, for the first fortnight and after that 4 quarts per day each man. You also engage with me Thomas Stebbing to do all the aforesaid harvest work in a good, workmanlike manner, pick the corn up clean, cut the stubble close (not higher than 8 inches), make small sheaves, bind them tight, set the tucks inwards and keep the sheaves set up till the field is finished cutting, but not to bind or cut when wet. And, when at cart, you are all to help clean and bate the horses well. And each man shall forfeit, for every day he loses through drinking or getting drunk, six shillings per day and 3/- for half a day so lost. And should any man fall ill and obliged to lose time, another man will be put in his place during his illness.

As witness our hands this 27th day of July, 1847,

Thomas Stebbing, Master, John Pool, Foreman [and 8 others].

## 5. *Household Goods*

The following inventories record the goods belonging to recipients of poor relief. *Original spelling retained.*
Wickham Bishops Overseers' Miscellaneous Papers (D/P 236/18).

[Wickham Bishops. Not dated] An Acount of Coote's goods

Six chairs
2 Brass Boilers
eaight puter plats
a chest of drawers
2 beds
one ovel table
on Square table
a kneading trough
a clock

a fender
a warming pan
a weel and real
2 flat irons
a pair tongs and poker
2 candle sticks
a trunk
a cubard
a tramel

a pair of bellowes a gridgion a frying pan

Great Bentley Overseers' Miscellaneous Papers (D/P 171/18).

November the 16, 1724 An acount of Elizabeth Collers Goods

2 Scilletes
on Basonladel
on worming pan
6 Trenchers
on Iron porridg pott
on Gridg Iron
a pair of Tongs
6 puter plates and Dishes
on weele
on rele

on Sive
2 Tables
a Driping pan
a Box
a Cubard
a Chest
on Beed and ye furnituer
on Boyler
a Neading trofe
2 chairs

and other Implyments . . .

| | |
|---|---|
| The 3 plats and dishes are sould for | 00 . 04 . 08 |
| More for a table | 00 . 04 . 00 |

Colne Engaine Overseers' Accounts (D/P 193/12/2).

Coln Engain, 6th day of April, 1795
An Inventory of the Goods and Chattles of Ann Bacon at the Workhouse taken this day.

9 Chairs
1 skep-baskitt
1 Hutch
1 Cradle
1 Trunk
1 Bedstead
1 Flock Bed
4 sheets

2 bolsters
2 pillows
1 Coverlid
1 Cubboard
2 Wheels
1 Reel
1 Kneadingtrough
1 pail

1 pr of Bellows
1 pr Tongs
2 Wood$^{n}$ Bottles
2 Glass D$^{o}$
1 Wash Keeler
1 Wash Stool
2 Tables
1 Tin Kettle

a Linnen dryer

## 6. *The Wages of Domestic Service, 1763, 1791*

Audley End Archives (D/DBy A14).

| | 1763 | 1791 |
|---|---|---|
| | £ s. d. | £ s. d. |
| House Steward and Butler (Butler, 1763) | 20. 0.0 | 63. 0.0 |
| Game Keeper | | 59. 4.0 |
| Cook | 12. 0.0 | 50. 0.0 |
| Bailiff | | 50. 0.0 |
| Valet | | 30. 0.0 |
| Groom of Chambers | | 30. 0.0 |
| Coachman | 21. 0.0 | 26. 5.0 |
| House Keeper | 16. 0.0 | 25. 0.0 |
| Kitchen Gardener | | 25. 0.0 |
| Porter | | 21. 0.0 |
| Lady's Footman (Upper Footman, 1763) | 10. 0.0 | 18. 0.0 |
| 2nd Coachman (Upper Postillion, 1763) | 15. 0.0 | 16.16.0 |
| Groom | 15. 0.0 | 16. 0.0 |
| Under Butler | 10. 0.0 | 16. 0.0 |
| Lord's Footman (Upper Footman, 1763) | 10. 0.0 | 12. 7.0 |
| Lady's Woman | 8. 0.0 | 12. 0.0 |
| 1st Laundry Maid | | 10.10.0 |
| Kitchen Maid | | 10. 0.0 |
| Housemaid (Upper) | 7. 0.0 | 9. 9.0 |
| Do. | | 9. 9.0 |
| 2nd Laundry Maid | | 9. 9.0 |
| Postillion | 7. 0.0 | 9. 9.0 |
| Houseboy | 6. 0.0 | 9. 9.0 |
| Dairy Maid | | 9. 0.0 |
| House Maid | 5. 0.0 | 8. 8.0 |
| Pantry Boy | | 8. 8.0 |
| House Maid | 3. 0.0 | 7. 0.0 |
| Stillroom Maid | 3.16.0 | 7. 0.0 |

# *NINETEENTH CENTURY CHANGES*

## 1. *The Decline of Paternalism*

The following is an extract from an article by the chief agricultural correspondent of the *Chelmsford Gazette*.

*Chelmsford Gazette*, Oct. 4, 1822 (E.R.O.).

We have heard very lately of several farmers who have come to the good resolution of boarding every labouring man whom they shall in future have occasion to employ. Such resolutions have our hearty prayers for their universal success; they look like the spirit, which was once diffused among the Essex farmers, being again revived, when each labourer as well as servant was regarded as one of the farmer's own family, for whose good conduct and appearance the master was in some degree accountable and for whose success in life, if he conducted himself properly, he was never entirely indifferent. In those days a half-starved set of labourers and masters of cottages and of families, who are themselves just prematurely escaped out of leading-strings, were things almost unknown and undreaded. For the farmers' good counsel could then be the means of preventing the appearance of many such miserable subjects of regret. With modern times the labourer went to live by himself in the best way that chance directed, with no one to advise or control, with no regular master; it cannot create surprise that, thus situated, many of the peasantry of this county have, for years past, reaped little but ill-advised speculations—miserable reward.

### 2. *A Rural Friendly Society, 1826*

The following are extracts from the draft rules of a society set up by local gentlemen in 1826.

Quarter Sessions, Rules, Aldham Friendly Society (Q/RSf 5).

1. The intent and design of this Society is to promote and establish Union, friendship, and mutual assistance among the members of it and to promote a comfortable subsistence in time of sickness and old age.

2. Every person who shall become a member shall be between the age of fourteen and forty years, and in perfect health.

4. Each member shall pay one shilling for his entrance, and one shilling and sixpence on the last Saturday evening in every month to the Steward of each parish, who shall in the course of the day deliver the same to some honorary member residing in the parish, who shall on the Monday morning following deliver the same to the Treasurer.

5. No member shall receive any money from the stock of this Society till he hath paid to the same one whole year, after which time, if any member shall become sick, lame, or blind (except by quarrelling, drunkenness, or debauchery, or any other disorderly practice) whereby he is rendered incapable of working, he shall be paid seven shillings per week from the Society during his indisposition. If any person breaks a limb, as a leg or arm (except by quarrelling, drunkenness, or other disorderly practice), he shall

receive two pounds from the Society, over and above his weekly allowance, towards paying a surgeon.

9. No member shall receive a pension from this Society in consequence of old age, until he has passed his sixty fifth year. He shall then receive five shillings per week for the remainder of his life if the funds of the Society are sufficiently large.

12. If any member has contributed to the Club six years without having received any thing from it, he shall, provided he does not marry till he has passed his twenty eighth year, receive five pounds from the funds of the Society.

13. When any member dies after he has been in and contributed to the Society for the space of five years, forty shillings shall be paid from the funds for his funeral charges and three pounds to his widow and, in case of no widow, to his children if he has any. Every member who has subscribed to this Society five years shall on the death of his wife receive forty shillings.

19. This Society shall not be dissolved or broken up so long as any three members thereof shall stand and abide by these articles.

21. It is requested that the members of the Club shall meet together at the Church in Aldham every Whit Monday at eleven o'clock to hear Divine Service. They shall afterwards dine together at one o'clock, alternately every year at the Queen's Head and Coopers' Arms, Ford Street; the other members in each district under their respective stewards at such places as the majority of the members shall think fit. Each member shall pay one shilling extra towards the expense of the dinner before he enters the room. The rest of the expence shall be paid from the Society's funds. Each man shall be allowed one quart of ale and no more.

### 3. *Allotments for Labourers, 1833*

*Essex Mercury*, Sept. 10, 1833 (E.R.O.).

In the parishes of Saffron Walden, Littlebury, and Wendon, the number of allotments has now extended to 255, by which about 1000 individuals are benefitted, taking, what is admitted to be a fair average, about four to each holding. The system, which originated in these parishes in the year 1829 with Lord Braybrooke and has been since promoted with great zeal by his lordship and several benevolent individuals, has been watched over with attention. Their opinion is that, if managed with common discretion, it cannot fail of producing great and lasting advantage to the parties interested. Among the benefits incidentally resulting from the allotments, it may be noticed that five sessions have been held consecutively in Saffron Walden, including the eventful winter of 1830, without a single prisoner; the rents are punctually paid; the numerous tenants conduct themselves with propriety, and lately a clothing bank has been established under the patronage of Lord and Lady Braybrooke, to which there are already nearly 300 contributors.

### 4. *The Labourers' Diet, 1834*

In 1834 parish officers were asked whether labourers could live on their wages.
*Report of Poor Law Commission,* 1834, App. B.1.

Great Baddow. Yes; on the best bread, some cheese, vegetables, bacon.

Little Bardfield. A family with four children could not subsist on their Earnings without assistance.

Bocking. Bread chiefly and potatoes.

Bulmer. They could, on flour, a little pork, and potatoes.

Clavering. They cannot subsist.

Great Coggeshall. Yes and on wholesome food, if always employed.

Castle Hedingham. They may subsist; principally on bread.

Kelvedon. They could not subsist on these earnings, buying clothes and paying rent.

Lawford. They can; and on the best wheaten bread.

Rochford. They do subsist, principally on bread, potatoes, tea, milk, occasionally a little meat and beer.

Stansted. When house-rent, firing, clothing, and other necessaries are taken into account, it may be decidedly said that the family cannot without the strictest economy, subsist on these earnings, unless they debarred themselves from wheaten bread, and potatoes were generally their sustenance.

Stebbing. Yes, on bread and potatoes.

Thaxted. Yes, provided flour does not exceed 8s 6d per bushel, on bread and potatoes, with an occasional piece of meat or cheese. A great deal depends on the management of the wife . . . many women, for want of industrious habits, instead of baking the bread themselves, prefer buying it of the baker.

Thorpe. They could only procure bread and coarse tea.

Great Waltham. They could not subsist on these earnings (as they generally live on bread, cheese, some butter, some tea and sugar, with a very little pork or meat) without parish relief.

Wickham Bishops. They cannot subsist with four children without relief.

## 5. *Rural Housing, 1850*

The following report is by a journalist of the *Morning Chronicle,* quoted by the *Essex Standard.*

*Essex Standard,* Jan. 18, 1850 (C.B.L.).

Along the whole line of country from Castle Hedingham to Clavering there is an almost continuous succession of bad cottages. Among the worst of these might be mentioned those in the neighbourhood of Sible Hedingham, Wethersfield, Bardfield, Wicken and Clavering. Great numbers of these cottages are situated in low and damp situations, and their heavy and grass covered thatches appear as if they had almost crushed the buildings down into the earth. Little or no light can ever find its way into the wretched, little windows, many of which are more than half stopped up with rags and pieces of paper. In point of fact there are many of them which, but for the possession of a chimney, would be nothing superior to many of the most wretched cabins which I have witnessed in Tipperary and many other parts of Ireland. At Manningtree also there are a considerable number of wretched one-room cottages, and those which are larger are generally tenanted by as many families as there are rooms.

## 6. *A Witham Labourer looks back*

Rider Haggard records the reminiscences of an Essex labourer.

Haggard, *Rural England,* 1906, Vol. I, pp. 458-9.

Not far from Blunt's Hall I saw an old labourer named John Lapwood, whose life experience, which I verified by enquiry, is worth preserving. For half a century or more he worked on the Post Hall and Oliver Farms in Witham, and now, by the help of some kind friends, was spending his last days in a little cottage, where he lived with his wife . . . He told me that in his young days wages for horsemen used to be down to 9s. a week, and for daymen to 8s., when the weather allowed them to be earned. During the Crimean War, bread cost him a shilling a loaf, and other food a proportionate price. He stated that for months at a time he had existed upon nothing but a diet of bread and onions, washed down, when he was lucky, with a little small-beer. These onions he ate until they took the skin off the roof of his mouth, blistering it to whiteness, after which he was obliged to soak them in salt to draw " the virtue " out of them. They had no tea, but his wife imitated the appearance of that beverage by soaking a burnt crust of bread in boiling water. On this diet he became so feeble that the reek of the muck which it was his duty to turn, made him sick and faint; and often, he said, he would walk home at night from the patch of ground where he grew his onions and some other vegetables, with swimming head and uncertain feet. I asked if his children of whom there were eight, lived on onions also. He answered no; they had generally a little cheese and butter in the house, but he could not put it into his own stomach when they were hungry and cried for bread. "Things is better now", he added.

Well, things are better now; indeed, it is scarcely too much to say that, in many cases today, the labourer has more than his share of the rather plumless agricultural cake. But with such a record behind him, knowing what his fathers suffered, is it wonderful that he should strive to drive home the nail of opportunity and sometimes to take advantage of the farmers who in the past too often were so merciless?

Let us try to understand his case and be just. Think, for instance, of this poor man Lapwood, whose condition was but that of ten thousand others, day by day forcing his hated food into a blistered mouth, starving that his children might be full. Think of him with his 9s. a week and ten souls to feed, house, and clothe, while bread stood at a shilling a loaf. Remember, too, that from this lot there was no escape; that labour was in overflowing supply; and that to lift his voice against an employer, however tyrannous, meant instant dismissal and the hell of a poor-house—it was little better in those days—or the roadside ditch to lie in. Is it strange that, remembering these things, he—or rather his sons—should wax fat and kick, that they should be haunted also by the fear that the evil might return upon them, and bear in their hearts resentment, cloaked but very real, against those classes at whose hands they received that evil of which no subsequent kindness can obliterate the memory? With the agricultural labourer, as I believe, this resentment against past suffering, at any rate as yet, is deeper than gratitude for present benefits.

## *FARM LABOURERS' MOVEMENTS*

### *1. A Labourers' Strike, 1800*

*Ipswich Journal,* June 14, 1800 (C.B.L.).

Last night were committed to our gaol, by the Rev. H. B. Dudley, Clerk, Thomas Crisp and Joseph Perry, charged on oath with tumultuously assembling on Wednesday last, in the parish of Steeple, with various other persons, who have absconded, and forcing the workmen of several farmers to join them, in order to raise a body of men with a view forcibly to prevent any work being done in Dengey Hundred, till their wages were raised or provisions lowered. Several of their accomplices were committed to the House of Correction by the same Magistrate, to be admitted as evidence against the ringleaders.

### 2. *Action against the 'Swing' Riots, 1830*

Quarter Sessions Order Book, Michaelmas 1831 (Q/SO 32).

Constables' Staves. Thomas Warren. £2.2.0.

It is ordered by this Court that the Treasurer of the Eastern Division of this County do pay to Thomas Warren the sum of two pounds two shillings for painting and numbering constables' staves for the parishes of Wickham Bishops and Great Totham in the said County, ordered respectively by Peter Wright and Oliver Hering Esquires, two of His Majesty's Justices of the Peace, as by bills now produced to and allowed by this Court . . .

### 3. *Rules of Tendring Agricultural Labourers' Union, 1836*

Tufnell, *Address to Agricultural Labourers* (C.B.L.).

1. Every person desirous of becoming a member of this Union shall pay two shillings and sixpence entrance money; and from the second day of July, 1836, one shilling per month to be reckoned from that day, etc, etc.

2. No able-bodied labourer, who is a member of this Union, shall work for less than two shillings per day, or twelve shillings per week, with beer; and if beer be not found him by his master, then to have in addition to two shillings a day, or twelve shillings a week, three half-pence in the shilling, or eighteen pence per week; such wages to be considered as the fixed scale when flour is two shillings and twopence per peck; and to rise and fall with the price of flour, according to the above scale; and any able-bodied member of this Union who shall refuse to work at a less rate of wages than the above and who shall leave his work in consequence, shall be allowed from the funds of this Union one shilling per day . . .

4. No member of this Union shall work or assist to work a thrashing machine; nor shall he be allowed to work for any master or on any farm, where any thrashing machine is used. Nor shall any member of this Union work for any master who employs any man or men who are not members of the same; except such men were employed previous to the first day of April last, in which case the members of the Union may use their own discretion.

### 4. *Incendiarism at Ardleigh, 1844*

*Suffolk Chronicle,* Feb. 3, 1844 (C.B.L.).

The spirit of incendiarism has manifested itself in this neighbourhood in a manner almost unexampled. On Monday night, no less than three fires were burning within sight of each other, the distance apart being less than two miles. The first broke out at a quarter past ten upon a farm situated on Bromley Heath, in the occupation of Mr J. Vince. The property destroyed consists of two stacks of wheat, one of barley, and a large barn recently erected and partly filled with oats. The second occurred in Badley Hall in the parish of Ardleigh . . . While the above was still raging, flames were discovered proceeding from a barn about a mile off, belonging to Mr David Cooper, of Ardleigh Bounds . . . Thus, in the short space of one hour, were three fires burning, the heavens for miles round were lighted up, awaking people from their sleep, and causing indescribable anxiety to the neighbouring farmers . . . A considerable number of labourers witnessed the fires, but we regret to say that, with few exceptions, their conduct was most heartless and disgraceful; many of them, instead of rendering assistance, frequently endeavoured to obstruct the firemen and openly exulted in the fearful progress of the flames.

### 5. *Joseph Arch in Essex, 1872*

Joseph Arch and a South Ockendon labourer addressed a meeting near Wethersfield in 1872.
*Chelmsford Chronicle,* Aug. 2, 1872.

Our readers will be interested to know what manner of men such phenomena as the labourer orators are. Both, then, had the general appearance of labourers, in truth and in deed, but labourers of the best sort. Perhaps the reader will understand what we mean when we say that they looked like a couple of farming foremen got up to take the 'missus' on a shopping expedition on a Saturday night. Arch's dress in particular was strongly suggestive of such a mission. He wore a black, felt billycock hat, rough dark coat and vest, and 'corduroys'. Redsell, who spoke first, has a ruddy, intelligent countenance, with hard lines in it, standing out like so many iron bands . . . Redsell spoke for about twenty minutes, Arch for about an hour, and very well they acquitted themselves. In each case the thought was sustained and well worked out, the language terse and vigorous, the illustrations homely and full of point, and the delivery lusty and well modulated. Both men quoted somewhat largely from Scripture and now and then made use of a phrase leading to the belief that at some time or other they had preached in village pulpits.

### 6. *Criticism of the Union*

The following is an extract from the speech of Col. Brise, M.P., to the Braintree Agricultural Society.
*Essex Standard,* Nov. 22, 1872.

There were some of the objects of the union which he approved. The union wished to better the condition of the agricultural labourer—so did he ; the union wished to abolish the system of privileges—so did he ; the union wished to regulate the supply of labour throughout the country—so did he. But he disagreed with the union on other points, viz. the method they adopted, which was to engender a bad feeling between master and servant. A man could not serve two masters. And he protested against the indiscriminate abuse levelled at all employers of labour and all who happened to be placed in a different position from those who agitated this question. Not only so, but he also protested against the revolutionary principles which were advocated by some, and by some only, of the delegates of the Labourers' Union.

### 7. *'The Rural Exodus'*

With the assistance of their Union, many Essex labourers found better paid employment in the North of England. One group of them, who had joined the Liverpool police, sent back the following account of their new life.
*Halstead Times,* June 22, 1872.

Sir, Liverpool, June 15, 1872.

We now take the Pleasure of thanking you for your Trouble you are takeing for us. Three of us revive at 3 o'clock, and 3 at seven o'clock. We had a good round the station and then we had the beef we should not have at home. Then see the Magor and he sent a man round the streets to show us about. on Tuesday we were swareing in as constables, and 2 suits of good clothes, and then the drill came. we can do that better than hopping over clods all day. we get a lb of beef every day and a good bed to lie upon. we had a grand set-out on Friaday. there were six or seven hundred policemen met together and a fine band play at the march, which we should not have seen there, and we hope all that goe away may prosper as we believe we shall, as we seem to like it, so we are yours truly, *POLICEMEN*

### 8. *The Labourers' Interest in Politics*

The Member for Saffron Walden speaks in Parliament.
*People's News,* April 29, 1887 (T/P 68/38).

Mr Gardner said his object was to give rural voters the opportunity of hearing both sides of the question at Parliamentary elections. There were villages, hamlets, and out-of-the-way places, where the greatest number of rural electors resided, and no place where the people could meet. In his own division, there were 80 villages, and in only five of them a place where a meeting could be held. The majority of his constituents were agricultural labourers, not having more than 12s. a week, and he cited a case in which one of them had walked seven or eight miles after a hard day's work to attend a political meeting. It was a great hardship that rural voters should be put to so much inconvenience when schoolrooms receiving a parliamentary grant were standing empty.

### 9. *The Smallholdings Movement*

Wilkin, *The Tiptree Small Holdings*, 1908 (E.R.O.).

The start for Allotments and Small Holdings began at the very bottom. In 1870 great excitement prevailed amongst the labourers as to the improvement of their condition and, owing to the action of the Agricultural Labourers' Union, a strong demand was presented to the employers that the men should have a small share of the land to cultivate for themselves. To this demand some of the employers cheerfully agreed, and that concession had such a good effect in pacifying the men that the majority of them settled down quietly to their old work with a new interest in life. Continuing their usual employment and living upon their wages, year by year they accumulated capital from the proceeds of the new land. The crops were good, the expenses small, and the men worked with newborn vigour, early and late—often during part of meal times—occasionally getting a day off by the goodwill of their employers. In three or four years a few had saved as much as £100 each, some more than that, and were so inspired with confidence in their new venture that they relinquished their work for wages and hired ten or twenty acres of land, one or two of them went so far as to hire little farms . . . The principal pioneer in this work was Mr John Parish, who was engaged by the writer as working foreman in the new seed-growing industry, which he was then introducing to the district . . . They had moreover a Cooperative Society of their own founding, which was a bond of union and encouragement. It now numbers something like a thousand members and turns over nearly £20,000 per annum . . . There would not have been many Small Holdings in this favoured spot, but for the happy circumstances that seed-growing had long been instituted at Coggeshall and Kelvedon, and therefore some seed merchants lived near by, who gave out contracts to small holders, when they found the men were competent to carry out the difficult work which it involved.

# TRANSPORT

Under Tudor legislation each parish was still in 1750 responsible for the upkeep of its roads and was liable to be fined by Quarter Sessions for their neglect. Parishioners were obliged to work on the roads in person under the supervision of unpaid Surveyors of the Highways, chosen by the Vestry. Increasingly, however, Essex Vestries had accepted money in place of labour service and had used the resulting income to employ paid road workers.

Essex roads, though better than many, could not have carried the increasing load of corn waggons, stage-coaches and other vehicles, if long stretches of main highway had not been managed by Turnpike Trusts and repaired from the proceeds of toll-gates. By the early nineteenth century Essex turnpike roads were in good repute, though cross-country roads remained poor under parish control. Meanwhile the continued improvement of Essex rivers facilitated and cheapened the carriage of agricultural produce to London and the import of coal from North-East England. After 1840 railways spread through Essex, firstly the two main lines to Ipswich and Cambridge, and later branch lines to most parts of the county.

## *THE PARISH AS HIGHWAY AUTHORITY*

### *1. Experiment in Highway Management, 1738*

Many Essex Vestries found it more effective to employ paid workers on the roads than to rely upon the obligatory labour of the parishioners.

Lambourne Vestry Minutes (D/P 181/8/2).

We, the parishioners of Lambourne, met at our Vestry this day, do order and agree as hereafter followeth . . .

Whereas for several years last past, besides the duty of teams and labourers enjoined by Act of Parliament, we have been obliged to raise large paid rates for the support [of] our highways ; yet still our roads are in a bad condition and the parish is in danger of being indicted for them; we therefore now voluntarily and unanimously agree for this present year, instead of all duties, to levy, by an equal paid rate on the land holders and inhabitants subject to do duty in the road, such a sum as shall be deemed sufficient; that every one that pays to this rate shall be allowed to earn, at the rates which the Surveyors shall affix, for carting and labouring in the highways, provided they work at the times and places the Surveyors shall appoint, of which they shall give notice the Sunday before; and we do allow the Surveyors of the Highway a rate of ninepence in the pound which we promise to pay.

## 2. *Aveley Highway Duties, 1807*

Extracts from a list detailing highway duty and composition money to be paid.

Aveley Surveyors' Accounts (D/P 157/21/1).

| Rents | Inhabitants | Days | Composition | 6d. in £ |
|---|---|---|---|---|
| £ | | work | £ | £ s. d. |
| 146 | Sir Thos. Lennard, Bt. | 12 | 46 | 1. 3.0 |
| 400 | Jos. Joyner | 48 | | |
| 115 | Willis Fitch | 12 | 15 | 7.6 |
| 80 | John Curtis | 6 | 30 | 15.0 |
| 20 | Thos. Bird | — | 20 | 10.0 |
| 15 | Widow Keeling | — | 15 | 7.6 |
| 6 | John Standish | — | 6 | 3.0 |
| 6 | John Simpking | — | 6 | 3.0 |
| 5 | Thos. Livermore | — | 5 | 2.6 |
| 3 | David Ashfield | — | 3 | 1.6 |

## 3. *Road Maintenance, 1794-5*

The following extracts are from the accounts of a typical rural parish in North Essex.

Great Sampford Surveyors' Accounts (D/P 289/21/1).

| 1794 | | £ s. d. |
|---|---|---|
| Mar. 15 | John Harrington, 4½ days in pit | 5. 3 |
| | Ditto, two sons, 3½ days ditto | 1. 9 |
| 22 | William Joyce, 6 days scraping roads | 7. 0 |
| 29 | Richard Whybrew wife, 2 loads stones | 2. 0 |
| | John Harrington, stubbing and sifting 10 load gravel | 5. 0 |
| Apr. 25 | John Harrington, emptying Ware Fuller's ditch | 6 |

| | | | |
|---|---|---|---|
| May | 4 | A wire sieve | 5. 6 |
| | 13 | Robert Pryor, 2 days work in the road | 2. 4 |
| | 17 | John James for spreading gravel | 6. 6 |
| | 26 | 8 bushels lime | 5. 8 |
| | | 300 bricks | 10. 0 |
| | 26 | 4 pounds white lead | 2. 4 |
| | | 1½ linseed oil | 10½ |
| | | ½ pound nails | 2 |
| | | Making a rate | 1. 0 |
| | | Journey to Sessions | 5. 0 |
| | | Isaac Goulet cleaning drains | 1. 2 |
| July | 29 | Gravel out Butt's pit, 67 load at 6d. | 1.13. 6 |
| Dec. | 5 | John Gray, repairing the bridge | 2. 6. 0 |
| 1795 | | | |
| Mar. | 4 | Repairing new Sampford bridge | 2. 0 |
| | 13 | Horses and man in How Lane | 4. 0 |
| | 31 | Mark Coote making a ditch | 5. 9 |
| Apr. | 6 | Paid John Willett for the Instructions | 4. 0 |
| Aug. | 29 | Beer bill | 15. 2 |

## 4. *Inspection of Parish Roads, 1713*

A J.P. made the following report to Quarter Sessions.

Quarter Sessions Bundle, Easter 1713 (Q/SBb 56).

I, John Cressenor, Esq., one of her Majesty's Justices of the Peace, do upon my own view present the highway between Great Coggeshall and Earls Colne against the cottage of John Tibball. A very deep hole, now twelve foot deep in water, is dug in the ditch of Richard Brewer in Great Coggeshall, and near a quarter part of the highway is fallen in and is so very dangerous that her Majesty's liege people cannot pass and repass as they ought to do ; and that Richard Brewer ought to repair, amend and fill up the same ; and do give him time to do the same until the 24th day of June next ensuing, upon pain of 40s.

## 5. *Enforcement of Better Standards, 1765*

Quarter Sessions often used the threat of a fine to compel parish Vestries to maintain their roads.

Quarter Sessions Order Book (Q/SO 11).

It is ordered by this Court that a fine of £100 be set on the inhabitants of the Parish of Toppesfield upon a presentment against them for not repairing their highways, but that the same be not levied until after the next general Quarter Session.

### 6. *Improvement under Pressure*

Quarter Sessions Bundle, Michaelmas 1725 (Q/SBb 92).

These are to certify that we two Justices of the Peace have viewed the piece of road called Peny Lane, lying in Great Coggeshall near a farm called Hovells, which was some time since indicted as being ruinous and much out of repair, but we do now find the same to be well and sufficiently repaired. [Signatures of two justices.]

## *ATTEMPTS TO IMPROVE THE ROADS*

### 1. *The Neglect of Main Roads, 1716*

Many Vestries were unable or unwilling to repair main roads passing through their parish.

Quarter Sessions Bundle, Epiphany 1716 (Q/SBb 67).

Upon the humble petition of the parishioners of Widford near Chelmsford showing that their parish is so small that there are no more than two teams therein and that the high road to London is near two miles in length in the said parish, which they are unable to repair without some help, and humbly praying assistance from the turnpike, it is ordered by this Court that it be referred to the Justices of the Peace for the Chelmsford Division to examine and enquire into the matter and make report thereof at the next Sessions.

We, whose names are hereunto subscribed, Justices of the Peace, pursuant to the above order, have viewed the said highway and do find the matter of complaint set forth by the said petition to be true. We do think the parish of Widford ought to be allowed fifty pounds towards mending the said highway.

Samuel John Guyon. E. Williamson.

### 2. *Essex Roads in the 1760's*

*Ipswich Journal,* Dec. 27, 1766 (C.B.L.).

Yesterday, as a Foreigner was walking to Colchester in his way for Holland, a Stage-Coach overtook him in the Lexden Road and he, in endeavouring to get up a Bank to avoid it, fell down, and the Coach, going over both his Legs, broke one of them, and much bruised the other. He was immediately taken care of by the Officers of St Mary's Parish.

*Ipswich Journal,* March 18, 1769 (C.B.L.).

This Day an Inquisition was taken at Ingatestone on the Body of Richard Aimes, when it appeared the Deceased was thrown from his Horse, a little on this Side Ingatestone, into a Ditch and was suffocated by Mud and Filth.

### 3. *Restriction of Traffic*

Parliament banned types of traffic considered detrimental to road surfaces.

*Ipswich Journal,* Jan. 31, 1761 (C.B.L.).

By an Act of the 30th of his late Majesty King George the Second, it is enacted "That it shall not be lawful for any Waggon or Wain, having the Fellies of the Wheels thereof of less Breadth or Gage than nine Inches, to pass upon any Turnpike-Road or thro any Turnpike Gate or Bar, if the same be drawn by Horses, or Beasts of Draught, in Pairs, and not by Oxen"; It is ordered that Mr Griggs, our Clerk (as Trustees of the Essex Turnpikes), do prosecute all Persons that shall offend herein, by Indictment or Information; that this notice be fixed upon all the Turnpike-Gates and Advertised in the Ipswich News Papers for four Weeks. —Signed at a Meeting held at Chelmsford, Jan. 15, 1761

Chest Moor Hall, Chairman.

*Ipswich Journal,* June 7, 1766 (C.B.L.).

It having been the custom of several Persons lately to watch the Number of Horses in narrow-wheel Waggons, Yesterday Morning a Woman at Baddow, perceiving five in one of them, took the fore Horse off and Yesterday applied to a Justice in order to have it allowed as her Property, agreeable to Act of Parliament; which was accordingly done. It seems her Husband had followed the practice some time ago, but he laying it aside, she said it was too lucrative to go out of the Family.

### 4. *A Turnpike Trust at Work, 1834*

Essex Turnpikes Trust, extracts from Minutes (D/TX 7/1).

24th March, 1834. At a General Annual Meeting of the Trustees held at the George Inn in Halstead.

Ashurst Majendie, Esq., was nominated and appointed a Trustee in the room of his father.

H. H. Carwardine, Esq., one of the Committee appointed to inspect the bridge at Earls Colne with a view to its repair, reported that such repairs as were found requisite to be done had been completed at an expense of £188 . 13 . 6.

Mr Carwardine also reported that since the last meeting he had made application to the Trustees of the Chelmsford Division of the Turnpikes for a Donation of £300 in order to enable this Trust to discharge their debt and lower the tolls; that the said Trustees declined to accede to such application, but that they had agreed to advance such sum upon mortgage for six years without requiring interest for the same, which offer he had accepted on behalf of the Trust.

It is ordered that Mr Holmsted of Aldham, miller, be allowed to compound at the Aldham Gate for £4 . 10 from Lady Day to Lady Day and that Mr Hawkes of Ford Street be also allowed to compound for his horse and cart at the said Gate at £1.

It having been reported to this meeting that an improvement might be made on the road near Mr Seymour's gate in the parish of Sible Hedingham by widening the same, it is resolved that a committee be requested to see such improvement carried into effect.

In consequence of information received by this Trust that Mr Hellen of Bouncers Hall had given permission to various persons to pass along a carriage on his farm in order to avoid the payment of toll at the Aldham Gate, and Mr Hellen having stated that he had given permission by the authority of his landlord, Mr Western, it is ordered that the Clerk to this Trust do forthwith write to Mr Western and request him to state whether or not there be any truth in such an assertion.

It is also ordered that the Clerk do ascertain what number of horses parties driving waggons with six-inch wheels are entitled to use.

5. *Turnpike Tolls, 1837*

Essex Turnpikes Trust Minutes (D/TX 7/1).

The Trustees having [considered] the expediency of advancing the tolls at the Toll Gates of Halstead, Aldham, Gosfield and Yeldham, did advance the said tolls, in manner following :—

| | From | To |
|---|---|---|
| For every stage coach licensed to carry 6 or more inside passengers drawn by 4 horses | 1 . 6 | 2 . 0 |
| Waggon or other such 4 wheel carriage with 9-inch wheels, drawn by 8 horses | 2 . 6 | 3 . 0 |
| Dray, Cart or other such two-wheeled carriage with 9-inch wheels drawn by 5 or 4 horses | 1 . 0 | 1 . 0 |
| Ditto by 3 do. or any less number | 7 | 9 |
| Dray etc. with 6-inch wheels drawn by 3 horses | 9 | 1 . 0 |
| Dray with wheels less than 6 inches drawn by 3 horses | 10 | 1 . 0 |
| Horse, Mare, Gelding or Mule, laden or unladen and not drawing | 1 | 1½ |

Drove of Oxen, Cows or Neat Cattle, 10d per score and so in proportion

Drove of Claves, Hogs, Sheep or Lambs, 5d per score and so in proportion

### 6. *Farming the Tolls, 1809*

The Turnpike Trustees lease the gates to a Middlesex contractor.
Essex Turnpikes Trust Records (D/TX 3/46).

The Trustees agree to let and John Colson to hire the tolls which after 29 September shall be payable from Lexden Gate for two years at the yearly rent of £875. Colson shall be at all the expense of collecting the tolls, viz. salary of the toll collectors, tickets, coals, candles ; the Trustees providing toll house, gate and fixtures and keeping the house, bars and gates in good repair. Colson shall be obliged to keep proper persons as collectors always on duty and [their] names painted on a board in large letters on the door of the toll house. And the Trustees shall at the request, costs and charges of Colson prosecute persons guilty of defrauding or evading payment of tolls at the gate. Such toll tickets shall be provided as shall be approved of [by] the Trustees and the Clerk, Surveyor and other servants of the Trust and persons carting materials for the repair of the turnpike road [shall] be allowed to pass toll free.

### 7. *Turnpike Trusts borrow Money*

*Chelmsford Chronicle,* May 18, 1787 (E.R.O.).

Epping Turnpike Road.

*NOTICE* is Hereby *GIVEN,* That a *MEETING* of the *TRUSTEES* appointed for repairing the road from the North part of Harlow Bush Common, in the parish of Harlow, to Woodford, in the county of Essex, and for repairing and widening the road from Epping, thro' the parishes of Northweald Bassett, Bobbingworth, High Ongar, Chipping Ongar, and Shelley, to the Four-Want-Way, in the said parish of Shelley and from thence thro' the parishes of High Ongar and Norton Mandeville, to the parish of Writtle, in the said county, will be held by adjournment at the Red Lion at Chipping Ongar, on Saturday the ninth of June next, at Twelve o'clock at noon, to view the New Turnpike Road, and make such orders for the repair thereof as shall appear to be necessary ; and a meeting of the Trustees will also be held at Epping-Place Inn, in Epping, on Monday the 25th of June next, at the same hour, in order to borrow and take up at interest, a further sum of money on the credit of the Tolls, when and where the Trustees are requested to attend. John Jessop, Clerk to the Trustees.

## *8. Opposition to Toll-Gates, 1850*

Dunmow Parish Records (D/P 11/28/17).

To the Trustees of the Essex Turnpikes.

The memorial of the landowners, ratepayers and others resident in the town of Great Dunmow and its neighbourhood sheweth

That your memorialists have heard with considerable surprise that a proposal is again made to erect a Toll Gate at the South end of the High Street.

That a large amount of public business connected with the Petty Sessions, the Board of Guardians & the public taxes is transacted at Dunmow and that the effect of erecting a Toll Gate will be to exact toll from persons who are compelled to come into the Town on these accounts or that it will cause them to neglect these important duties—as they travel on roads maintained at the cost of their respective parishes until within a few hundred yards of the town, and that from the peculiar situation of Dunmow the traffic [passes] through from Clare, Bumpstead, Bardfield, Finchingfield, Wethersfield, Thaxted, Braintree, Felsted, Stebbing, etc, in the direction of the Roothings.

That another effect on such a proceeding will be to drive away from the town many persons who are in the daily habit of coming into it from the South and who cannot enter it without passing over a small portion of the Turnpike Road.

For these Reasons your memorialists submit that the erecting a toll gate in the town or its immediate vicinity will be most unjust and oppressive and will cause a certain injury to the property of the town & considerable annoyance and inconvenience to the inhabitants without materially increasing the revenues of the Trust, particularly as notice has been given for the introduction of a measure for the general management of our public roads.

## *9. Macadamising the Roads, 1833*

*Essex Mercury*, Oct. 22, 1833 (E.R.O.).

Mr M'Adam has already made a very great improvement in the road between Shenfield and Chelmsford, for which he has contracted. Since the representations made by the post-masters and coachmen to the commissioners as to the road from Shenfield to London, a great alteration and improvement has been effected in that line.

## *10. Praise for Essex Roads, 1807*

Young, *General View of Agriculture in Essex,* 1807, Vol. II, p. 384.

It is impossible to say too much in praise of the roads of most of the districts in Essex. All through Tendring hundred I found them excellent and, wherever they branched off, all carried the same appearance. In Dengey hundred they are incomparable; every lane seemed to rival the finest turnpikes; yet I was informed at Latchingdon, that the gravel, wherewith they were made and are repaired, cost 4s. the load of 24 bushels. The roads of this hundred ought not to be mentioned without assigning the merit where due. It was the unwearied exertions of the Rev. H. B. Dudley that affected the marvellous change experienced; from being as bad as I described others in this county in 1767, his attention as a magistrate made them equal to any in the world. What he effected there instigated others to similar endeavours, and the result has been a general blessing to the county.

## *11. Minor Roads Still Poor, 1850*

Alderman Mechi urges the farmers in the Tiptree area to invest in better roads.
*Essex Standard,* Jan. 4, 1850 (C.B.L.).

It is impossible not to be struck with the present gross mismanagement of our cross-country roads. There are, of course, exceptions, but these are few and far between. First, one sees the direction-posts in a state of decay and illegibility—surveyors appearing to forget that these were intended to guide the wandering stranger, who knows nothing of the country; next, we see the roads concave instead of convex, having high shoulders covered with grass and which effectually retain the water in the road, much to its injury . . . How frequently do we see a hilly road deeply furrowed in the middle by the descending force of the accumulated water (a sheet of ice in winter), for the want of proper outlets all the way down the hill, beginning them near the top and keeping the crown of the roads higher than the sides. In fact, we have only to look to our turnpike roads to see how differently these things are managed. Generally speaking, the ditches, openings under gateways and pathways are either choked up or insufficient for the passage of the water. Another nuisance is the projection of great, round, unbroken stones, like half a large cricket ball, sticking up just high enough to catch the toe and break the knees of a tired or lazy horse or fracture an axle-tree in frosty weather . . . It would be well if our agricultural friends would trim some of their enormous road-side fences, for they ruin the roads by excluding sun and air, keeping them always wet and soft, whilst on an open heath they are almost always dry. Depend upon it, these neglects touch the farmers' pockets, for in roads, as in other matters, a stitch in time saves nine; many an old waggon and cart would crack on for years, but for the jogs, jounces and staunces of our mismanaged cross-roads, the wheelwrights' best friends.

## *COACHING, CANALS AND RAILWAYS*

### *1. Chelmsford to London in Five Hours, 1754*

*Ipswich Journal,* Sept. 14, 1754 (C.B.L.).

Chelmsford Machine Fly sets out on Monday, Sept. 16, from the Coach and Horses at Chelmsford at Seven o'Clock in the Morning, to go every Day (except Sunday) to the Spread Eagle in Gracechurch-Street, and will be there at Twelve in the Forenoon; and returns the same Day at Two o'Clock in the Afternoon. Passengers will be detained no longer than to take fresh Horses at Rumford. The same Person has a Stage-Coach sets out from the Coach and Horses at Chelmsford aforesaid, at Nine o'Clock in the Morning, every Monday, Wednesday, and Friday, to the Cross Keys in Gracechurch-Street; and returns from London at Nine o'Clock in the Morning, every Tuesday, Thursday, and Saturday. To go by the Coach for Three Shillings a Passenger.
N.B. Any Person may be furnish'd with Coaches, Hearse, or Chariot, with able Horses, to any Part of England, at reasonable Rates.

Perform'd, if God permit, by Deborah Gooding.

### *2. Maldon to London, 1787*

*Chelmsford Chronicle,* April 6, 1787 (E.R.O.).

Maldon Machine sets out from Maldon every Monday, Wednesday, and Friday morning at Seven o'clock to the Blue Boar Inn, in Whitechapel, London; and returns from thence every Tuesday, Thursday, and Saturday morning during the summer season at Twelve o'clock.

Inside passengers to pay nine shillings and to be allowed 20 lb weight of luggage and to pay 6d per score for all above that quantity. No allowance can be made for children, excepting those on the lap, for whom half price is to be paid. Outside passengers to pay five shillings.

The proprietor will not be responsible for any parcels, unless entered and paid for at two-pence in the pound sterling; he also returns his sincere thanks to his friends at Maldon and Baddow, and the public in general, and hopes for a continuance of their favours, assuring them no expence shall be spared to make every accommodation agreeable.

Performed by their humble servant, Richard Ward.

### 3. *Faster Coaching, 1823*

*Chelmsford Gazette,* May 9, 1823 (E.R.O.).

The drivers of the two new Colchester Coaches were on Friday last fined 3*l.* 7*s.* each, including costs, for furiously driving. At the time they were observed by the worthy magistrate, who for the general good of the public enforced the penalties, the coaches were going at the extraordinary rate of from 14 to 15 miles an hour.

### 4. *Steam Coach, 1828*

*The Sickle,* Oct. 16, 1828 (E.R.O.).

Essex Steam Coach. It may startle the coach-proprietors and horse-owners along the great eastern road to learn that there is something like a serious intention of trying the practicability of a conveyance by steam betwixt London and Colchester. Although we mention the rumour, as it reached us from pretty good authority, yet we imagine that the parties most deeply interested in the matter have but little reason to apprehend such a thing being carried into effect. There are certainly but few roads in England that present fewer inequalities of surface than this; in the whole 50 miles there are only three or four hills, the ascent of which is gradual; but it will be long before the public mind can be relieved from the fear of an explosion . . . It would not be very difficult to prove that ninety-nine persons out of a hundred in Essex would give the preference to Mrs Nelson's or Ned Cracknell's team of bays or greys, rather than to Gurney's or Burstead and Hall's steam coaches. Willing as we are to allow all due credit to the invention of those gentlemen, and sensible as we are how much has already been accomplished by the application of steam power, in various mechanical operations, there are some objections to its being employed in land conveyance. In the first place, it is not wholly without risk of human life; that, in the next, it would lessen the value of horses and take away the demand for hay, oats, and other fodder—but what we consider as the chief objection is, that, if suddenly adopted, it would have the effect of throwing thousands of poor fellows out of employment.

## 5. *Coaching on the Eve of the Railway Age, 1838*

Shortly before the railway reached Chelmsford, a census of traffic was taken at Shenfield tollgate, from which the following is an extract. Petre Archives (D/DP O18/3).

Wednesday, March 7th, 1838

| To London | Number of passengers | | From London | Number of passengers | |
|---|---|---|---|---|---|
| Names of Coaches | Inside | Outside | Names of Coaches | Inside | Outside |
| Royal Mail | 2 | 3 | Yarmouth Star | 2 | 10 |
| Telegraph | 0 | 4 | Phenomena Norwich | 2 | 5 |
| Chelmsford | 4 | 10 | Shannon Ipswich | 1 | 10 |
| Chelmsford 3 Horses | 2 | 2 | Wellington Colchester | 4 | 11 |
| Braintree | 3 | 6 | Bury | 1 | 4 |
| Coggeshall | 1 | 10 | Chelmsford ½ 12 p.m. | | 3 |
| Burnham and Maldon | 2 | 4 | Ipswich Blue | 3 | 8 |
| [a]Wellington Colchester | 1 | 8 | Sudbury New | | 4 |
| Sudbury | 2 | 7 | Colchester | 3 | 9 |
| [b]Ipswich Blue | 1 | 8 | Coggeshall | | 6 |
| Bury | 3 | 3 | Braintree | 2 | 6 |
| [c]Shannon Ipswich | 2 | 7 | Chelmsford 3 Horse | 1 | 2 |
| Chelmsford ½ 4 p.m. | 2 | 7 | Chelmsford | 1 | 6 |
| Phenomena Ipswich | 1 | 2 | Telegraph | 3 | 5 |
| Colchester | | 10 | Royal Mail | 3 | 1 |
| [d]Times Norwich | 1 | 6 | | | |
| Yarmouth Star | 2 | 7 | | | |

a, b, c, d, 2 Extra Horses

## 6. *The End of Coaching*

*Essex Standard,* Nov. 17, 1843 (C.B.L.).

Colchester. On Saturday last the "Golden Path" coach, which was started by Messrs Clary and Shuttleworth on the discontinuance of the "Old Wellington" from Colchester to London, ceased running, leaving no other public conveyance between this town and the metropolis than the railroad trains. We cannot but regret . . .

## 7. *The Cheapness of River Transport, 1766*

Sage Collection 413 (E.R.O.).

*TO THE PUBLIC*

There is now a convenient Wharf opened at Illford Bridge for the Sale of Newcastle Coals, which are unloaded from Colliers at Barking Creek's Mouth and brought up the river Rodon to Illford, the Navigation of the said River being made safe and easy, upwards of 150 old Piles or Stumps having been drawn out of the Bottom of the River for that Purpose.

As this is the first Attempt ever made to unload Coals at Barking Creek's Mouth and convey them to Illford, by which Means the Country round about have the Opportunity of getting the best sort of Newcastle Coals as cheap as at Raynham, Barking, or Stratford, and Many Buyers will save Four Miles in every Journey ; it is therefore humbly apprehended that all public-spirited Gentlemen will give suitable Encouragement to the Adventurers in so useful an Undertaking.

At a moderate Distance (if required) Coals will be delivered in Sacks stampt with the City Mark. At the said Wharf are sold the best sort of Scotch Coals and fine White Sand.

By John Webb and Co.

### 8. *Opposition to the Chelmer Canal, 1793*

Chelmer Navigation Papers (D/Z 1).

Observations on the Chelmer Navigation Bill.

It is worthy of Notice, That in the Year 1733, a Plan of a Navigation from Maldon to Chelmsford was made by Mr J. Hoare, an eminent Surveyor, and at an Estimate of £9,355. Proposals, stating the supposed Utility, were printed for Consideration, but not being found satisfactory, the Scheme was abandoned.

In 1765, the Project was revived. Proposals were again printed ; and an Act was obtained in 1766, for making the River Chelmer navigable from the Port of Maldon to the Town of Chelmsford . . . This Act directed that the Sum of £13,000, the then Estimate for making this Navigation, should be subscribed before any Part of the Act should be put into Execution. And though the Commissioners, Persons of the first Consequence and Property in the Country, held several Meetings for the Purpose, such Subscription could not be obtained . . .

The present Rage for Canals has again revived this Subject . . . It may now be reasonably asked, What new Sources of Manufactures or Commerce are opened that can, upon any Ground of Public Utility, justify the diverting the established Trade from the ancient Town and Port of Maldon, and the Intrusion on Private Property, at the enormous Expence of from £40 to 60,000 allowed to be raised by this Bill ?

It may be necessary here shortly to advert to the Conduct of the Promoters of this Navigation . . . A Committee was appointed, and they were directed, when the Plans, Estimates, etc, were prepared, to call a General Meeting to report a State of the Business. The Inhabitants of Maldon and those who conceived that their Property might be affected by this Navigation waited patiently for the promised public Meeting. No such Meeting was called. But a Meeting was convened of " The Friends of the Navigation, for the special Purposes of signing a Petition to Parliament and to subscribe towards the Expences of carrying it into Execution"—A Navigation very different from what had hitherto been in Contemplation, as will be evident by adverting to the Bill. The Navigation before proposed was from Maldon upwards, but the present one is from Chelmsford downwards to Colliers Reach, below Maldon, and running by Heybridge, deserting Maldon altogether.

### 9. *Opening of the Braintree—Maldon Railway, 1848*

*Essex Standard,* Aug. 18, 1848 (C.B.L.).

On Tuesday last the Maldon, Witham and Braintree Railway was opened for goods traffic, pursuant to notice given; on the 1st of September next, we see . . . it is expected the line will be ready for passenger traffic. This event is anxiously looked forward to by a large class of merchants and traders whose attendance is frequently required at neighbouring towns and markets. The electric telegraph is already laid down, and in a few days the towns of Maldon and Braintree will possess the advantage of an almost instantaneous communication with the great metropolis, in addition to increased facilities for personal attendance. One of the leading questions with parties conversing on the subject of this branch railway is "Will it pay?" From our knowledge of facts in connexion with the district through which the line passes, we have no hesitation in saying it *will pay.* This may not be the case just at first, because all the complicated arrangements for bringing traffic on the line cannot yet be fully developed. These in part consist of the formation of copious and convenient docks at the Maldon terminus and also the deepening the course of the Black-water River, by which vessels of a larger tonnage than heretofore will be able to come up and unship their cargoes into the very trucks upon the line, by which they may be carried to their place of destination, or nearly so. Then we have to look to the large extent of country lying out beyond Braintree. The large quantities of grain brought from these parts and shipped at the port of Maldon is perhaps not known to many of our readers. But it is sufficient to lead the directors of the Eastern Counties Railway to contemplate . . . the ultimate extension of this line to the neighbourhood of Saffron Walden. But without waiting for this extension, there is every reason to suppose that the exporters of this large extent of agricultural produce will avail themselves of these new branches, and in return will avail themselves of the opportunity of obtaining coals, limes, oil-cake, and other useful commodities, at a much lower rate than they have hitherto done.

# LOCAL GOVERNMENT

In 1750 the parish Vestry had several important public functions. Its Overseers of the Poor provided a rudimentary system of social security. Its Surveyors of the Highways were obliged to repair the roads by means of the compulsory labour of the parishioners. Its Constables were responsible for order. Its Churchwardens undertook civil as well as ecclesiastical duties, giving poor relief or representing the parish on important business. The Vestry itself, as occasion demanded, carried out diverse and sometimes costly activities on its own account.

The Justices of the Peace administered some services at Quarter Sessions, maintaining certain bridges, for instance, and employing inspectors of weights and measures. In their individual capacity and in their own neighbourhood they exercised even greater influence. They maintained order, appointed parish officers from nominees of the Vestries, checked parish accounts, heard appeals from applicants for poor relief, reported to Quarter Sessions cases of neglected roads and in other ways decisively shaped parish policy. Borough magistrates likewise supervised parish officers within their jurisdiction. Municipal corporations were dignified bodies, but in Essex they no longer displayed much energy either in economic regulation or in the provision of public services.

The eighteenth-century system was modified in several ways before being replaced by new institutions in the nineteenth century. Many Essex parishes, for instance, elected special committees to supervise poor relief in detail or employed full-time officials to assist their unpaid Overseers and Surveyors. Ratepayers, by paying money in lieu of compulsory road service, enabled Surveyors to employ labourers in their place. Turnpike Trusts improved main roads, while in towns special authorities were set up to provide neglected services. Despite these developments the old system was judged unsuitable to nineteenth-century needs. Poor Law expenditure soared, in Essex as elsewhere. Cross-country roads continued poor. Parish Constables remained inefficient. Nonconformists contested the levy of a church rate. Democrats denied the right of non-elected Justices to rule the county or unrepresentative Corporations the town. Cholera in 1831 and 1848 and Parliamentary reform in 1832 reinforced the critics.

The New Poor Law of 1834 diminished the influence of both Parish and Justices, by removing administration of relief to a district board and its supervision to the central Poor Law Commission. The parish lost other functions, the appointment of Constables, power to levy a compulsory church rate and, where district highway boards were established as in some parts of Essex, the upkeep of its roads. Quarter Sessions set up its county police, but otherwise gained little new influence. Municipal corporations, though made elective in 1835, at first acquired few new functions.

The establishment of Boards of Health in some towns under the Act of 1848 was an important step towards modern local government. Parliament conferred fresh sanitary powers both upon these Boards and also upon Municipal Boroughs and Boards of Guardians. In 1872 Boards of Guardians became Rural Sanitary Authorities, and Boards of Health were renamed District Boards. Cities were now undertaking the supply of gas, water and other services. Further Parliamentary Reform Acts led to a wider municipal franchise and also to the transformation of local government in rural areas. In 1888 elected County Councils were set up and in 1894 Parish Councils. In 1894 also Rural Sanitary Authorities became Rural District Councils, and District Boards became Urban District Councils. The structure of modern local government was virtually complete.

## *THE GOVERNMENT OF THE COUNTY*

### 1. *Preserving Order*

The following extract is from a letter written by the Earl of Rochford to the Clerk of the Peace for Essex.

Quarter Sessions Bundle, Epiphany 1772 (Q/SBb).

I have been informed from the Secretary at War that application has been made to him from the Magistrates of Colchester and its neighbourhood for troops to be sent to Colchester to assist in preventing the riots that have lately happened, such as seizing waggons loaded with wheat and flour. It is therefore incumbent on me, as Lord Lieutenant of the County, to recommend to the Magistrates of Colchester and its neighbourhood, particularly those nearest to the place, to use their utmost endeavours to stop these riots and to be as expeditious as possible in seizing some of the people concerned ; the making early examples of such as shall be found guilty will be the means of preventing further mischief . . . I wish to hear from you, by the return of the post, whether this disturbance has subsided.

### 2. *Manning the Navy, 1770*

Quarter Sessions Bundle, Michaelmas 1770 (Q/SBb).

To our very good Lord, William Henry, Earl of Rochford, Custos Rotulorum of the County of Essex, After very hearty commendations to your Lordship, whereas his Majesty's service doth at this time require a speedy supply of seamen to man his Majesty's fleet which is now fitting out, we do therefore . . . pray and require your Lordship to call upon the Justices of the Peace . . . to cause all straggling seamen, who are fit to serve on board his Majesty's ships, to be taken up and sent by proper persons from place to place until they shall be brought to the Clerks of the Checque of his Majesty's Yards at Deptford . . . Plymouth or Harwich, or to any of his Majesty's ships appointed to procure men at other ports . . . and that there be paid to the persons who shall be entrusted with the conducting them, by the aforesaid Clerks of the Checque, twenty shillings for each seaman fit for his Majesty's service and sixpence for every mile they respectively travel, not exceeding twenty miles . . . From the Council Chamber at St James's, the 12th day of October, 1770.

### 3. *Prison Administration*

Quarter Sessions Order Books, 1750, 1752, 1791 (Q/SO 9, 15).

It is ordered by this Court that Rebecca Woodall of Halstead . . . doth succeed John Woodall, her late husband, as Mistress at the House of Correction at Halstead.

---

It is ordered by this Court that it be referred to Sir John Cross, Baronet, Thomas Bramston, Esquire, and the Reverend Mr John Tindal to order sufficient and necessary conveniences and pumps to be made in the rooms that are now building at the House of Correction at Chelmsford, as they shall think proper, at the charge of the County, whereby the prisoners that shall from time to time be committed to the same may be kept sweet and clean.

---

It is ordered by this Court that the Clerk of the Peace do write a letter to Robert Baker, Keeper of the House of Correction at Newport, informing him that complaint has been made to this Court that the punishment ordered to be inflicted by him on Thomas Joyce was not duly inflicted and requiring that he will in future pay strict attention to his duty.

### 4. *Inspection of Prisons*

Quarter Sessions Bundle, Midsummer 1794 (Q/SBb).

The report of . . . two of his Majesty's Justices of the Peace [on] Newport House of Correction.

State of the building—But little has been done towards the reparations ordered at present, in consequence of not being able to procure sufficient workmen.

Prisoners—On enquiry of the Keeper respecting the behaviour of the prisoners, he reported that they conducted themselves peaceably and orderly, except Theophilus Graves who has been very refractory during his confinement, tearing his apparel to pieces and making such noises as to disturb the rest of the Keeper and also the prisoners confined with him.

Keeper—On enquiry of the prisoners respecting the behaviour of the Keeper towards them, they reported that they had no cause of complaint against him.

### 5. *Maintenance of County Bridges, 1790*

The following is a report by a Quarter Sessions committee appointed to inspect one of the bridges for which the county was responsible. Quarter Sessions Order Book, Easter 1790 (Q/SO 14).

We, having attended Mr Johnson the County Surveyor to inspect the state of the bridge at Ramsey, found that the wharfing is very much decayed so as to require the same and the piling thereof to be entirely new, the posts and railing of the bridge in a decaying state, the standard bearers and planking in a pretty good condition. We think, agreeable to the opinion of the Surveyor, that it should be of advantage to the County that the wharfing should in future be built with brick, which, if executed in this manner, would not require to be made more than one third part of its present length. We proceeded from the bridge to a tide mill about half a mile above the same belonging to — Garland Esquire and found from the account of the miller that the same was of little value and that it had been in the contemplation of the late Mr Garland to make an embankment to prevent the tide from flowing beyond the present bridge. The present owner of the estate being a minor about the age of eighteen years, we recommend that no material repairs be done to the bridge till the said minor comes of age, not doubting but he will consent to join the County in the charge of an embankment which would materially benefit his estate and render a bridge in future unnecessary.

### 6. *The Beginnings of a Paid Staff*

Quarter Sessions Order Book, Easter 1718 (Q/SO 5).

Whereas by long experience it appears that the county hath been notoriously abused and put upon by the workmen of several trades employed in the repairs of the public bridges belonging to this county and in other public works and repairs . . . for want of a proper officer to take care therein, for remedy whereof this Court doth appoint Edward Turner to be the public surveyor.

### 7. *Licensing of Alehouses*

Quarter Sessions Bundle, Midsummer 1713 (Q/SBb 57).

We, her Majesty's Justices of the Peace, do allow and license Nicholas Bacon of Lawford, victualler, to keep a common alehouse and to sell bread and other victuals, beer, ale and other exciseable liquors . . . for the space of one whole year . . . so as the true assize of his bread, beer, ale or other exciseable liquors be duly kept and no unlawful games, drunkenness or any other disorder suffered in his house, yard, garden or backside, but that good order be maintained . . .

### 8. *Licensing of Dance Halls*

Quarter Sessions Bundle, Michaelmas 1772 (Q/SBb).

At the General Quarter Session held at Chelmsford, we, being four of his Majesty's Justices of the Peace, upon application to us made by several of the inhabitants of the parish of Waltham Holy Cross do license the house known by the sign of the Cock Inn . . . to be kept for public dancing, music and other entertainment of a like kind upon condition that . . . such room or place in the said house as shall be kept for the purpose aforesaid be not opened before five in the afternoon.

### 9. *Supervision of Apprenticeship*

Quarter Sessions Order Book, Midsummer 1763 (Q/SO 10).

Whereas by indentures of apprenticeship . . . Joseph Francis did put himself apprentice to John Curtis of Tolleshunt Darcy, cordwainer, to learn his art and with him after the manner of an apprentice to serve . . ., now at this General Quarter Session . . . the said Joseph Francis appearing and praying to be discharged from his master, for that the said John Curtis has failed and left his business and not provided the said Joseph Francis with necessaries, this Court doth order that the said Joseph Francis be discharged.

### 10. *Preserving the Peasantry, 1740*

The law requiring the attachment of four acres to every new cottage was rarely enforced in the eighteenth century.

Quarter Sessions Bundle, Michaelmas 1740 (Q/SBb 150).

The presentments of the Grand Jury at the General Quarter Sessions . . . We also present Frances Pratt of Boxted for erecting a cottage in the said parish and not laying four acres of land thereto.

### 11. *Supervision of Moral and Spiritual Welfare, 1786*

Quarter Sessions Order Book, Midsummer 1786 (Q/SO 14).

It appearing unto this Court that of late on the Lord's Day several disorderly persons do expose for sale wares and merchandise, that drovers, waggoners, butchers, higglers and their servants do travel and that tradesmen, artificers, workmen, labourers and other persons exercise worldly labour of their callings and that the religious observance of the Lord's Day hath been notoriously profaned and neglected in violation of the laws divine and human, in contempt of order and decency, and to the great scandal of our most holy religion ; now this Court . . . do recommend it to his Majesty's Justices of the Peace strictly to put the laws in force for the better observance of the Lord's Day . . . And it is ordered that the chief constables of the several hundreds, as also the petty constables, headboroughs and other peace officers . . . take effectual care to prevent all persons keeping taverns, chocolate houses, coffee houses and other public houses from selling wine, chocolate, coffee, ale, beer or other liquors or permitting guests to be in their houses at the time of divine service . . . And the Justices do hereby earnestly exhort all masters of families, more especially such as have apprentices, that they together with their families and apprentices duly attend divine service on the Lord's Day.

### *12. Suppression of Profanity*

Quarter Sessions Roll, Midsummer 1761 (Q/SR 745).

Be it remembered that, on the 13th day of June in the first year of the reign of his Majesty King George the Third, Thomas Adams of St Leonard at the Hythe in Colchester, limeburner, was convicted before me of cursing five profane curses. Geo. Wegg.

### *13. The J.P. as an Appeals Tribunal*

Coggeshall Overseers' Miscellaneous Papers, 1812 (D/P 36/18/1).

Whereas Hannah Nicholls of Great Coggeshall hath made oath before me . . . that she is poor and impotent and not able to work, and that she did apply to the Overseers of the Poor of the said parish to be relieved but was refused to be relieved by them ; and whereas the acting Overseer, being present and required to show cause why relief should not be given, has not made any sufficient cause to appear ; I do therefore order the Churchwardens and Overseers to pay unto Hannah Nicholls the sum of two shillings and sixpence weekly . . . Chas. Dalton.

### *14. Mobilising Parish Constables*

J.P.s had no staff of their own but acted through local constables and other parish officers.
Coggeshall Constables' Papers (D/P 36/10).

To the Constables of Great Coggeshall . . . These are in his Majesty's name to require you to apprehend the bodies of Mary Spinck [and four others] and bring them before me or some other of his Majesty's Justices of the Peace to answer the complaint of the Churchwardens and Overseers of the Poor of the parish touching their living idly at their own hands and refusing to take themselves to service . . . 5th day of March, 1741. Robt. Tweed.

## *THE MUNICIPAL CORPORATION*

### *1. A Municipal Corporation at Work, 1813*

The following extracts indicate the limited functions of many municipal corporations in the eighteenth and early nineteenth centuries.
Maldon Borough Assembly Book, Feb. 1813 (D/B 3/1/32).

At this meeting Edward Chase, Esquire, the Mayor of this Borough, having at the request of the united parishes of All Saints and Saint Peter convened this present meeting for the purpose of requiring their concurrence to a grant or sale of a piece of waste ground of this borough called the Town Dunghill for the purpose of converting the same into an additional burial ground for the use of the said parishes and the barracks . . ., the Court are unanimously of opinion that it would be extremely injurious to the inhabitants resident near that spot to alienate the said land and do therefore decline selling the same.

It is ordered that the Town Clerk doth give immediate notice to Mr Brewster to take down a shed which now stands on the same ground . . . or the same will be ordered by the Court to be forthwith pulled down.

It is also ordered that the sum of 6s. 8d., heretofore demanded of every foreigner exercising any trade within the said Borough, be forthwith demanded by the sergeants at mace.

It is ordered that this Court doth meet at the Town Hall on Monday, the first day of March next, for the purpose of going the boundaries of the Borough.

It is also ordered that the ancient rolls and papers belonging to this Borough and the records of the same be kept in the Town Hall and that suitable places for their custody be prepared.

### *2. Enforcing Moral Welfare, 1786*

The borough magistracy was often a more active force in urban life than the corporation itself.
*Ipswich Journal,* April 29, 1786 (C.B.L.).

Colchester. An intimation being given to the Justices that the pernicious practice of gaming having prevailed in many public-houses in this town, the constables were sent out to inspect the same and returned with the Nine-hole table, Devil amongst the Taylors, etc. (games played by working hands to the destruction of themselves and families) which were ordered to be publicly burnt, and the order was accordingly put into execution on Tuesday last before the gaol; and a charge was given to the constables, in their respective parishes, to inform the justices if any such practices were in future suffered by the landlords on their premises.

### 3. *Protecting Local Tradesmen, 1792*

Harwich Borough Records, Bundle 114/1.

To his Majesty's Justices of the Peace holding the General Quarter Session of the Peace for the Borough of Harwich, 16th April, 1792.

We, shopkeepers residing within and paying great rates and taxes for the parish of St Nicholas, beg leave to represent to your Worships that we have for long sustained great injuries to our respective trades by the intrusion of diverse persons, who bring into this parish various commodities in which we deal and hawk the same from door to door; and which persons frequently bring such commodities as are of qualities inferior to the prices they demand and often obtain for the same; whereby, and by their taking ready money from the town without having contributed to the taxation thereof or support of the poor therein, every person of trade residing in the said town is proportionally injured.

We therefore humbly request that an Order of Court may be made, restricting all hawkers and pedlars of every article of manufactory and, whether such persons have Travelling Licences or not, from offering to sale in this town any part of their goods to any other persons than those who are shopkeepers therein and who buy the same by wholesale to sell again.

### 4. *Supervising Parochial Administration, 1761*

*Original spelling retained.*
Maldon Borough Sessions Papers, 1761 (D/B 3/3/441).

Maldon. The Presentment of the Jurors sworn to inquire for our Lord the King in a Court Leet holden for the said Borough on Monday the Thirteenth Day of April 1761

We present the parrish of Saint Maries for the Lane tooe of the well oposet Mr Daneses timber yard not Bening in in Repare Dangerous for Cheldren folen in

We present the parrish of Saints peeters for the foot parth not being in Repare opeset Mr Eliegoods Shope

We present Mr Robert Patyson for not haven a foot bridg at the botam of Grate hill mash Which is the third mas in the foot parth Going from mauldon to mundon.

### 5. *Vested Interests in Municipal Government at Harwich*

*Commission on Municipal Corporations*, 1834, App. Part IV, pp. 2271-2.

The guildhall, gaol, school and other buildings, already specified as a part of the corporate property, though yielding no revenue, are kept in repair at the expense of the corporate funds. This forms part of the sum headed "tradesmen's bills" . . . Some of the tradesmen employed are members of the council; and till a recent change in the mode of letting the property their bills were annual charges of considerable amount. An examination of the accounts of former years shows that they were in the habit of receiving large sums from the fund they were appointed to control. The office of Chamberlain . . . was for many years held by a carpenter. During that period the corporation estates appear to have been constantly in want of carpenter's work, and the chamberlain's accounts constantly present his own bills.

A sinking fund has been established, which, by gradual accumulations, had amounted in 1822 to a sum exceeding £538 invested in the public funds. In that year it was found necessary to sell out this stock for the payment of outstanding bills, and the greater part of the proceeds was shared by the chamberlain and another member of the corporation in part liquidation of their claim for repairs.

In 1824 a new debt of £400 was incurred to pay off the remainder of the chamberlain's claim.

This head of expenditure has been materially reduced by the better management of the estates. The repairs formerly done by members of the corporation are now done by their tenants, and the chamberlain is no longer a carpenter.

The change appears to have been introduced about the time when the present mayor became the head of the corporation.

### 6. *Colchester Improvement Commission, 1781*

In the following passage are described some of the powers given to the Colchester Lighting, Paving and Navigation Commission, a type of 'ad hoc' authority set up in many towns to provide services neglected by existing authorities.
*Colchester Lighting Act*, 1781 (D/DR O6).

That in case the Owner of any House, Shop, Warehouse, or other Building, now adjoining or contiguous to . . . any of the Streets or Lanes within the said Town, shall not, at their own Costs, within one Month next after Notice in Writing shall be given . . . cause all Water to be conveyed from the Roofs, Eaves, Cornices, and Penthouses of his House, Shop, Warehouse into the Common Channels or Drains by sufficient Pipes or Trunks . . . or otherwise shall not cause all Water to be conveyed . . . into their own respective private Grounds; it shall be lawful for the Commissioners . . . to cause the same to be done, and to levy the Costs attending the same by Distress . . .

That if any Person shall run, drive, draw, carry, or place . . . on any of the Foot Ways in any of the paved Parts of the said Streets and Lanes any Wheel or Wheels, Sledge or Carriage whatsoever, or shall roll any Cask, or wilfully ride, drive, or lead any Horse or other Cattle in any of the said Foot Ways, other than in Case of Necessity, such Person shall forfeit any Sum not exceeding 20s.

That the Commissioners may cause such Glass Lamps to be erected and set up in the said Streets and Lanes and to fix so many such Lamps as they shall think proper to any House or other Building, making good the Damage which shall be done thereto . . . That if any Person shall wilfully break, throw down, or otherwise damage any of the Lamps . . . or any of the Posts, Irons, or other Furniture thereof, or shall extinguish any of the said Lamps, it shall be lawful for any Justice of the Peace for the said Town to issue a Warrant for apprehending the Party accused.

## *THE SCOPE OF PARISH GOVERNMENT*

### *1. Perambulating the Parish, 1818*

The Vicar of Kelvedon made the following record.
Kelvedon Vestry Book, 1811-79 (D/P 134/25).

1818. On the 30th of April, Ascension Day, I set off to go the bounds of the parish, accompanied by the following persons ; Mr Jos. Baker, Mr Geo. Wm. Cole, Churchwardens [and twelve others]. We had performed that part which takes in Ewell Hall, Highfields, etc., when it came on to rain so very hard that we were obliged to defer the remainder of the walk till Saturday, May 2nd, when we completed it and afterwards dined at the Angel.

### *2. Parochial Pride, 1789*

Chelmsford Vestry, an efficient body by contemporary standards, was loth to surrender its functions to any newly created public authority.
Chelmsford Overseers' Rate Book (D/P 94/11/2).

At a meeting of the inhabitants of the town of Chelmsford and that part of the hamlet of Moulsham which will be affected by a Bill now before Parliament for lighting and watching the said town and hamlet and paving the footpaths, held this 20th day of April, 1789.

Resolved. That the said Bill, so far as respects the lighting and watching and preventing nuisances and encroachments, will be of general advantage.

Resolved. That the footpaths are in a very good condition and do not require paving and that the pavement thereof will be a great and unnecessary expense and extremely oppressive . . . the present rates being already very heavy.

Resolved. That the public street in the centre of the town and the back street and also a considerable part of the hamlet of Moulsham are so narrow that the paving the foot paths there will be attended with great inconvenience to persons passing through with carriages.

Resolved. That application be made to the committee, who have the conducting the said Bill and the passing the same through Parliament, that the powers therein given for paving the foot paths may not be included in the said Act.

### 3. *Parishioners allocate Pews, 1725*

Thaxted Vestry Minutes in Overseers' Accounts (D/P 16/12/3).

Whereas, when the old pews were standing, they were not capable to contain the people, many being very much thronged and others forced to sit in the alleys for want of room and there being as yet no new pews erected upon any new ground, we do therefore agree, for the better convenience of the people, that more pews be built in that large and vacant space between the cross aisle and belfry. And as upon the building of the pews, that are to stand betwixt the bottom cross aisle and the belfry, the pulpit would stand at too great a distance from them, we do therefore approve of the removal of the pulpit to the next pillar downwards in order to the placing it as near as conveniently may be in the middle of the congregation.

Whereas there is nobody pleads any prescription to any seat or ground where the pews are erected, which pews have been built out of the late Lord Maynard's Charity, and whereas the seats in the body of the church we look upon to be the most proper for gentlemen, farmers and other housekeepers who pay to the Churchwardens' rate and contribute towards the repairs of the church, we therefore think it very unreasonable that any person should presume to place his servants in any of these chief seats, there being very decent pews in the north and south aisle provided for them.

### 4. *Administration of Charity Schools, 1750*

Wethersfield Vestry Minutes (D/P 119/8/2).

Wethersfield . . . At a meeting held by the trustees for the Free School . . . the gift of Thomas Fitch, Gent., we the Churchwardens and Overseers of the said parish and trustees of the said school do appoint Thomas Carpenter of the said parish to be school master.

### 5. *Enforcing Sabbath Observance, 1818*

Chelmsford Vestry Minutes (D/P 94/8/3).

Vestry Room, Chelmsford, 7th July, 1818. At this monthly meeting it was unanimously resolved by the parishioners present, in conjunction with the Rev. I. G. Ward, the Rector, to exert themselves for the correction of abuses which have crept into practice in this town and operate strongly against the due observation of the Lord's day, and especially that of partially opening shops on the morning of that day and exposing for sale the necessaries of life in breach of the statute law. And this meeting doth order that the Beadle, Sidesman and all other officers respectively be very vigilant in giving such information as may lead to putting the statutes in force against all persons found offending after due notice of this resolution is publicly circulated through the parish, and for that purpose the Vestry clerk do have a sufficient number of copies of this order printed and cause one to be forwarded to every shopkeeper and trader resident in the parish.

### 6. *Chelmsford's Vaccination Campaign, 1821*

Chelmsford Vestry Minutes (D/P 94/8/3).

Resolved that the following Notice be printed and distributed about the town.

"Whereas it appears that the prevention of that dangerous disease, the smallpox, by means of vaccination has been lamentably neglected in very many families resident in this parish—the Select Vestry, fully convinced of the great utility of vaccination in preventing altogether in most cases, and universally in mitigating, the contagion of small pox, do most urgently recommend to the inhabitants (and to the poor in particular) to vaccinate without delay such of their children as are still exposed to that loathsome and fatal disease. I. G. Ward, Chairman."

### 7. *Dunmow Fire Brigade, 1831*

Dunmow Select Vestry Minutes (D/P 11/8/5).

I hereby agree to attend the fire engines for the year ensuing as follows.

To take the engines out three times in the year, to procure and pay men for the same, to oil the pipes and buckets, cleanse the valves, suckers, tubes, etc, to take the acting part as fireman, should such accident happen and also to take out the engines after the same to cleanse as aforesaid, at the sum of three pounds per year. W. Wright.

## 8. *Recruiting, 1795*

Little Clacton Overseers' Papers (D/P 80/17).

Essex, District of Tendring . . . Whereas the returns of the whole number of men appointed to be raised by the parishes of Great Holland, Little Clacton and Frinton have not been made within the time limited to you for so doing, this is therefore to require you [the parish officers] to appear before the Justices of the Peace at a Petty Sessions to be holden on 11th May next at the Bell Inn in Thorpe to answer for your default. Hereof fail not. John Bridges, M. Thompson.

---

9th April, 1795. I, John Warren, now or late of Ramsey, do hereby consent to serve for the parishes of Great Holland, Frinton and Little Clacton and do promise to attend the Justices at Mistley Thorn on Monday next for that purpose, and I do acknowledge to have received of Mr William Baker, Overseer of Great Holland, 5s., part of £26 . 5s., the whole bounty to be paid me.

The mark of X John Warren.

[Endorsed] Warren. Regulated and approved of by me at Harwich this 14th April, 1795. Wm. Collis, Regulating Officer.

## 9. *Aiding Home Defence, 1798*

Castle Hedingham Vestry Minutes (D/P 48/8/1).

At a meeting of householders, inhabitants of Castle Hedingham . . . it was unanimously resolved :—

That, in the present serious situation of public affairs, it is the duty of every honest man and loyal subject to step forward in the defence of his country.

That an armed association consisting of a troop of cavalry be immediately raised from amongst the householders, and the parishes of Sible Hedingham, Great Maplestead, Little Maplestead, Great Yeldham and Gestingthorpe be invited to enter in the same.

That any person residing within the above parishes, not being a householder but recommended by two householders, may be admitted into the association.

That the troop shall be under the command of Lewis Majendie, Esq., . . . that the troop shall not be called out, except in case of actual invasion, nor be called upon to act out of the Hundred of Hinckford ; that all expenses except for arms and ammunition be defrayed by the parties associating.

That the association will upon every occasion strenuously exert itself in the support of the civil authority and for the suppression of riot and tumult.

## 10. *The Parish against Napoleon, 1803-5*

The following are selected entries from printed parochial invasion preparations schedules completed in MS. by the overseers of Great Coggeshall. *Original spelling retained.*

Coggeshall Militia Records (D/P 36/17/5).

SCHEDULE No. 1

Live and Dead Stock

| Names | Live Stock | | | | | Horses | | | | Average Amount of Dead Stock | | | | | | | |
|---|---|---|---|---|---|---|---|---|---|---|---|---|---|---|---|---|---|
| | Oxen | Cows | Young Cattle and Colts | Sheep and Goats | Pigs | Riding | Draft | Waggons | Carts | Wheat, Quarters of | Oats, Quarters of | Barley, Quarters of | Beans and Pease, Quarters of | Hay, Loads of | Straw, Loads of | Potatoes, Sacks of | Malt, Quarters of |
| Osgood Hanbury, Esq. | 40 | 8 | 10 | 150 | 30 | 4 | 12 | 3 | 6 | 200 | 100 | 120 | 100 | 150 | 50 | 40 | 10 |
| Filmer Honywood, Esq. | — | 4 | — | — | 10 | 1 | 9 | 4 | 4 | 70 | 20 | 100 | 50 | 10 | 20 | — | — |
| Messrs. Townsends | 8 | 10 | 1 | 49 | 20 | — | 7 | 2 | 6 | 80 | 10 | 120 | 20 | 10 | 20 | — | — |
| Messrs. Brightwens | — | 4 | — | — | — | 2 | 8 | 2 | 1 | -- | 50 | 100 | 20 | 20 | — | — | 100 |
| Mr Stephen Unwin | — | — | — | — | — | 1 | 1 | — | 1 | — | 100 | 200 | 20 | 4 | — | — | 200 |
| Mr Fisher Unwin | — | — | — | — | — | 2 | — | 1 | 2 | 15 | — | 30 | 5 | 10 | 10 | — | — |
| Mr Richd. White | 20 | 4 | — | 50 | 10 | 2 | 6 | 3 | 4 | 100 | 10 | 40 | 20 | 20 | 10 | — | — |
| Mr Thos. Allaker | — | 12 | 7 | 40 | 20 | 1 | 7 | 2 | 3 | 60 | 20 | 36 | 10 | 20 | 10 | — | — |
| John Prior | — | — | — | — | — | — | 1 | — | 1 | — | — | — | — | — | — | — | — |
| Wm. Gazard | — | — | — | — | — | — | 1 | — | 1 | — | — | — | — | — | — | 100 | — |
| [and 11 other names] | | | | | | | | | | | | | | | | | |

## SCHEDULE No. 2

Overseers and Persons appointed for the Removal of Waggons, Cattle, Horses, and Live Stock, as well as to take Charge of the Dead Stock . . . It is recommended to the Proprietors to mark their Cattle, not only with the Initials of their Names, but also to add some distinctive mark common to the whole Parish, that Confusion may be avoided if the Stock of several Parishes should join in one Body.

| Persons appointed for the Removal of Horses and Waggons, conveying such persons as are unable to move themselves | Overseers appointed to superintend this Service | Persons appointed for the Removal of Cattle | Overseers for the same | Persons appointed for the Removal of Sheep and other Live Stock | Overseers for the same | Persons appointed to take Charge of the Dead Stock, and to be stationary |
|---|---|---|---|---|---|---|
| James Thompson<br>Haddon Rudkin<br>Thos. Harris<br>George Beard<br>Thos. Hines<br>Robt. Matthews<br><br>[No names omitted] | Thomas Andrew, Sen. | Jonathan Hervey<br>Thos. Hassenden<br>F. Harrisson<br>John Harrison<br>John Winkle<br>John Evans, Jun.<br>John Browning | John Gurton, Sen. | Abm. Tyler<br>Jas. Bailey<br>Jacob Anthony<br>Willm. Kirkham<br>Richd. Clark<br>Chas. Willshire<br>Abm. Chapman | Thos. Allaker, Sen. | Richd. White<br>Richd. Appleton |

## SCHEDULE No. 3

Persons between the Ages of Fifteen and Sixty, willing to serve with Arms, and who will agree to assemble in Troops or Companies, under such Persons as are chosen from amongst themselves, and approved of by the Civil Authority of the said County.

It is recommended that before the Meeting separates, the People who have so signed, should class themselves into Troops and Companies, or where the Number of Cavalry and Infantry does not admit of a distinct Service, into a Joint Body ; and on forwarding their Return to the Lieutenancy, they should propose the Names of their Leaders for their Approbation, at the rate, as nearly as possible, of one to twenty-five or at most thirty-five Men.

N.B. It is earnestly recommended to all who voluntarily offer to appear with Arms, to provide a Bullet Mould for the Calibre of their Gun or Pistol, a small Bag for Bullets, and a Powder Horn, lest the Bore of their Arms being smaller than those of the Army should prevent their using the Ammunition made up for the King's Troops, in which case, a Delivery of Lead and Powder will be made to them.

| Names | On Horse Back | On Foot | How Armed | | | | Remarks |
|---|---|---|---|---|---|---|---|
| | | | Cavalry | | Infantry | | |
| | | | Swords | Pistols | Firelocks | Pitchforks | |
| Saml. Harrison Jun. | 1 | Foot | 1 | 1 | — | — | Leaders :— |
| Chas. Plaistow | — | Do. | — | — | 1 | — | Willm. Swinbourn |
| Matt. Nickols | — | Do. | — | — | 1 | — | Willm. Potter |
| Saml. Sach | — | Do. | — | — | 1 | — | Richd. Williamson |
| James Boag | 1 | — | 1 | 1 | — | — | Goodey Pudney |
| Henry Skingley | 1 | — | 1 | 1 | — | — | Refused :— |
| Isaac Rogers | — | Do. | — | — | 1 | — | Peter Rowland, Jun. |
| Fisher Appleby | — | Do. | — | — | 1 | — | Joseph Winterflood |
| [and 17 other names] | | | | | | | |

[Also 129 names of persons to be provided with arms]

## SCHEDULE No. 4

Persons between the Ages of Fifteen and Sixty, willing to act as Pioneers or Labourers, and willing to be classed in Companies under such Leaders or Captains, from their own Body . . .

| Names | Implements they can bring | | | | | | Other Instruments Pioneers may bring | Remarks |
|---|---|---|---|---|---|---|---|---|
| | Felling Axes | Pick Axes | Spades | Shovels | Bill Hooks | Saws | | |
| Stephen Leaper | 1 | | | | | | | Leaders :— |
| Matt. Stuck | | | | | | | Pike | Thos. Powell |
| Abm. Metcalf | | | | | | 1 | | Saml. Sprayne |
| Robt. Humphry | | 1 | | | | | | Thos. Baines |
| Benj. Deal | | | | | 1 | | | Whitlock |
| John Allerton | | | | | | | 1 Cudjgel | Captains :— |
| John Hayward | | | 1 | | | | | Saml. Sach |
| Willm. Surry | 1 | | | | | | | Jos. Everett |
| [and 155 other names] | | | | | | | | |

## SCHEDULE No. 5

| Persons appointed to act as Guides, being mounted and chosen from amongst the most intelligent Residentees in the Parish | Remarks |
|---|---|
| Stephen Unwin | Osgood Hanbury Esq. Quaker |
| Jordan Unwin, Jun. | Saml. Harrisson Do |
| Thos. Andrew, Jun. | John Hamson Do |
| Saml. Rudkin | Isaac Brightwen Do |
| Northey Rowland | F. Hills Do |
| [No names omitted] | |

## SCHEDULE No. 6

We the undersigned Nobility, Gentry, and Yeomanry, having taken into our Consideration a Plan recommended to our Attention by the Magistrates of the County aforesaid "For an Association to supply such Number of Waggons, Carts, Horses, Drivers, and Conductors, in aid of the Provisions made by the Mutiny Act, as may be necessary for carrying on his Majesty's Service, as also to contribute towards the Supply (when required) of his Majesty's Forces with Flour, Wheat, Oats, Hay, Straw, and Fuel, in Case of an Invasion", Do hereby declare our Concurrence in the same : And we do faithfully promise and engage to furnish Waggons and Carts, provided with able Horses, Drivers, and Conductors, and also such Quantities of Flour, [etc.] as may be required of us, when it is in our Power so to do, upon receiving a Requisition from the Commissary General of the Army, or other officer duly authorized by him, desiring our Aid, and specifying the Quantity and Quality of the Articles called for ; a Receipt to be given by him at the Time of Delivery, afterwards to be paid for at such a Rate as shall be fixed by the Deputy-Lieutenants or Magistrates of the County . . .

| SUBSCRIBERS' NAMES<br>Those who cannot furnish Tilts should . . . mark, "No T" | Waggons with Tilts and | | Carts with Tilts and | | Persons appointed to act as Servants with Teams | Conductors for the same, in Proportion of One to every Ten Waggons | General Agent for the Parish to whom Requisition is to be made to call forth the Carriages or Waggons |
|---|---|---|---|---|---|---|---|
| | Four Horses or more | Three Horses | Three Horses or more | Two Horses | | | |
| Fisher Unwin | One, "N.T." | | | | Two | | |
| Thos. Allaker | One, "N.T." | | | | Two | | |
| Saml. Harrisson | One, "N.T." | | | | Two | | |
| John Gurton | One, "N.T." | | | | Two | | |
| Richd. White | One, "N.T." | | | | Two | | |
| Osgood Hanbury, Esq. | One, "N.T." | | | | Two | Jacob Pattisson | Peter Good |
| Henry Skinsley | One, "N.T." | | | | Two | | |
| Richd. Townsend | One, "N.T." | | | | Two | | |
| Goodey Pudney | One, "N.T." | | | | Two | | |
| Thos. Denton | One | | | | Two | | |
| Steph. Unwin | — | | | | One | | |
| Haddon Rudkin | — | | | 1, "N.T." | One | | |
| [and 5 other names] | | | | | | | |

SCHEDULE No. 7

We the undersigned Millers do faithfully promise and engage to deliver such Quantities of ready-made Flour as we may happen to have in Hand, over and above the immediate Wants of our Customers ; and also to prepare and deliver such Quantities of dry, sweet, and clean Flour made of good marketable English Wheat . . .

| SUBSCRIBERS' NAMES | Names and Situations of Water Mills | Names and Situations of Wind Mills | Will the Subscribers provide the Wheat or not ? |
|---|---|---|---|
| John Prior | — | New | Yes |
| Richd. Stammers | — | Roots | — |
| John How | — | Thompsons | — |
| [No names omitted] | | | |

SCHEDULE No. 8

We the undersigned Bakers, in case of an Invasion, do hereby faithfully promise and engage to bake and deliver such Quantities of good wholesome well-baked Bread, as our Stock of Flour in Hand at the Time may enable us to furnish, over and above the Ordinary Consumption of our Customers ; and also to bake and deliver good, wholesome, well-baked Bread, out of such Flour as may be delivered to us for that Purpose, whenever we may be required so to do, to be afterwards paid for [as in Schedule No. 6].

| SUBSCRIBERS' NAMES | Loaves of Three Pounds to be furnished by each Subscriber, every Twenty-four Hours | | For what Kind of Fuel the Ovens are calculated | What Quantity is required for every Twenty-four Hours, to keep each Oven constantly at Work, supposing Six Batches to be baked | Whether Fuel is abundant or not ? |
|---|---|---|---|---|---|
| | For a Constancy | On an Emergency | | | |
| John Prior | 300 | 400 | Wood | 6½ Cwt | No |
| Will. Appleford, Jun. | 300 | 400 | Wood | 6½ Cwt | No |
| Widow Prior | 300 | 400 | Wood | 6 — | No |
| Will. Appleford, Sen. | 200 | 300 | Wood | 5 — | No |
| Rich. Coe | 200 | 300 | Wood | 5 Cwt | No |
| [No names omitted] | | | | | |

### *11. The Coggeshall Volunteers*

*The C—ll Volunteer Corps, A Farce,* Colchester, 1804.

Scene 1. A Room. Mrs. Dashit at a Glass, adjusting her Head Dress : Mr Dashit enters hastily.

Mr D. My dear, would you think it, I am a lieutenant, a lieutenant 'pon honour, a most respectable meeting, there was I myself, and twenty or thirty more gentlemen, all the heads of the town, six captains, the rest all lieutenants, three companies, hundred in a company, uniform superfine scarlet lined with blue, silver edging, gold epaulets, kerseymere waistcoats and pantaloons, bearskin helmets, and ostrich feathers, swords and side knots ; all is settled, all settled. Don't you think I shall cut a fine figure ? But I can't stay, for we are all going out to canvas for privates. Must come forward. But they are all waiting : there's I *myself,* twenty or thirty more gentlemen, heads of the town all going out a' canvassing for privates. Everything is settled, quite settled ; six captains, the rest lieutenants, three companies, a hundred in a company ; no expence ; develish well managed, however ; find their own clothes ; so good bye, dearee. Lord, lovee ! what an elegant figure I shall make ; scarlet, lined with blue, silver edging.

### *12. Voluntary Food Rationing, 1800*

Moreton Vestry Minutes (D/P 72/8/1).

At a Vestry purposely convened to promote the measures of economy recommended in his Majesty's proclamation, we the principal inhabitants of Moreton have unanimously agreed during the present scarcity to reduce the consumption of bread in our respective families by at least one fourth of the quantity consumed in ordinary times, that we will abstain from the use of flour in pastry, and moreover carefully restrict the use thereof in all other articles than bread ; we do also covenant carefully to restrict the use of oats and other grain for the subsistence of our horses, especially horses for pleasure, as far as our respective circumstances will admit.

## *THE PARISH OFFICERS*

*The work of the* Overseers of the Poor *and of the* Surveyors of the Highways *is illustrated on pp. 102-19 and pp. 52-5 of this book.*

### *1. Obligatory Service in Parish Offices, 1755*

All Saints, Colchester, Vestry Minutes (D/P 200/8/2).

All Saints Parish in Colchester, 26th December, 1755. At a meeting of the parishioners in vestry assembled it was unanimously agreed that, in regard the present Surveyors of the Highways have not sufficiently discharged the duty of the said office, that the said Surveyors, John Sparrow and Robert Brown, together with John Walker and John Paine be returned to the Justices for their appointment of two of them to be Surveyors of the Highways for the year ensuing.

## 2. *The Work of the Constables*

Upminster Constables' Accounts (D/P 117/9/1).

| 1788 | | £ s. d. |
|---|---|---|
| Mar. 24 | Relieved 2 paupers with passes | 0.2.0 |
| May 28 | Summoning the Jury to Foxhall | 0.6.0 |
| Sep. 22 | Attending the Vestry when choosing Surveyors | 0.2.6 |
| Oct. 6 | Going to Brentwood with Freeholders' list [etc.] | 0.8.6 |
| Nov. 1 | Collecting the names for Militia and making the list | 0.5.0 |
| Dec. 19 | Taking Mary Vale into custody and keeping her | 0.2.6 |
| 20 | Carrying her to House of Correction | 0.5.0 |
| | Expenses for horse, cart, turnpikes, prisoner, etc. | 0.8.6 |
| 1789 | | |
| Mar. 2 | Taking John Blatch into custody and keeping him in hold 4 days and 3 nights | 1.5.0 |
| | Paid for assistances 4 days and 3 nights | 0.7.6 |
| Sep. 7 | Going to Brentwood on Licence day | 0.5.0 |
| Dec. 8 | Taking Thos. Snell and detaining him till was married | 0.7.6 |
| 12 | Going to Aveley after a pair of orders to remove him | 0.5.0 |

## 3. *The Work of the Churchwardens*

Wivenhoe Churchwardens' Accounts (D/P 277/5/2).

| 1797 | | £ s. d. |
|---|---|---|
| Apr. 8 | To the Minister for attending Visitation | 0. 5. 0 |
| 15 | Mr West's bill for work at the Church | 0.16. 0 |
| | For parish clerk (John Barrel) | 3. 0. 0 |
| | For winding up the clock | 0.10. 6 |
| | Sarah Chiswick for cleaning the Church and linen | 1. 1. 0 |
| | Mr Lays for wine for the Sacrament | 1. 0. 0 |
| | For 24 weeks for instruction in Church music at 3/- per week | 3.12. 0 |
| | To a bill from Barrel for Sacrament bread and sundries | 0.12.11 |

| | | | |
|---|---|---|---|
| Jun. | 14 | To eight briefs paid at the Visitation | 0 . 8 . 0 |
| | | To a form of thanksgiving for Sir J. Jervis's victory over the Spanish fleet, Feb. 14 | 1 . 0 |
| | 27 | To expenses going to Colchester to swear M. Davis's residence | 4 . 0 |
| | 28 | Relieved a soldier with a pass | 0 . 1 . 0 |
| July | 22 | To expenses going to Colchester on parish business | 0 . 3 . 0 |
| Oct. | 16 | When Admiral Duncan obtained the victory over the Dutch fleet, for ringers | 0 . 5 . 0 |
| | 30 | To two bell ropes | 0 . 14 . 0 |
| | | Relieved Edward Cole | 0 . 1 . 0 |
| 1798 | | | |
| Feb. | 12 | To expenses and sending a man to Colchester, at Hempson's settlement, at the Falcon | 0 . 9 . 0 |
| Apr. | 6 | Paid West, bricklayer's bill, for work done to the Church and porch | 8 . 5 . 0 |
| | | Paid Mrs Mason's bill for work at the Church | 3 . 3 . 0 |
| | | For allowance of beer cleaning the Church | 0 . 1 . 0 |

### 4. *Lambourne Surveyor called to Account, 1745*

Lambourne Vestry Minutes (D/P 181/8/2).

At a Vestry held the 24th Dec. 1745, it was agreed . . . That the Surveyor of the Highways hath not complied with the order made the 20th June, in respect to the people that have been employed in the highway ; that he do it upon oath before a magistrate and that he likewise give the parish the same satisfaction in respect to the quantity of stones that have been gathered, whether they are all laid on the roads or not ; and that he is by order of Vestry to have no more than 2s. 6d. for every journey to Harlow and that he show reason why Squire Lockwood was not called on to do his highway work.

Whether bringing stones out of his own ground and ordering them to be laid on the waste before his own yard be doing highway work ? That he give account why the ditches that are in the roads, as also all ditches leading from them to the river, were not cleared in order to drain the roads. If the persons to whom the ditches belonged refused to clear the ditches, why he did not oblige them, or else do it himself and charge them for it ? By what power he charges Matthew Steel and Richard Saintpier one guinea each in lieu of their highway work ?

For the above reasons it is that we, the parishioners present, cannot agree to sign the Surveyor's accounts.

## *THE SUPERSESSION OF THE PARISH POLICE*

### *1. The Nomination of Chief Constables*

*Original spelling retained.*
Quarter Sessions Bundle, Easter 1719 (Q/SBb 68).

Abberton 7 April, 1719.

Samuel Lusse one of the Cheife Constables of the Hundred haveing Sarved the offis three years desiers the faver of this Court to apint one in My place whare of I have given in a List

James Sabrook magna wigbrow
John Harvey Eastmarsy
John Snelling fingringho

### *2. Parish Constable aids Smugglers?*

Quarter Sessions Bundle, Michaelmas 1713 (Q/SBb 58).

The informations of John Cripps and Lucy Fisher . . . taken upon oath this 22nd August 1713, before us, Hope Gifford and John Potter, Esqs., two of her Majesty's Justices of the Peace, do say as follows.

That they, being Surveyors and Gagers of her Majesty's Duties of Excise in and about Wivenhoe, had information of some foreign brandies being run and lodged at or near the house of Peter Weston in Wivenhoe, whereupon these informants, the better to discharge their office, did require John Turner, one of the Constables of Wivenhoe, to be aiding them in the keeping the peace whilst they made search for the brandy. And the Constable did readily go along with them till they came to Weston's house and, when he saw they had a design to search the house of Weston, the Constable called to Weston and used these or like words, " Take care of the pigs in your cherry gardens ", which these informants believe was a sign for him to secure his brandies.

That Lucy Fisher knocked at Weston's door, that he might come down to let him into the house, but when the Constable did see the informants did design to search the house, he takes hold of Fisher by the collar and pushed him several times upon the breast and did swear by God that, if his hands were not tied, he would knock his brains out. And the Constable withdrew some distance from them, by reason of which the informants were afraid to make any search after the brandies. And then these informants went back to the Constable and told him that they expected his assistance and did wonder he should leave them. And thereupon the Constable did again take Fisher by his breast and did swear again by his God that, if his hands were not tied, he would beat his brains out.

### 3. *Anarchy in Dengie Hundred*

Without a J.P. to direct and co-ordinate them, parish constables often failed to maintain elementary order.
*Ipswich Journal,* Dec. 19, 1767 (C.B.L.).

It is scarcely to be conceived the Hardship the People undergo in Dengy Hundred for want of an Acting Magistrate in that Division, they being over run by Beggars and Thieves, who have been driven into that Quarter from other Places. Scarce a Night passes without some Robbery being committed by these Strollers and Vagrants. On Monday Night last Mr Smith of Burnham had a fine fat Sheep stolen from his Grounds, and killed and stripped in a neighbouring Field, and his House has several Times been beset this Winter.

### 4. *Highwaymen Active, 1765-9*

*Ipswich Journal,* Nov. 23, 1765 (C.B.L.).

Chelmsford. Last Friday Evening as Mr Pinneck, Farmer, was returning from this Market to Ingatestone, he was knocked down a little beyond Widford-Bridge by a Foot-pad . . . who demanded his Money, declaring he had seen him receive some at the Saracen's Head. Mr Pinneck immediately rose up and, a Battle ensuing, he soon got the Fellow under him ; on which an Accomplice came up and attempted to shoot him with a Pistol, but, it only flashing in the Pan, Mr Pinneck attacked them both and would in all probability have mastered them, had he not unluckily dropt his Stick, which obliged him to make his Escape.

*Chelmsford Chronicle,* Dec. 26, 1768.

Yesterday morning the Colchester coach was robbed between Stratford and Ilford by a single highwayman, who took four guineas from the inside passengers but took no manner of notice of those on the outside.

*Chelmsford Chronicle,* Jan. 20, 1769.

Yesterday morning, about 7 o'clock, the Norwich Post Coach was stopped near Romford Gallows by a young highwayman, extreamly well mounted, who robbed one of the inside passengers of two guineas and the other of about thirty shillings. His hand trembled while he held the pistol, but he behaved with the greatest politeness.

### 5. *The Parish Constable's Shortcomings, 1837*

*Colchester Gazette,* June 17, 1837 (C.B.L.).

Chelmsford Petty Sessions. James Horsnail, constable of Springfield, appeared to answer a complaint preferred by Mr Neale, the Governor of the Convict Gaol, for misconduct in the performance of his duty. Last week a man named Richardson was committed by the Bench for stealing greens, and Horsnail was directed to take him to prison; he ought to have taken him in the afternoon, but Mr Neale stated that he did not arrive until a quarter past nine at night, and he should say that both had been drinking, as the prisoner staggered. Mr Neale asked him why he did not come before and the constable replied, "There is no harm done, he has been to several places with me". The constable admitted he had done wrong, but denied that Richardson was intoxicated; the prisoner, he said, had lived 45 years close to him and was, besides, his cousin, and he did not like to hurry him to gaol, as he wanted to make arrangements for a child which otherwise might have been left without anyone to take care of it.

### 6. *The Penal Code in Operation, 1785-6*

The following is an extract from a list of executions for crimes committed in Essex.

Tufnell Archives (D/DTu 235).

| Date | Persons executed | Offence | Where committed |
|---|---|---|---|
| 1785 | | | |
| Mar. 12 | Robert Wright | Murder | Paglesham |
| Mar. 18 | John Godfrey | Burglary | Hatfield Peverel |
| | William Dobson | Burglary | Hatfield Peverel |
| Mar. 26 | William Grace | Stealing in house | Avery Hatch [Ilford] |
| | George Ingram | Horsestealing | Shenfield |
| July 22 | William Jones | Burglary | Dagenham |
| | Williamson | Burglary | Dagenham |
| | J. Morgan, Wheeler | Highway Robbery | —— |
| | Michael Wadcock | Ditto. | West Ham |
| | William Moore | Ditto. | West Ham |
| | Edward Smith | Assault and robbery | Southminster |
| | Thomas Littler | Stealing from a calico ground | Waltham Abbey |
| | Thomas Abrams | Sheepstealing | Waltham Holy Cross |
| | Edward Green | Highway robbery | Wansted |
| 1786 | | | |
| Mar. 24 | William Brooks | Burglary | Writtle |
| | John Sparrow | Highway robbery | —— |
| | John Wells | Highway robbery | —— |
| | Thomas Brett | Burglary | Stansted |
| Aug. 11 | Samuel Riglin | Leather | Ballingdon |
| | John Cornell | Horsestealing | Finchingfield |
| | Thomas Jaggard | Highway robbery | Littlebury |

### 7. *Voluntary Night Watchmen in Colchester, 1801*

*Ipswich Journal*, March 21, 1801 (C.B.L.).

A regular nightly patrole is established among the principal inhabitants of the several parishes in this town, who, chiefly by themselves or approved substitutes, patrole the streets for the protection of their property from depradations.

### 8. *The Bow Street Runners, 1797*

*Ipswich Journal*, Jan. 7, 1797 (C.B.L.).

Colchester. On Tuesday night, the 27th of Dec. last, the dwelling-house of Mr Thos. Cooper, of Langenhoe Hall, near this town, was burglariously broken into and robbed of bank-notes and cash to the amount of £450 and upwards, besides other property. And on Saturday last, through the exertions of Messrs Fugion and Taylor, of the public office, Bow St., assisted by Mr Bullock, high constable of Winstree hundred, Mr Wood of Heybridge, Mr Wells of Peldon, and others, a person of the name of Avis was apprehended upon suspicion of being concerned in the said robbery; who, being strictly questioned by the Bow-street Officers, confessed he was one of the party; and upon his information Mr Fugion, at 12 o'clock at night, set off from Heybridge to Ostend (near Cricksey Ferry) and recovered of Avis's assister 15 guineas and a half of the cash, etc, stolen.

### 9. *Calling in the 'Peelers'*

Coggeshall Vestry Minutes (D/P 36/8/7).

Great Coggeshall, Essex,
4 Nov., 1833.

Gentlemen,

Depradations to some considerable extent having of late been committed in this parish and suspicion having fallen upon several persons on whom property has been found, supposed to be stolen, we the undersigned . . . shall feel obliged by your sending down an intelligent police man at your earliest convenience, and the expenses attending the same we shall most readily discharge.

To Cols. Rowan and Mayner, [Signed by parish officers.]
Police Office, Scotland Yard.

### 10. *County Police established, 1839*

In 1839 Essex Quarter Sessions debated the adoption of powers to establish a rural police force.
*Essex Standard*, Nov. 29, 1839 (C.B.L.).

Lord Braybrooke—All are disgusted with the ignorance and neglect of the constables. I have seen instances of prisoners being brought before me in a state of intoxication, while the constable himself has not been sober. As to the execution of a search warrant, I have almost trembled to grant them . . .

Mr Disney—A poor man says, I know not where to go if my cottage is robbed. If I go to the constable, perhaps he is the pot companion of the thief and I must go to Billericay or to some other distant place, where an active police officer resides . . . They are driving all the thiefs out of London into Essex, and I told a gentleman of Suffolk the other day, " I am going to drive all the thiefs out of Essex into your county; you must drive them into the next, and so on till they are driven into the sea ".

Mr Shaen—I have the fortune to have an excellent constable, a most respectable man, and in consequence of a robbery a few days ago he was sent for; he went and condoled with the person who had lost the goods; but where were the robbers? Could he go after them? No, he had to attend to his business; if he went after them without catching them, he would get nothing for his trouble; and if he caught them, he would only get 5s. a day, while he could be making 10s. at home.

Mr Gurdon Rebow—In this county a short time ago, at Colchester, we had incendiary fires, and one was very near the town; we called a meeting of the gentry and neighbours round, and the result was the appointment of a secret committee, of which I had the honour to be one. We wrote to Sir F. Roe for a police officer, and he sent one. It was three or four days before he arrived; but when it was known that a London police officer was down, there were no more fires.

Mr Bramston—I can state a fact that was related to me by a man who was executed a few years ago. A burglary and murder had been committed. The constable went in pursuit, in his way traced the man, obtained the assistance of other constables, and they took him and he was convicted. While he was under sentence of death, he stated that the constable, when he came to him said, " Good God, Tom, is this you? If I had known it, you would have been the last man I should have taken "; for this man had been the constable's chief man as a poacher, and they had been in the habit of going out together.

## *FURTHER CURTAILMENT OF PARISH AUTHORITY*

### *1. Denominational Conflict, 1728*

The following passage records an early appearance of the Nonconformist movement which eventually led to the ending of the compulsory church rate.
Chelmsford Churchwardens' Accounts (D/P 94/5/2).

Chelmsford, Jan. 2nd, 1728. It was then agreed at a General

Vestry that there be no money allowed for the purchasing of pessoks [hassocks] in the church, and the officers of the parish are hereby required not to purchase any pessoks except by a special order of Vestry first obtained in writing. [Signed by 14 parishioners.]

Memorandum. I, Oliver Pocklinton, Rector of Chelmsford, was at this parish meeting when this order was dictated in a great measure by Mr Lucas and, when it was read, I expressed my dissatisfaction and said that I would not sign it; upon which, although I may safely say that there were thirty parishioners present, nay perhaps forty, if not fifty, yet all of them scrupled to set their hands to it until Mr Lucas set his hand to it, and then the rest followed, being fourteen in all, whereof five are dissenters.

2. *Opposition to Church Rates, 1839*

Sage Collection 670 (E.R.O.).

*TO THE INHABITANTS OF ROMFORD*

An address, under the formula of religious expressions, has been circulated in this Town, bearing the signature of " A. Grant, Vicar ". Its primary object is to impose a rate upon the inhabitants, for the building of (what is vulgarly called) a New Church. But with that I have nothing to do, as I esteem the Large and Small Tithes sufficient for that purpose, affording a good annual living after all. My object is to give a flat contradiction to the religious-like statistics the circular contains :—

1. That there are many Sanctuaries in this Parish, and that no Parishioner is doomed to spiritual destitution : and that an assertion to the contrary is a vulgar declamation to hoodwink the people.
2. That no man is cut off from the means of religious worship and instruction, excepting when he wilfully cuts himself off; and that a system of religion, which restrains man's free agency, is false, both in cause and effect, and altogether destructive of the birthright of the creature.
3. That the present state of the said Church is no discredit to the Town, but that it is a noble structure of the Gothic age; and that £500 would perfectly repair and beautify it : towards which, I am willing to contribute by way of subscription.
4. That the present state of the said Church is no seeming slight to the Most High ! And that to assert the contrary (considering the Being of a God who dwells not in Temples made by hands) is a grave and deliberate and pagan falsehood, and awfully at variance with the Divine Order ! !

*SAMUEL HANNA CARLISLE,*
Independent Minister.

Romford, Dec. 17, 1839.

### 3. *An Experiment in Highway Management, 1836*

Attempts to widen the area of highway administration decreased the power of the parish Surveyor.

Quarter Sessions Highways Returns (Q/AH 2).

At a Special Sessions of the Highways, held at the Bell Inn, Castle Hedingham, June, 1836.

We the undersigned, being the majority of the Magistrates assembled, having considered of the application of the chairmen of the several Vestries of the parishes mentioned in the margin hereof, to be formed into a District for the purpose of having one sufficient person to be the District Surveyor, to have the management of the funds to be raised under the provisions of an Act passed in the fifth and sixth years of the reign of his present Majesty . . . do hereby unite the several parishes into a District for the purposes of the said Act. And we do hereby appoint Henry Rose of Middleton, yeoman, as a fit person to be Surveyor at an annual salary of £52, to be paid to him by the Surveyors in the proportions set opposite the names of the parishes in the margin hereof. [Signed by three Justices.]

| *Parishes* | *Salary* |
|---|---|
| Ballingdon | £ 4 |
| Belchamp Walter | 10 |
| Borley | 5 |
| Bulmer | 10 |
| Foxearth | 10 |
| Gestingthorpe | 10 |
| Liston | 3 |

## *PUBLIC HEALTH AND LOCAL GOVERNMENT*

### 1. *Beginnings of Public Health, 1831*

In the cholera epidemic of 1831-2 the Government urged the establishment of local Boards of Health.

Hornchurch Vestry Minutes (D/P 115/8/2).

At a meeting of the Churchwardens, Overseers, Surveyors and other parishioners in the Poor House, convened this 15th Nov. 1831 . . . for the purpose of taking into consideration the most effectual means of preventing the introduction of the disease called the Cholera . . . Ordered—

That the Vestry Clerk be directed to write forthwith to the Surveyors of the 2 wards of this parish to have the ditches, drains, water courses and privies thoroughly cleansed and emptied and all nuisances removed and, if they find any impediment in so doing, they will immediately apply to the Magistrates for a summons . . .

That the Churchwardens and Overseers be directed to see that the Constables report to the Magistrates any licensed public house kept open after eleven o'clock at night . . . and likewise any shop for the sale of beer open after 10 o'clock . . . That the Churchwardens and Overseers give notice to each of the publicans and occupiers of shops for selling beer to be careful whom they take in as lodgers, that they harbour no common beggars, vagrants or any other disreputable persons . . .

The Constables be directed to warn all persons against begging alms and, if they do not desist from so doing, immediately to apprehend them . . . and that a person from the house, Samuel Stock, be appointed with a coat, etc, and staff to traverse the town and adjacent roads to caution all beggars and vagrants and suspicious characters to leave the place . . .

That the Workhouse be immediately lime or white washed from top to bottom and thoroughly cleansed and kept clean and ventilated. That the Select Vestry, in giving relief to families, enquire into the state of their dwellings and, if in the opinion of such Vestry they require cleaning, to employ a man to lime wash, clean the drains, gutters, etc, and where the parties are too poor so to do and the landlords after application refuse it.

That any person heading up or stopping any current of water be prosecuted.

That a Board of Health be established according to the circular received by Thomas Mashiter, Esq., from the Privy Council.

## 2. *Chelmsford Board of Health at Work, 1831-2*

Chelmsford Board of Health Minutes (D/P 94/24/1).

Dec. 15, 1831. The propriety of a barrel drain down the east side of New St. has been considered . . . The committee are of the opinion that no substantial good can be effected in Moulsham without public sewers being opened, as all the foul water, offal, etc, is thrown on the surface of the confined yards in this district . . . The cottages in New St., occupied by Porter, Turner and Chilvers, much more suitable for two, than three habitations . . . Cottages 8 feet by 7½ wide and 6½ feet high. In cottage No. 1—family 5 ; in cottage No. 2—family 4 ; in cottage No. 3—family 5 ; only two rooms in each cottage.

Jan. 12, 1832. Nothing done to Mr John Greenwood's premises, Page's privy, Dove's ditch, the Grammar School ditch or as to the removal of the privy of Drake's yard in New St. . . . No alteration having yet been made in the dung pit in Grave's yard, Back St., to render it more wholesome, it is agreed to allow the committee liberty to pay half the expense . . . There is typhus fever in Juniper's house, three persons being ill . . . The rain comes into the bed-chamber of Broid in Moulsham . . . Turner's family are crowded together, nine in number, into one small room, where they live by day and lodge by night.

### 3. *Petition for Sanitary Powers, 1848*

The following extract is from a Parliamentary petition, initiated during the cholera epidemic of 1848.

*Essex Standard,* Oct. 13, 1848 (C.B.L.).

That the town of Witham is increasing. That no general or public drainage exists, the only drains being private and very inefficient, the consequence of which is that the nuisance has reached such an extent as to render many of the houses in the neighbourhood of open drains unfit for habitation; and the evil is severely felt by inhabitants of many of the better class of houses from their being no proper and sufficient outlet for their own drains; and your petitioners firmly believe that, in the event of cholera appearing in the neighbourhood, the health of the inhabitants would materially suffer.

### 4. *The Constitution of Braintree Board of Health, 1850*

Solicitor's Official Papers (D/DO O3).

I, Augustus Charles Veley, Esq., . . . do hereby, in pursuance of The Public Health Act, 1848, give notice,

That the Number of Persons to be Elected as Members . . . is Nine.

That every Person to be Elected must be resident within the Parish of Braintree or within seven miles thereof and must be seized or possessed of Real or Personal Estate to the Value of not less than £500 or must be . . . rated to the Relief of the Poor upon an Annual Value of not less than £20.

That in the event of a Contest, every Rate Payer in respect of Property within the District will be entitled to vote according to the Scale hereinafter set forth.

That the Scale of Voting prescribed by the Act . . . is as follows,

| | |
|---|---|
| If the Rateable Value be under £50 | One Vote |
| If £50 and under £100 | Two Votes |
| If £100 and under £150 | Three Votes |
| If £150 and under £200 | Four Votes |
| If £200 and under £250 | Five Votes |
| If £250 and upwards | Six Votes |

## 5. *The Cost of Public Health*

A ratepayer of Halstead protests against the establishment of a Board of Health in the town.
*Essex Standard,* Jan. 21, 1853 (C.B.L.).

Sir, It surely is rather hard that the patriotism and loyalty of the middle classes on the memorable 10th of April in 1848, in rallying round our beloved Sovereign to defeat the attempt to overturn the Constitution, should have been rewarded by an Act to place a Napoleon, with powers to confiscate property and enslave persons, over every town in the kingdom . . . I call upon my countrymen to purchase Spottiswoode's edition of the Health of Towns Act, and to make themselves acquainted with the instrument of their destruction, common sense being generally sufficient to interpret it. Indeed this would be a redeeming feature, were it not for the awful nature of the apparatus; so that even this is an aggravation of the case, as it is like parading the fatal instrument of torture and death before the eyes of the devoted martyr. Take it all in all, 'tis a formidable weapon in the hands of Puseyites and Levellers. Halstead makes ten towns in Essex that have been victimised, for terrible to tell, *we* have passed the Rubicon. The last poor's rate for our parish has been laid at 18d in the pound, and now we are to have the Health of Towns Act, with its thousand and one charges, besides the number of place hunters, who, if they are successful, have a kind of life provision . . . Now, the question comes, and with tremendous force, who is to pay the fiddler? Who? why the farmer, the tradesman and the artizan . . . One consolation remains. They may tax us, but they cannot force us to submit altogether. If the present mania for imposing fresh charges continues, while the industrious classes are at present burdened almost beyond bearable point, the Gold Diggers of Australia must of necessity receive large accessions of adventurers from the middle classes of this country . . . Once more I ask—What can be done to save the towns from ruin?

## 6. *Improving Rural Sanitation*

In 1872 Boards of Guardians were given the status of Rural Sanitary Authorities.
Extracts from Maldon R.S.A. Minutes (E.R.O.).

1 May, 1883. Resolved that, subject to the approval of the Surveyors, a new well be made in the New Road, Burnham, to supply water for flushing the upper sections of the sewers but [if] the parish Committee should consider that it is more desirable to purchase a piece of ground near the New Road for a well and, if necessary, a reservoir, then Mr Brady to ascertain whether such

piece of ground can be obtained and to prepare estimates for the cost of wells of various dimensions and depths.

Dr Downes reported on new well near the Post Office, Great Totham, and it was resolved that owners be called upon to complete same.

Dr Downes also reported that a public spring at Tolleshunt Major on the New England Company's farm had been enclosed and it was resolved that the agent of the Company be communicated with upon the subject and an arrangement made for carrying the water to a pump or reservoir near the road side.

Dr Downes reported upon the water supply to two new houses at Tollesbury belonging to Mr John Banyard and it was resolved that upon his cleaning up a ballast hole near the well and filling up such hole with proper material that a water certificate be granted to him.

Dr Downes also reported on the proposed water supply to four new houses at Tollesbury built by Mr William Heard, two of which are occupied, and reported that he could not approve of the proposed water supply because it is a shallow well close to privies and it was ordered that the clerk do write to Mr Heard that, unless a proper water supply be provided, proceedings will be taken against him.

Ordered that proceedings be taken before the Witham Bench against each of J.T. and U.M. of Tolleshunt D'Arcy for a nuisance arising from a house so overcrowded as to be injurious to health and that Mr Brady, the Inspector of Nuisances to the Authority, do lay the necessary information in each case and appear on behalf of the Authority before the Justices.

Ordered that at the next meeting of the Authority to be held on 15th instant the question of the drainage of the Parish of Tillingham be considered . . .

Ordered that a contribution for general expenses at the rate of one halfpenny in the pound be made upon the Overseers of the several parishes of the Authority . . .

Ordered that a cheque for £35 be drawn to Mr A. C. Freeman for one year's salary as clerk.

## *LATER DEVELOPMENTS IN LOCAL GOVERNMENT*

### *1. Municipal Enterprise*

A Colchester newspaper advocates a municipal water service.
*Colchester Mercury*, Sept. 13, 1879 (C.B.L.).

Whether or not the concern were commercially remunerative

—and in Colchester no doubt upon this point can exist—it is the duty of the Corporation, as we have repeatedly pointed out, to assume control of a matter so intimately connected with the public convenience, the public health, and the public safety . . . Indeed so easy are the terms upon which money can now be obtained by Urban Sanitary Authorities, and so many are the advantages which discreet and judicious expenditure in public improvements brings with it, that we should rejoice to see the Corporation displaying a still more enterprising spirit. Why should it not avail itself of the additional statutory powers recently conferred upon it and "improve out of existence" some of the wretched hovels which exist at various parts of the town—aye! and even in the unsuspected alleys in the noble High St.

*Essex Telegraph,* Aug. 29, 1891 (C.B.L.).

At a meeting of the Harwich Town Council on Thursday, the first business on the agenda paper was to confirm a resolution passed at a previous meeting, that the Council apply for Parliamentary powers to light the borough with electricity . . . the estimated cost would be about £150.

## 2. *The County Rate in 1851*

*Essex Standard,* April 11, 1851 (C.B.L.).

Essex Quarter Sessions . . . The Committee recommended a general county rate of three farthings in the pound; a police rate for general expenditure at one farthing; and the following police rates for local expenditure:—Districts 1, 4 and 6, at a halfpenny; 2, 3 and 5, at three farthings; and district 7 at one farthing.

## 3. *The Movement for Elected County Councils*

The Chelmsford Board of Guardians passed the following resolution in 1851.

*Essex Standard,* Feb. 14, 1851 (C.B.L.).

That the County and Police Rates for the County of Essex have for many years been increasing and are now arrived at such an amount as to be a heavy burden to the ratepayers. That, during the last four years, your petitioners have been called upon to contribute out of the poor-rates of the several parishes of this union towards the cost of the police and the general county expenditure nearly one seventh of the whole amount expended by your petitioners out of the poor-rates; and over this portion of their expenditure your petitioners or the ratepayers in general have no control or supervision.

That your petitioners, some time since, called the attention of the Magistrates of the county of Essex (under whose sole and exclusive control the levying and expenditure of the county-rate is at present placed) to the heavy burden which in this shape now presses upon the ratepayers generally, and your petitioners urged upon the attention of the Magistrates the question whether some reduction might not properly be made in the expenditure of the county.

That this application proved ineffectual, and your petitioners have no expectation that the magistrates will make such reduction in the county expenditure as your petitioners think might safely and properly be effected.

That in order therefore to effect such a reduction in the police and general county expenditure, it is essential that the ratepayers throughout the kingdom should be permitted to have a supervision and control over the assessment and expenditure of the county rates.

That in the opinion of your petitioners this supervision and control would be obtained, and might advantageously be exercised, by the introduction and establishment, throughout the kingdom, of county financial boards, to be composed of guardians and other ratepayers, chosen by the different boards of guardians, with a proportionate number of the magistrates of the county.

### 4. *Opposition to Elected County Councils*

When in 1853 Parliament discussed the creation of elected County 'Financial Boards', Essex Quarter Sessions put forward the following objections.

Quarter Sessions Committees Book (Q/ACm 6).

The provisions in this Bill hazard the moral control of the Counties being changed from where it is now placed . . .Those in whom election of Financial Boards would be placed have not a sufficient interest or knowledge in the Counties and certainly not in so great a degree as those in whom the control of expenditure is now placed . . . In cases where concurrent jurisdiction is given, conflicts must ensue, causing great delay of business, confusion and additional expense . . . It would be a subject of great regret to see the expenditure of the county brought under the control of government . . . The Constabulary of the County being interwoven with all the judicial proceedings, it will be impossible for the Justices to execute their duties, if the payment of the Chief and other Constables and the erection of Station Houses and Strong Rooms be transferred to any other jurisdiction than their own . . .

# THE OLD POOR LAW AND ITS PASSING

In their financial accounts and other records the parochial Overseers of the Poor have left a vivid picture of Eighteenth Century practice in local government and social administration. Under the 'Old' Poor Law these officials were selected annually from the larger ratepayers. Supervised by the Justices of the Peace and scrutinised by the parish Vestry, they had a wide range of duties to perform, including the payment of allowances to old people and widows, the care of orphans and the maintenance of a rudimentary health service.

A rising poor rate during the Eighteenth Century led to many attempts at economy, especially in Essex. Vestries established their own workhouses, appointed paid officials to administer relief and elected small committees of ratepayers to watch expenditure. Parish workhouses were particularly numerous in Essex. Nevertheless the poor rate continued to rise steeply during the Napoleonic Wars and it remained high during the post-War depression, when many ratepayers were themselves in financial difficulty. Critics of the 'Old' Poor Law received increasing public support, especially for their opposition to the so-called Speenhamland system, by which many rural parishes in Essex and other southern counties supplemented labourers' wages with small family allowances from the poor rate.

The 'New' Poor Law of 1834 quickly followed the first Reform Act. It established a more stringent system of relief and transferred responsibility for its administration from the parish to a district Board of Guardians. The Justices of the Peace lost their supervisory powers to a national Poor Law Commission. These changes, coinciding with a period of social discontent, provoked much popular protest and contributed greatly to the rise of

Chartism. Only in the more prosperous years after 1850 did the Poor Law question fall from prominence as a major political issue.

## *THE CONSTITUTIONAL PATTERN*

### *1. Choosing the Overseers*

The Easter Vestry nominated several of the larger ratepayers as possible Overseers of the Poor. From these nominees the local Justices of the Peace selected two or more for office, usually by placing some mark against their names.
Theydon Garnon Vestry Minutes (D/P 152/8/1).

Officers chosen at a Vestry held this 20th day of April, 1772, for the parish of Theydon Garnon for the ensuing year

| | | | |
|---|---|---|---|
| Edward Smith<br>Thos. Bishop | Churchwardens | John Gilderson<br>Thos. Searl | Constables |
| ✓ Edwd. Welch<br>Willm. Gardiner<br>✓ Saml. Lake, junior<br>Elizabeth Archer | Overseers | John Collop<br>Richd. Hyde | Surveyors |

Allowed and confirmed this 23d April, 1772, by us, W. Kerrich, Wm. Altham.

### *2. Rota for the Office of Overseer*

Since the Overseer's duties were onerous and unpaid, some parishes drew up an obligatory rota of service.
Stondon Massey Vestry Minutes (D/P 98/8).

Easter Monday, 1798

Order of rotation for the office of Overseer as agreed upon this day :—

| | | | |
|---|---|---|---|
| Patmore's Farm | — | Murkin's Do. | Robt. Sumner |
| Cannon's Do. | Jos. Clark | Little Myles's Do. | John Crabb |
| College Do. | John Seach | Hall's Ford Do. | John Ayley |
| White's Do. | — | Shiver's Do. | Wm. Coe |
| Soap House Do. | Jos. Clark | Manor Farm | John Cooper |
| Stondon Lands Do. | John King | Hill House Farm | Jos. Knight |

### *3. The Overseer's Paraphernalia*

A newly elected Overseer signs for the receipt of official documents.
St. Runwald's, Colchester, Weekly Pay Book (D/P 177/12/8).

The following Books and articles were received by me from Mr. John Devall, 16th Sept., 1831.—H. G. Woodcock.

Rate Book; Weekly Pay Book; Disbursments etc.; Nolan's Poor Laws (2 Vols.); Burns' Justice (5); Old Check Books (5); New Check Books (2); Old Vestry Meeting Books (2);

Examination, Register of Apprentices, old Weekly Pay Book, and Vestry Meeting Book, 1831.
Skip, Watering Pot and Hoes.

### 4. *Estimating the Rate*

These extracts are taken from evidence given before a Commission of Enquiry in 1834.

*Report of Poor Law Commission,* 1834, Appendix B.1.

Stisted . . . The Poor Rate of this Parish is settled quarterly. The amount is determined by a Vestry, duly summoned by a notice published at the Church six days before the proposed meeting. At this meeting the Overseers produce their books, accounts, and expenditure, for the inspection and examination of the Ratepayers present, in which the number and the names of the poor claiming and entitled to receive relief are stated ; and from that statement the exigency for the ensuing quarter is determined.

Castle Hedingham . . . The part which the Overseers and Vestry take in these matters is so nearly the same, that it is hardly possible to state in what manner or degree they respectively interfere ; perhaps from their more immediate acquaintance with the business of the parish, the Overseers may be said to propose what the Vestry confirms. It should be added that the Churchwardens at present and very often take the office of the Overseers upon them.

### 5. *How to Levy a Poor Rate*

An experienced Overseer records some information for the guidance of his successors.

Colne Engaine Vestry Book, 1745-1805 (D/P 193/8/2).

A proper title to a poor rate.

Colne Engaine. An assessment for the necessary relief of the poor and for the other purposes in several Acts of Parliament mentioned relating to the poor of the said parish of Colne Engaine in the said County of Essex, made and assessed — day of —, being the first rate at — in the pound for the present year.

| Rents | | | | |
|---|---|---|---|---|
| £20 | AB | .............. | o | .............. |
| £30 | CD | .............. | o | .............. |
| £40 | EF | .............. | o | .............. |
| and so forth | | | o .. o .. o | |

Assessors

| | | | |
|---|---|---|---|
| AB<br>CD | Churchwardens | EF<br>GH | Overseers |

Parishioners consenting

JK LM NO PQ

Then get the rate allowed by two Justices and give notice on the Sunday following in church of such allowances and proceed to collect.

## 6. *Some Sources of Parish Income*

Paupers in Stansted Mountfitchet helped to pay for their keep by spinning and other work. *Original spelling retained.*
Stansted Mountfitchet Overseers' Accounts (D/P 109/12/6).

|  | |  |  |
|---|---|---|---|
| 1787 | | | |
| May | 7 | Rec$^{d}$ of Samuel Rogers on Spining note up to April 2d 1787 | 5. 6. 0 |
| July | 2 | Rec$^{d}$ a Spining Note up to May 23 | 5. 0.10 |
| Aug. | 13 | Rec$^{d}$ of Sam$^{l}$ Rogers one Spining Note up to June 26$^{th}$ | 4.12. 2 |
| Nov. | 5 | Rec$^{d}$ for the W$^{d}$ Savills Goods | 4. 9. 5 |
| 1788 | | | |
| May | 5 | Rec$^{d}$ of W$^{m}$ Warwick for the Workhouse Orchard | 0.10. 0 |
| July | 7 | Rec$^{d}$ of Mr Headland for J$^{no}$ Marshall's work | 0.12. 0 |
| Dec. | 3 | Rec$^{d}$ of Rev$^{d}$ Mr Grant for Boy's Work | 1. 2. 6 |
| | | Rec$^{d}$ from Henry Pledger on ac$^{t}$ of Girl | 2.15. 0 |
| 1789 | | | |
| Oct. | 5 | By Cash of Slaughter for Wood sold | 0.12.11 |
| | | By D$^{o}$ for Apples | 0.16. 6 |
| | | By D$^{o}$ for Work at W. Welch's | 0.10. 6 |
| | | By Cash for Gravel | 2.10. 0 |
| 1790 | | | |
| June | 7 | Rec$^{d}$ of Mr. Woodley for Weeding | 0. 6. 0 |
| July | 6 | Of Mr Packer for Workhouse Child$^{n}$ Work | 0.12. 0 |
| 1791 | | | |
| Dec. | 5 | Rec$^{d}$ for Daniel Larns work 55 Days at 8d p$^{r}$ Day | 1.16. 8 |
| 1792 | | | |
| April | 4 | Rec$^{d}$ of Mr Nash for 31 lb fatt at $3\frac{1}{2}^{d}$ | 0. 9. 0 |
| | | Rec$^{d}$ of Mrs Levey for 30 lb seam at 5d | 0.12. 6 |
| June | 4 | Rec$^{d}$ for Spining of Silk | 0.14. 5 |
| July | 2 | Rec$^{d}$ of Mr Phillips for pulling Docks | 0. 0. 8 |
| Sept. | 5 | Rec$^{d}$ of Webb for 4 Boys 2 Days | 0. 4. 0 |
| Dec. | 5 | Rec$^{d}$ of Robt Bull for 540 faggots | 4.10. 0 |

### 7. *The Sovereign Ratepayers*

The Thaxted Vestry of 1725 asserts itself.

Thaxted Overseers' Accounts (D/P 16/12/3).

Memorandum that if the account for the workhouse be brought without Bills to justify the same, it will not be passed nor allowed in the agreement of this present vestry.

The Vestry of All Saints, Colchester, sometimes exercised detailed supervision of Poor Law administration.

Colchester, All Saints, Overseers' Accounts (D/P 200/12/8).

Aug. 5, 1793. At a General Monthly Meeting held at the house of Sarah Green, it was agreed

1st. That in consequence of the Surgeon reporting to the parish the case of Charlotte Hamilton, she be allowed the same pay as before for one week longer, and then her pay to be reduced one shilling per week, and afterwards as the Overseers shall deem necessary.

2d. That Elizabeth Johnson be allowed an apron and shift.

3d. That Mrs Prike be allowed a sheet.

4th. That a Bill of expenses which this parish has been at for John Stuck (owing for the parish of St Giles) be made out and the Overseers take every proper and immediate steps for the payment thereof.

5th. That a notice be sent tomorrow morning informing B. Angier, Esq., that the parish in consequence of the late perambulation have thought proper to rate his land in the parish fifteen pounds rate instead of what he has been used to pay.

### 8. *Repelling 'Foreigners'*

Vestries impeded the entry into their own parish of poor people from outside, who by working or residing for certain periods could acquire a 'settlement' in it and entitlement to receive assistance from its rates. In order to prevent such immigration, Theydon Garnon Vestry in 1776 threatened to invoke the obsolete law requiring the attachment of four acres of land to newly-built cottages.

Theydon Garnon Vestry Minutes (D/P 152/8/1).

At a Vestry held at the Parish Church of Theydon Garnon on Thursday, the 11th day of April, 1776, it being represented to the gentlemen and inhabitants . . . there assembled that Richard Palmer of Epping, bricklayer, hath begun to erect . . . cottages for habitation of poor persons within this parish without having or intending to lay four acres of land to each of the said cottages ; and whereas we are of opinion that the building of such cottages will bring great charge to this parish by the poor persons that will be brought to inhabit therein —— Resolved that, in case such cottages are built, a prosecution be commenced against him for erecting the same. But, Mr Palmer being present and agreeing not to go on with the building of the said cottages, the further consideration of this matter is adjourned.

### *9. A Settlement Examination*

Parish officers could bring 'intruders' before a J.P. to be examined about their parish of settlement and to be sent back to it by his order.

Woodford Settlement Papers (D/P 167/13/4A).

The Examination of George Monk now residing in the parish of East Ham and chargeable thereto taken on oath touching the place of his last legal settlement.

Who saith that he is of the age of 47 years and was born at Woodford Bridge in the parish of Woodford at which time his parents belonged there as he hath been informed and believes, and that his mother after the decease of this examinant's father received a regular weekly allowance from the parish officers of Woodford amounting to 3s 6d per week which they continued to pay her until her death which took place about nineteen years ago, that he the examinant was never bound apprentice nor hath he ever let himself as a yearly servant or hired a house of ten pounds a year or done any act whatever to gain a settlement in his own right, and that about 27 years ago he was lawfully married by banns to Sophia his present wife in the parish church of Woodford by whom he hath 5 children living born in wedlock, namely Maria aged 21 years who is emancipated, George aged 19, Emma aged 14, William aged 9 and Nathaniel aged 7.

Sworn this 19th day of June 1830 — The mark X of
Before Rich. J. Brassey — George Monk

### *10. A Settlement Certificate*

To enable a parishioner to seek work elsewhere the parish authorities would give him a certificate admitting his 'settlement' in their own parish and their consequent responsibility for his maintenance during unemployment, sickness or other misfortune.

Little Clacton Parish Records (D/P 80/13/1).

Essex. We, James Minton and William Hoy, Churchwardens and Overseers of the Poor of the parish of Holland Parva, do hereby own and acknowledge Thomas Pettican, his wife and family, to be inhabitants legally settled in the parish of Holland Parva aforesaid.

Attested by [four parishioners].

## *THE SCOPE OF THE POOR LAW*

### *1. The Overseer's Routine Business*

The following extracts from a Stansted Overseer's accounts show allowances being paid to old people, widows and the foster-parents of orphan children. *Original spelling retained.*

Stansted Mountfitchet Overseers' Accounts (D/P 109/12/1).

| | | |
|---|---|---|
| October, 1748 | | |
| 7 | tu sheoats [two shirts] to welses boy | 0. 4. 2 |
| | mary savel a gound | 0. 5.10 |
| | for bearring of georg vinson | 0. 9. 6 |
| 10 | wed larn | 0. 1. 6 |
| 14 | william plail | 0. 2. 0 |
| 17 | wed larn | 0. 1. 6 |
| 21 | wilam Plail | 0. 2. 0 |
| 25 | for cloatheing of the tu galls at the weder gefens | 0.13. 2 |
| 26 | for bareing of felopsis child | 0. 6. 0 |
| | the wid larn for wood | 0. 2. 6 |
| November | | |
| 17 | a Petey coate to the wed worreck | 0. 2. 6 |
| 28 | three yards and a haf of lensey [linsey] and tu Payer of stokens for the tu gals at the wed wits | 0. 5. 5 |
| December | | |
| 14 | three hunderd and a hafe of fagots to the Pore | 2.12. 6 |
| 19 | Paid haf a cround for the wed welsis rent | 0. 2. 6 |
| 30 | for making the wrate | 0. 2. 0 |
| January, 1749 | | |
| 5 | a goney to the seshens | 0. 2. 6 |
| | Paid the corttregde [quarterage] | 1. 7. 6 |
| 20 | a learther ceoate for wil Plail | 0. 6. 9 |
| 30 | a wescoate for Jobas | 0. 2. 6 |
| February | | |
| 6 | Three hundred and a haf of fagots to the Pore | 2.12. 6 |
| 10 | for goneys and charges for the setelment of betty marten | 1.17. 6 |
| | spent at the tound meating | 0. 3. 0 |
| March | | |
| 24 | Paid ruls rent | 0. 5. 0 |
| | paid ould skolens rent | 0. 5. 0 |
| 25 | fener rel charges for will Plail | 0.19. 0 |
| | and a Payer of breches for Jobas | 0. 4. 6 |
| | and for stuf for the eago [ague] | 0. 1. 0 |

## 2. *'The Weekly Collection'*

The following extract is taken from the list of those authorised to receive a weekly allowance at Coggeshall in 1733. *Original spelling retained.*

Coggeshall Overseers' Accounts (D/P 36/12/1).

| | |
|---|---|
| Wido Bennington | 0.2.0 |
| George Coney for Nickolds Child | 0.0.6 |
| Mary Calf | 0.0.6 |
| Wido French | 0.1.6 |
| Matthew Faireds Wido | 0.0.6 |
| Old Tho French | 0.2.0 |
| Wido Foster | 0.1.0 |

## 3. *A Parish Pensioner, 1777*

*Chelmsford Chronicle,* Jan. 24, 1777.

About four weeks since died at Maldon, in the 102nd year of her age, a poor woman who had been chargeable to the parish of Ulting near 50 years; during which time she regularly received from four to five shillings per week.

## 4. *The Care of Orphans*

Moll Flanders, heroine of Defoe's novel, receives the treatment usually given to Colchester orphans.

Defoe, *Moll Flanders,* Chapter 1.

It was at Colchester, in Essex, that those people left me; and I have a notion in my head that I left them (that is, that I hid myself and would not go any farther with them), but I am not able to be particular in that account; only this I remember, that being taken up by some of the parish officers of Colchester, I gave an account that I came into the town with the gypsies, but that I would not go any farther with them, and so they had left me, but whither they were gone that I knew not, nor could they expect it of me; for though they sent round the country to inquire after them, it seems they could not be found.

I was now in a way to be provided for; for though I was not a parish charge upon this or that part of the town by law, yet as my case came to be known, and that I was too young to do any work, being not above three years old, compassion moved the magistrates of the town to order some care to be taken of me, and I became one of their own as much as if I had been born in the place.

In the provision they made for me, it was my good hap to be put to nurse, as they call it, to a woman who was indeed poor but had been in better circumstances, and got a little livelihood by taking such as I was supposed to be, and keeping them with necessaries, till they were at a certain age, in which it might be supposed they might go to service or get their own bread.

This woman had also a little school, which she kept to teach children to read and to work; and having as I have said, lived before that in good fashion, she bred up the children she took with a great deal of art, as well as with a great deal of care.

But that which was worth all the rest, she bred them up very religiously, being herself a very sober pious woman, very housewifely and clean, and very mannerly and with good behaviour. So that in a word, excepting a plain diet, coarse lodgings, and mean clothes, we were brought up as mannerly and as genteelly as if we had been at a dancing school.

I was continued here till I was eight years old, when I was terrified with the news that the magistrates (as I think they called them) had ordered that I should go to service . . .

### 5. *The Village Foster Mother*

Earls Colne Vestry Minutes (D/P 209/8).

17th April, 1727. I then agreed with the Churchwardens and Overseers of the poor of Colne Earls to take and keep Eliz. Bewers, a poor child of the said parish, for the term of two years, allowing and paying of me the sum of ten shillings a year and at the end of the said two years I do agree to deliver the said Eliz. Bewers unto the Churchwardens and Overseers with one new suit of apparel and all other necessaries and as good as when I received her.

Witness my hand. The mark of Mary X May wife of H. May

### 6. *A Start in Life for Pauper Children*

*Ipswich Journal*, May 31, 1760 (C.B.L.).

To be lett as yearly Servants, or placed out as Apprentices by the Churchwardens and Overseers of the Poor of the Parish of Bocking . . .

Six strong, stout, healthy Lads, from the Age of 12 to 15 years; and four Girls, from 14 to 16 years old; all desirous of going to Service and likely to make good Servants.

N.B. None of these children shall be put to any Persons who shall not bring a Certificate from the Parish where he resides, as to his Character, and Ability to take and keep an Apprentice or Servant.

Wickham Bishops Apprenticeship Indentures (D/P 236/14).

[1781] This indenture . . . witnesseth that Peter Warden, Churchwarden of the parish of Wickham Bishops in the County of Essex and Josiah Smith and Thomas Francis, Overseers of the Poor of the said parish, by and with the consent of his Majesty's Justices of the Peace whose names are hereunto subscribed, have put and placed, and by these presents do put and place, Richard Burchell, a poor child of the said parish, apprentice to Daniel Burchell of the parish of Mundon in the said County, blacksmith, with him to dwell and serve . . .

## *THE VILLAGE HEALTH SERVICE*

### 1. *The Cost of Disease*

This was not the only case of smallpox in Thaxted in 1717 for which the parish paid the expenses.

Thaxted Overseers' Accounts (D/P 16/12/3).

Widow Norris's having the small pox

| | |
|---|---|
| Pd for bread and cheese and flour | 1. 4. 7 |
| For beer, strong and small | 1. 3. 6½ |
| For small goods | 1. 6. 3 |
| For milk | 0. 2. 9½ |
| For wood | 0. 8. 8 |
| Pd John Saward for carrying things to them | 0.12. 0 |
| Pd to John Saward's wife for nursing | 1. 9. 0 |
| Pd for tripes 12d, beans 15d, roots 2d | 0. 2. 5 |
| Pd to John Hills a bill of meat for them | 0. 7. 6 |
| Pd more for wood | 0. 0. 6 |

### 2. *The Salaried Doctors, 1747*

Chelmsford Churchwardens' Accounts (D/P 94/5/2).

We whose names are hereunto subscribed, being the apothecaries chosen by the parishioners as by the above ballot, do agree . . . to take care of the poor of the said parish at the rate of two pounds, ten shillings per quarter and . . . to visit any poor parishioner when ordered by the Overseer . . . in any neighbouring parish not exceeding two miles from the town of Chelmsford, but, if ordered to visit at a further distance, to be allowed half a crown every journey made.

Benj. Pugh, Abra. Griffinhoofe, Thos. Cookes, Theoph. Greene, F. Tomlinson.

### 3. *A Doctor's Bill, 1777*

Stansted Mountfitchet Overseers' Accounts (D/P 109/12/14).

The Parish of Stansted Dr. to Geo. Welch.

| | | | | |
|---|---|---|---|---|
| March | 19 | A corroborating mixture | Emd. Dench's child | 1.6 |
| | | A regrigerating lotion | | 1.0 |
| | | Two purging powders | Rd. Phillips | 1.0 |
| | 20 | A balsamic mixture | Gillby's daughter | 2.0 |
| | 24 | A cathartic electuary | Rd. Markwell | 2.0 |
| | | Antirheumatic drops | Rd. Wright's wife | 1.0 |
| April | 21 | Bleeding | Rd. Turner | 0.6 |
| May | 18 | Bleeding at home | H. Griggs | 1.0 |
| | 24 | A nervous mixture | ——— | 2.0 |
| July | 17 | A cephallic mixture | Plumb's wife | 1.0 |
| | 28 | Drawing a tooth | Mary Saville | 0.6 |

### 4. *An Isolation Hospital*

Many parishes established pest houses for the reception of small pox cases.
Great Bentley Vestry Minutes (D/P 171/8/4).

Great Bentley. At a parish meeting held this 27th day of August, 1781, It is unanimously agreed to take a house called Gunn's, for the purpose of a Pest House . . . for the term of twelve years at £4 . 4s. per year, . . . commencing on Michaelmas Day, 1781, ensuing, and expires on Michaelmas Day, 1793 . . .

Samuel Heckford, jun., Churchwarden; Thos. Carrington, Overseer.

### 5. *A Great Bentley Pauper's Funeral, 1756*

*Original spelling retained.*
Great Bentley Vestry Minutes (D/P 171/8/3).

| | |
|---|---|
| for a quert of ould bear and a pint of gin for the widow orsbin | 0.11 |
| for going for Mr hunt to the wid orsbin | 1. 0 |
| for fetching the nurs from wivener to the widow orsbin | 1. 6 |
| for a pint of wine and pearl barley and harts horn for the widow orsbin | 1. 3½ |
| for the Coffin for the widow orsbin | 7. 0 |
| for Carring of the widow orsbin to the ground in a tumbril | 1. 0 |
| to the minister | 2. 6 |
| for the affedave [affidavit of burial in wool] | 0. 6 |
| to the sexton | 3. 0 |
| for bear at the bering of the Widow orsbin | 4. 0 |

## *THE PARISH WORKHOUSE*

### *1. Setting up Earls Colne Workhouse*

From the early 18th century many Essex parishes set up their own workhouses in an attempt to check the rising Poor Rate.

Earls Colne Vestry Minutes (D/P 209/8).

March the 16th, 1723. Then agreed at a Vestry meeting . . . to agree with the inhabitants of the parish of Halstead to take such poor persons from the parish of Colne Earls as we or some of us at any of Vestry meetings for the future shall in their discretions think fit to send to the workhouse of the said parish of Halstead, in witness whereof we have hereunto set our hands . . .

At a Vestry held the 7th July, 1740, We, the parishioners of Earls Colne, do consent and agree that the Minister, Churchwardens and Overseers . . . shall call in two hundred pounds (being part of the three hundred pounds left to this parish for the use of the poor by the last Will of Mrs Mary Pointer deceased) lent to John Sympson of Lamarsh . . . and that the said sum of two hundred pounds shall be laid out in building a workhouse for the use of the poor of the said parish, and also . . . that the Churchwardens and Overseers do mortgage the following tenements, viz : the tenement in the occupation of John Paine, the tenement in the occupation of Francis Martin, glazier, the three tenements on Colne Green in the several occupations of Jacob Green, Joseph Fell and William Smith, and also the said now intended Workhouse, as the security for the said two hundred pounds and legal interest. And in order to repay the said two hundred pounds and interest we do also consent and agree that our Poor Rates shall not be less than thirty quarters for the whole year till the same shall be repaid . . .

### *2. The Workhouse Master*

Colne Engaine Overseers' Accounts (D/P 193/12/2).

Colne Engaine. Dec. 4th, 1786

An agreement made this day between the Churchwardens and Overseers . . . and John Spurgeon of Halstead, now living in Box Mill Lane, for he the said John Spurgeon and his wife to take care of the poor in the said Parish Workhouse, and to be a Governor of the same for one year, and he the said John Spurgeon is to receive . . . twelve pounds, and if any disputes shall arise between either of the parties, whoever desires to dissolve this agreement shall give a month's warning or pay a month's wages.

N.B. The said John Spurgeon and his wife are to find their own tea and sugar. Mark of X John Spurgeon

Parishioners consenting [ten signatories].

### 3. *Who Lived in the Workhouse?*

A number of Essex parishes were asked in 1834 whether they possessed a workhouse and, if so, who were its inmates. Here are some of the answers.

*Report of Poor Law Commission,* 1834, App. B.1.

Rochford Parish. Yes. Its inmates chiefly old infirm Men and Women, the children of convicts, and orphans. Six men, between 60 and 82 years of age; six boys between four and fourteen; two Women, 23 and 43 years of age; 5 girls between 1 and 17.

Castle Hedingham. There is no Workhouse.

Fryerning. Eight persons in the Workhouse, seven Males and one Female; all old and infirm.

Braintree. We have; containing 12 Males of the ages of 81, 80, 75, 70, 70, 61, 38, 22, 20, 18, 12 and 7; and 6 Females, aged 80, 66, 60, 24, 14 and 12.

Witham. Yes. Its inmates consist of eight old Men, four old Women, and two boys, besides the Governor and his family.

Stansted. A Workhouse, the inmates of which are two Females 80 years of age; one, 78; one, 70; one, 60; one, 55; one, 35, and two about 20 who cannot be prevailed upon to go out to service; one Male, 70; two, 65; two, 60; one, 10; one, 8; one, 5; and one 3 years of age.

### 4. *Workhouse Diet, 1817*

The Chelmsford authorities were exact in their provision for workhouse inmates, but they were not ungenerous.

Chelmsford, Minutes of Poor Law Committee (D/P 94/8/12).

| Day | Breakfast | Dinner | Supper |
|---|---|---|---|
| Sunday | Soup made from the bones the day before | Beef with Suet Pudding & Vegetables | Bread & Cheese |
| Monday | Soup made from the meat the day before | Bread & Cheese | Bread & Cheese |
| Tuesday | Milk Pottage | Cold Meat & Vegetables | Bread & Cheese |
| Wednesday | Milk Pottage | Beef & Vegetables | Bread & Cheese |
| Thursday | Soup from the Meat the day before | Pork with Vegetables | Bread & Cheese |
| Friday | Milk Pottage | Ox Cheeks & Vegetables | Bread & Cheese |
| Saturday | Soup from the ox cheeks the day before | Soup made from the bones that was left all the week | Bread & Cheese |

N.B. No Bread with Vegetables—No Cheese for Children's Suppers—No Small Beer for Do.

Chelmsford Select Vestry Minutes (D/P 94/8/4).

Oct. 13, 1823. An application was made by some of the aged women in the House to have half a pint of beer daily and fourpence per week allowed them, which was agreed to be taken into consideration forthwith.

Oct. 27, 1823. Six aged women in the Poor House were ordered to have a pint of strong beer each per day and fourpence a week gratuity.

## *THE 'SPEENHAMLAND' SYSTEM*

### *1. Food Subsidies in Wartime*

In the early years of the war with France many Essex parishes adopted the practice described in the following extract, but they soon abandoned it in favour of family allowances.
Chelmsford Overseers' Accounts (D/P 94/12/11).

Chelmsford, June 29, 1795.

At a Vestry meeting then held . . . it was resolved that it is the opinion of the parishioners here present that the poor of this parish do stand in need of some relief and assistance owing to the present high price of provisions.

Resolved that the best mode of relieving the poor at this juncture will be by providing household flour for them at 2/4 per peck and bread at 2/8 per peck loaf and so in proportion.

Resolved and ordered that the price of flour beyond 2/4 per peck and of bread beyond 2/8 per peck loaf be defrayed by the Overseers . . . out of the Poor Rates for such of the Poor of this parish as shall receive proper tickets or orders for that purpose from the Overseer and that the quantities of flour and bread to be provided as aforesaid be limited as follows :—to every poor man having a wife and two children two pecks of flour or two peck loaves weekly and for every poor man having a wife and four children three pecks of flour or three peck loaves weekly and so in proportion for every poor family consisting of a greater or smaller number.

### *2. 'Speenhamland' in Essex*

Most rural parishes in the early 19th century were paying family allowances to labourers, according to a means test, to enable them to meet the increased price of food.
*Report of Poor Law Commission,* 1834, p. 13.

Division of Chelmsford, 1821.

At a special meeting of the Magistrates . . . held at the Justice Room, in the Shire Hall, on Friday, the 15th day of June, 1821.

It was resolved that the undermentioned scale of relief, for the assistance of the overseers of the poor within the said division in relieving the necessitous poor, be recommended : that they do provide each person in every family with the means of procuring half a peck of flour per week, together with 10d. per head for other necessaries, if the family consist of two only ; 8d. per head, if three ; 6d. per head if four ; and 5d. per head if more than four.

N.B. The above mentioned sums are exclusive of fuel.

### 3. *The Prevalence of 'Speenhamland'*

The system of family allowances described in the following reports seems to have been general in rural Essex in 1834.
*Report of Poor Law Commission,* 1834, App. B.1.

Thorpe le Soken . . . In this part of the country a direct payment of Wages out of Rates does not prevail, though the relieving those employed, in proportion to the size of their families, seems indirectly to have the same effect. An allowance on account of family, when made, will be given according to the wages a man earns, and the price of flour. If his wages are 9s, it will begin at four children ; if 10s at five.

Great Waltham . . . To all Families, small or large, Allowance is made from the Poor Rates ; to the whole number beginning from the first. Work done for individuals has been partly paid for by the parish, in a few instances, but, I believe, not any now.

Little Waltham . . . There is an allowance universally on account of families ; and not only when the families are large, but it frequently begins with the first child, and generally with the third. Wages are not paid out of the rates ; but when the wages are inadequate, the Poor Rates are taxed with the remainder.

Wickham Bishops . . . Allowance is usually made where there are four children.

Witham . . . Relief has been refused to able-bodied Labourers. They complained to the Magistrates, and Orders of Relief were made upon the parish.

### 4. *The Speenhamland Scale, 1834*

The scales described in the following extracts represent the parishes' estimate of the minimum income necessary for a labouring family's subsistence. Allowances were given to enable labourers to achieve this minimum.
*Report of Poor Law Commission,* 1834, App. B.1.

Great Baddow . . . A half peck of bread flour, together with 10d a head for other necessaries, if the family consists of two only ; 8d a head if three ; 6d if four ; and 5d if more than four.

Barking . . . No fixed scale.

Boreham . . . According to a Scale recommended by the Magistrates.

Braintree . . . Generally according to the following Scale (exclusive of fuel) : flour being 2s a peck.

| | | | | | |
|---|---|---|---|---|---|
| No. in family | 2, | the price of half a peck | of flour and | 10d. each, | 3s 8d |
| Ditto | 3 | Ditto | Ditto | 8d | 5s 0d |
| Ditto | 4 | Ditto | Ditto | 6d | 6s 0d |
| Ditto | 5 | Ditto | Ditto | 5d | 7s 1d |

Clavering . . . Scale is, single Man, 3s 6d a week ; Women 2s 3d ; Families with four children and upwards, the price of two quartern loaves per head.

St. Giles, Colchester . . . No Scale.

Epping . . . 2s per head for the number of the Family, including the Father and Mother.

## *ATTEMPTS TO ECONOMISE*

### 1. *Poor Law Expenditure in Certain Parishes*

Printed Parliamentary Poor Law Statistics, 1803 and 1818 (E.R.O.) and *Report of Poor Law Commission,* 1834, App. B.1.

| | *1776* | *Average 1783-5* | *1803* | *1813* | *1814* | *1815* | *1821* | *1831* |
|---|---|---|---|---|---|---|---|---|
| | | | | (In £s) | | | | |
| Bocking | 1240 | 1630 | 4878 | 4079 | 4112 | 3047 | 4072 | 3452 |
| Boreham | 250 | 317 | 650 | 1366 | 1079 | 757 | 1076 | 935 |
| Braintree | 948 | 919 | 2209 | 2450 | 2557 | 2155 | 2207 | 1966 |
| Bulmer | 115 | 166 | 285 | 884 | 676 | 510 | 487 | 775 |
| Chelmsford | 742 | 1076 | 2155 | 2727 | 2516 | 2729 | 3615 | 3008 |
| Gt. Coggeshall | 659 | 830 | 1500 | 2571 | 2418 | 2075 | 2696 | 2357 |
| Gt. Maplestead | 223 | 251 | 398 | 826 | 640 | 419 | 611 | 704 |
| Hatfield Peverel | 201 | 372 | 626 | 1540 | 1253 | 886 | 1029 | 1154 |
| Lawford | 155 | 156 | 492 | 874 | 645 | 580 | 634 | 561 |
| Sible Hedingham | 543 | 176 *(sic)* | 2691 | 4025 | 2884 | 1727 | 1758 | 2956 |
| Stansted Mt. | 341 | 476 | 1316 | 1714 | 1439 | 872 | 1103 | 1160 |
| Wickham Bishops | 62 | 119 | 354 | 373 | 369 | 364 | 364 | 411 |

### 2. *A Parish Committee*

Colne Engaine Overseers' Accounts (D/P 193/12/2).

Colne Engaine Sept. 30th, 1783.

We whose names are underwritten do agree to meet at the Workhouse every Monday morning at 10 o'clock, in order to hold a Committee to consult about the parish affairs, for their better management and to make a good provision for the poor, and whoever absent himself (except in case of illness) shall forfeit sixpence, and to continue their meeting until Easter, 1784. [Nine signatories].

### 3. *Braintree Select Vestry at Work*

Under an Act of 1819 parishes might elect committees called Select Vestries to supervise poor relief in detail.

Braintree Vestry Minutes (D/P 264/8/10).

13 June, 1825. By Order of Committee,

No more rents to be paid by the parish after Quarter day, 25th September, 1825—Notice to the above effect be given to different landlords.

It was unanimously agreed to send down to Norwich to see, enquire and ascertain the state of the paupers there belonging to Braintree . . .

29th August, 1825. It was unanimously resolved that all persons keeping dogs, not paying the Duty, shall henceforth be chargeable to the Poor Rate, and also be taxed, by a return of the Assessors. And all persons taking parochial relief will be struck off the pay book who keep dogs—or who have inmates keeping the same . . .

12th October, 1829. It is resolved that the applications to pay the extra Constables at the late Fair be not complied with . . .

### 4. *An Efficient Parish, 1834*

Chelmsford's Select Vestry received the mild commendation of a very critical Commission of Enquiry.

*Report of Poor Law Commission,* App. A, Part I, pp. 233-4.

Chelmsford was a considerable barrack station during the war. At the peace, pauperism was increasing rapidly ; a select vestry was established, which, by a close examination and a general knowledge of the poor, has been effectual in stopping its progress. The select vestry is well attended ; the rector takes part in its proceedings, and accounts for relief are audited every fortnight ; the names of all the paupers, with the sums received by them, are printed in an annual abstract, and this practice is thought very beneficial. The workhouse, as an asylum for the aged and orphan or deserted young children, is well managed . . .

### 5. *Differing Views about Select Vestries, 1834*

Opinions varied considerably about the efficacy of Select Vestries and paid Assistant Overseers.

*Report of Poor Law Commission,* 1834, App. B.1.

Braintree . . . We have a Select Vestry, but a very inefficient one : no Assistant Overseer. The Select Vestry had the effect of considerably reducing the rates for the first few years, since which it has not been so well attended. Although there is a Select Vestry . . . yet a parish meeting is always called early in every quarter to grant a rate to meet the expenses of the current quarter.

Castle Hedingham . . . There is an Assistant Overseer and the Accounts are very accurately kept. There is also a Committee of Accounts for the inspection of the parish accounts every quarter.

Copford . . . The Acting Overseer pays the poor every Monday morning at the Parish Workhouse, at which any of the parishioners that choose attend.

Stansted . . . No Select Vestry; nor does it appear necessary, as a Committee is formed, who attend weekly to the wants of the poor. An Assistant Overseer has for many years been employed and has performed his duty to the satisfaction of the parishioners.

Stisted . . . We have an Open Vestry, where all the principal occupiers attend and assist the Overseer, and prevent many impositions.

Little Waltham . . . An Open Vestry once a week, when the Overseer, under its control, pays the poor, and once a month to inspect his accounts is found sufficient. We had for a few years an Assistant Overseer; it was found highly beneficial.

Witham . . . We have a Select Vestry and an Assistant Overseer; the effect has been beneficial.

### 6. *Emigration No Solution, 1834*

*Report of Poor Law Commission,* 1834, App. B.1.

Great Henny . . . Last year the parish offered to enable any portion of the Labourers to emigrate who would go, or bind any of the lads apprentices to a trade at home, and there was not one who would take either offer, for they were aware that we must employ them or support them.

Kelvedon . . . We think any enactment encouraging emigration would in the end be bad policy, by reducing the natural strength of the country.

## *THE NEW POOR LAW AND ITS OPPONENTS*

### 1. *A Critic of the Old Poor Law*

An official investigator, acting on behalf of the 1834 Poor Law Commission, condemns the 'Speenhamland' system.

*Report of Poor Law Commission,* 1834, p. 33.

In Coggeshall, Essex, says Mr. Majendie, weekly wages are 8s, but by piecework a good labourer may earn 10s. Now, consider the case of labourers with four children, for the subsistence of which family (according to the Chelmsford scale, which is the law of that district) 11s 6d is required. Of this sum the good labourer earns 10s, and receives from the parish 1s 6d. The inferior labourer earns 8s, and receives from the parish 3s 6d. The man who does not work, and whom no one will employ, receives the whole from the parish.

## 2. *A Reform Candidate Demands a Change*

The following is an extract from the Election address of W. P. L. Wellesley at the Election of 1830.

*Report of the Proceedings at the Essex Elections,* 1830.

Revision of the Poor Laws, and Amelioration of our Civil and Criminal Code.

Upon these important topics of National policy I am only anxious to see such Amendment as may make the labourer less dependent on the Overseer of the Poor, and secure to industry and frugality the chance of rising above the rank of a Pauper, of which in the present state of Agricultural depression, and the baneful practice of sending the labourer to the poor rates for his wages, there can be but little prospect.

## 3. *The New Poor Law in Operation*

Under the New Poor Law of 1834 parishes surrendered their Poor Law powers to District Boards of Guardians, which first curtailed and soon discontinued outdoor relief to able-bodied males. The former parish workhouses were replaced by a central workhouse, in which the diet was to be poor and the discipline severe.

Witham Board of Guardians Minutes—extracts (G/WM 1).

Witham Union. First Meeting of the Guardians of the Witham Union, comprising the parishes of Witham, Great Coggeshall, Kelvedon, Hatfield Peverel, Terling, Messing, Feering, Rivenhall, Little Coggeshall, Great Braxted, Inworth, Fairstead, Faulkbourne, Little Braxted, Ulting and Wickham Bishops, held at the Blue Posts Inn, Witham on Thursday, the 17th day of December, 1835.

Ex Officio Guardians : Hon. J. J. Strutt, W. W. Luard, Esq., Samuel Shaen, Esq., Rev. Charles Dalton and Rev. John Cox.

Elected Guardians : Witham, Messrs. John Crump, Thomas Butler and William Hutley; Great Coggeshall, Messrs. Fisher Unwin Pattison, Robert Jackson & Charles More; Great Braxted, Mr. William Jacobs . . .

It was resolved

That The Hon. John J. Strutt be Chairman.

That W. W. Luard, Esq., be Vice Chairman.

That Mr John Philbrick be Relieving Officer at a salary of £100.

That a weekly meeting of the Board of Guardians be held at the White Hart Inn, Witham, every Monday at 10 o'clock a.m.

28th December, 1835.

It was resolved . . . that Thomas James Bollingbroke and Elizabeth, his wife, be Master and Matron of the Witham Workhouse at a salary of £50 per annum, Workhouse diet allowed . . .

4th January, 1836.

Sixpence per head was taken off allowance for paupers in Witham Workhouse till further arrangements.

11th January, 1836.

The Guardians ordered out-relief to divers paupers in the parishes of Witham and Wickham Bishops and orders were given for admission of some paupers belonging to Wickham Bishops into the Witham Workhouse and that 2/6 be paid by that parish for maintenance.

It was determined that the New System be carried fully into effect at the Witham Workhouse by the 25th instant . . .

6th Feb., 1836.

The paupers belonging to the parishes of Fairstead, Rivenhall, Wickham Bishops, and Faulkbourne were separately examined by the Board and the relief regulated according to the merits of the particular cases. The paupers were had in singly before the Board and their cases minutely enquired into. The Out-relief Book was inspected and the chairman's initials put to each case.

15th February, 1836.

Appellants were heard from Great Braxted, Feering, Witham, Great Coggeshall, Little Coggeshall, Wickham and Rivenhall, Hatfield and Inworth and their allowances settled.

7th March, 1836.

It was determined to adopt the Dunmow Dietary and Clerk was directed to write to Poor Law Commissioners for consent.

25th July, 1836.

Mr. Hutley moved that outdoor relief (except in cases of affliction) be discontinued, and that the rule remain in force for three months . . . Mr. Hutley withdrew his motion respecting outdoor relief, and the Clerk was directed to write to the Poor Law Commissioners stating that at present with one exception no relief is afforded by this Board to able bodied persons . . .

17th October, 1836.

Mr. Orpen gave notice that he should this day fortnight bring before the Board the question of dividing the old married people in the Workhouse and should propose that the separation be discontinued . . .

31st October, 1836.

Mr. Orpen's proposal for not separating old married persons was lost . . .

27th February, 1837.

Petitions against any repeal or material alteration of the Poor Law Amendment Act were signed.

### 4. *Outdoor Relief Denied to Able-Bodied*

Witham Vestry Clerk's Letter Book (D/P 30/8/12).

Witham, December 2nd, 1836.

Mr. Lancaster,

I yesterday laid your letter before the Select Vestry of Witham and am desired to inform you that the new Poor Law Bill is in operation here and that no relief can be given you out of the workhouse.

Hoping you will see better days,

I am your Humble Servant,

Robert Bretnall, Vestry Clerk.

To Mr. Lancaster,
No. 18, Water Street,
Birmingham.

### 5. *A Progress Report on the New Poor Law*

*Second Annual Report of the Poor Law Commissioners,* 1836, p. 256 (E.R.O.).

Maldon Union. Dear Sir, The reduction of able-bodied pauperism in this Union is very considerable, and will no doubt be carried to a much greater extent; but we have thought it inexpedient to act at first too severely; still I flatter myself you will think we have neither been inattentive to the intention of the Legislature or the interests of the ratepayers.

Our reduction of expenditure is very large. The average payment of our rates for three years previous to forming this Union was 14,236*l*, and our quarter's disbursements ending 25th March were 1219*l*. 18*s*. 9*d*. showing a saving which must give general satisfaction; and I feel in no way has it been distressing to the deserving poor, who I am convinced are quite as well off as they were under the old system.

The habits and behaviour of the labouring classes are certainly improving. They feel they cannot now compel an overseer to relieve them as they used to do; they are consequently more cautious how they expend their earnings, and duly appreciate a good master; not captiously leaving their employ, as was too much the custom when they could demand relief from an overseer, without being subject to the searching inquiries they have now to submit themselves to . . .

Speaking generally, our Union works very satisfactorily; we are rapidly advancing towards the completion of our chief house, which when complete will, I have no doubt, be ample for the whole Union. Our applications for relief are decreasing, and our pauper population satisfied. I am, etc.

John Payne.

### 6. *A Refractory Pauper, 1836*

In the new central workhouses men, women and children were to be housed in different wards.
*Colchester Gazette,* April 30, 1836 (C.B.L.).

William Sallowes was put to the bar, charged with assaulting Joseph Dennis, one of the serjeants at mace, on Wednesday evening last. Mr. Roy, the governor of the workhouse at St. Mary at the walls [Colchester], stated that the prisoner with his wife and family were admitted into the house on Wednesday afternoon, and in a short time after their admission, the prisoner became very refractory, and refused to pay any regards to the rules and regulations of the house, and violently assaulted the son of the witness. He, witness, felt it necessary to call in the aid of the police, and on Dennis endeavouring to restore order, prisoner violently assaulted him. Dennis corroborated the evidence of Mr. Roy. The prisoner in his defence said, he was not aware that he struck anyone; he only objected to being separated from his wife and family, and he should like to know who made that law. His Worship told him such a law was in existence, and while he was a pauper, he must conform to it, or take the consequence. The fact of his having committed evident assault had been clearly established, and he must answer the charge at the Sessions. He was fully committed for trial.

### 7. *Support for the New Poor Law*

A Liberal newspaper, the *Essex Times,* defends the New Poor Law.
*Essex Times,* Feb. 9, 1838 (C.B.L.).

The principle of the new Poor Law is, we think, that the rights possessed by the poor, grounded on the 43d of Elizabeth previous to the new enactment, should be preserved to them. The change is not in the divestment of their rights, but in the change of the individuals intrusted with the guardianship and management of their rights. Formerly that guardianship and management was in the imbecile and ignorant, and interested, and sometimes intemperate hands of the overseers, subject to the superintendence and check of the local magistracy; under the misguided, vacillating, and capricious arrangements of such officials, this country was unquestionably travelling with frightful rapidity to its disorganisation and ruin. The Whig amendment of the law has placed that guardianship and management into much more enlightened and efficient hands . . . A man is now paid according to his work; he receives his money as honourable wages, and not as he did under the old system, in the degrading character of a pensioner. When the parish funds were forestalled to maintain fifty or sixty of the worst workmen for doing nothing, it was not to be wondered at that the employer, with his means thus unprofitably and perniciously wasted, endeavoured to indemnify himself by cutting down to the lowest possible figure, the just wages of the workingman. He had it in his power, too, to do this the more easily, for when a just, a fair remuneration for his labour was insisted upon by a sturdy peasant, the employer had nothing to do but to call into his service some of the parish pensioners always at hand, and a considerable portion of whose wages would be paid by the overseer, and instantly throw out of employment, and into a state of starvation or pauper dependence, the honest fellow who only demanded what was right, and perhaps, and most probably, what was less than his right. The case is now altered, the able-bodied labourer who has a parish pension is not at hand—his residence is in the poorhouse. The man who can and will work, has now no worthless pensioned competitor . . .

### 8. *Qualified Support for the New Poor Law, 1834*

The Tory *Essex Standard* was not entirely convinced of the New Poor Law's value.
*Essex Standard,* Aug. 29, 1834.

The Whigs, who are ever talking of their desire to give increased political power to the people, have by this measure destroyed much of that wholesome local influence, both political and social, which formed a connecting chain between the middling and lower classes. Hitherto it has been the policy of Great Britain to keep up a kindly intercourse among the various classes of society—to render them mutually dependent on each other, and more especially to confide the interests of the poor to the country gentlemen, the magistracy, and the parochial clergy. These three valuable classes of the community have the means of knowing the wants of their humble neighbours ; they have joyed with them in their joys, and sorrowed with them in their sorrows : to see the tenant of the cottage happy and prosperous has been the greatest pride and pleasure of the lord of the mansion, and of the minister of the church . . . The administration of the new Poor Law will furnish abundant evidence that the rich care for the poor. The administration of the Act will, necessarily, in many instances have the appearance of harshness ; but though official persons must act in obedience to the cold calculating precepts of political economy, the poor will still find that they have numerous warm and active friends, anxious to embrace every opportunity to succour the afflicted and to encourage and reward the virtuous and industrious. The fountain of public charity will not be so bounteous as formerly, but in proportion as that is diminished, we are satisfied that the efforts of private benevolence will be increased. We do not mean to condemn the new Act without its having had a fair trial : it is the opinion of some of the most benevolent and enlightened men that the measure will work both a moral and a political cure with regard to some of the most serious evils that at present afflict the country. We therefore earnestly hope that all persons appointed under the provisions of the Act will, to the best of their skill and knowledge, endeavour to advance the great objects which we are told it is intended to promote : viz to improve the spiritual and temporal happiness of the poor, to give them employment, to protect and encourage the industrious, to restrain and punish the idle and vicious, and to decrease the burdens which press so heavily on the country at large. We place the latter consideration last in the list of benefits, for in an enlarged point of view it is the least.

### 9. *Debauchery in the Workhouse?*

By 1841 the *Essex Standard* had become openly critical.
*Essex Standard,* Jan. 1, 1841 (C.B.L.).

This year the poor in the Union-houses of Chelmsford, Halstead, Maldon, and Rochford received an extra allowance on Christmas-day. At Braintree the inmates of the house had roast beef and plum pudding, a pint of strong beer for each adult, half a pint to each child ; pipes, tobacco and snuff were also given. Pretty doings at Braintree, truly ! At Romford, to the disgrace of the Guardians, the paupers, 400 in number, had 240 plum puddings, weighing in all 600 lbs. What an uproar these proceedings will make at Somerset House. Paupers eating plum-puddings on

Christmas Day ! What will this world come to ?

### *10. The View of the Labourers, 1837*

*Colchester Gazette,* July 1, 1837 (C.B.L.).

The humble petition of the Agricultural Labourers and others in the parishes of Little Waltham, Great Waltham, Leighs and Terling . . .

It is with feelings of pain and regret that your petitioners view in the operation of the new Poor Law Amendment Act the total frustration of their hopes, for while the professed design of the said law is to better their condition and raise them in the scale of society, its obvious tendency is to sink them into a state of the most abject poverty and destitution.

That your petitioners cannot refrain from stating most respectfully to your honourable house that they view the said law as unjust, inasmuch as it does not recognise that essential principle of just government, the protection of the weaker portion of the community against the tyranny and oppression of the strong, while it interferes with those relations of life which the Almighty has declared to be inviolable, and isolates those social and domestic feelings which distinguish us from a nation of savages.

That the administration of the said law has already been the cause of unexampled suffering to thousands, while it has established a system of terrorism in a manner which must prove truly injurious to the entire labouring population.

That your petitioners also complain to your honourable house that the power to afford parochial relief under the said law is denied to those who have the best knowledge of the local circumstances of the poor, and placed in the hands of those who are least likely to gain such knowledge, or who may derive it through a distorted medium, to the great injury of the poor.

Your petitioners beg also to state to your honourable house, that they do not wish to be relieved from the toil and duties connected with their humble station in society ; and whilst they wish at all times to pay due regard to all the just laws and institution of the country, they feel it a grievance that while the interests of the higher classes of society are scrupulously guarded by your honourable house, the poor should be treated as if they had no right to live on the land of their birth.

Your petitioners therefore pray that your honourable house will either totally repeal the said law, or make such alterations or amendments therein, as shall have a due regard to the wants and feelings of the poor; and your petitioners therefore pray that your honourable house will devise and adopt such measures as shall be the means of enabling them by honest industry to obtain the common necessaries of life; and while your petitioners assume that your honourable house is well informed on all subjects which concern the welfare of this country, they would humbly suggest that with a system of Poor Law founded on the just and unalienable rights of the poor, of small allotments of land to labourers to be cultivated with a spade for their own use and benefit, a well-regulated property tax, and the removal of all those imposts which tend to make provisions dear and labour cheap, are subjects with which the welfare and the prosperity of the country at large are closely connected, and which your petitioners pray may receive the most attentive consideration of your honourable house.

*11. Chartist Opposition*

From the speech of Samuel Everard, a Braintree tailor.
*Essex Mercury,* Nov. 20, 1838 (C.B.L.).

I, exclaimed the speaker, have a wife, and I am not ashamed to say now, as I have said before, that I love her, and sooner than I will be torn from the bosom that has yielded consolation to me in all my trials and difficulties; sooner than I will be torn from that wife and from the children we love, I will die in the public streets. (Immense cheering).

From the speech of W. G. Blatch, a Colchester shoemaker.
*Essex Times,* Sept. 15, 1838 (C.B.L.).

As for the Poor Law, the Houses of Parliament had no right to pass that Act, for it is contrary to Scripture and the feelings of humanity; and any laws that are contrary to these cannot and ought not to stand. It is a Malthusian law, and the disciples of Malthus have no sympathy with the people, but are only anxious for the saving of money. I am not the advocate of idleness, but no human being must be allowed to die of hunger, however worthless he may have been. I say, give him straw for his bed; for such beings let there be workhouses; but do not place the industrious labourer on a level with them. I know we are branded as bloody revolutionists, but is not the man a bloody revolutionist who supports such an abominable and unconstitutional measure? . . . Until we get a free and full system of representation, we shall never be enabled to do away with the absolute power of the three despots of Somerset House, but shall be always obliged to submit to them.

# EDUCATION

Prosperous Essex farmers and townsmen in 1750 were sending their children to private boarding schools. At these their daughters were taught the social graces and their sons might study book-keeping and mensuration as well as classics and dancing. Despite pretentious advertisements and high fees, teaching was usually poor. The grammar schools were no more efficient, and in Essex there were very few of the admirable Nonconformist academies found elsewhere. Children of small farmers and tradesmen might acquire some elementary schooling for a small weekly fee at a private day school.

Few poor children received instruction. Only a small minority were taught reading and good manners at charity schools, although these institutions were comparatively numerous in Essex. More attended the Sunday Schools which churches and chapels began to set up from about 1790. In Essex the Church of England was more successful than other denominations in the educational expansion that followed. By 1807 it had a growing number of day schools under its control. Soon afterwards it formed local branches of its National Society for the Education of the Poor and thereby enlisted powerful lay support for further expansion. By 1840 it had established schools in most towns and by 1860 in many villages.

The Nonconformists collaborated with the British School Society to found day schools in towns and some larger villages. Less numerous than their rivals, they suffered constant financial difficulty and partly for that reason tended to support the movement for public control of education which led to the Education Act of 1870 and to the establishment in some places of elected School Boards with power to levy a rate. Where they succeeded in having a School Board established, they usually transferred their British Schools to its control.

From 1850 teaching steadily improved. Government inspection and more enlightened public interest were partly responsible, but the chief cause was the higher quality of the teachers themselves. Better trained and better paid, they won public respect for their competence and conscientious service. With the extension of public control in education they gained greater independence and, through the local branches of the National Union of Elementary Teachers, a greater influence upon educational development.

Secondary education progressed more slowly. The grammar schools were gradually reformed and some private schools in mid-Victorian times seem to have offered an education as good as any available in the county. Technical education was almost non-obtainable, despite warnings by local newspapers against its neglect in a competitive world. Only in the 1890's were the newly created County Councils given responsibility for its development.

## *EARLY SECONDARY SCHOOLS*

### *1. A Schoolboy's Letter, 1732*

The Hon. T. Lennard Barrett writes to his aunt from Harrow. *Original spelling retained.*

Barrett Lennard Archives (D/DL C43/3/112).

Dear Aunt, March the 29, 1732

As you have always been exceeding good to me, for which I shall never be able to make you a Return, I beg you'd now please to grant me this Request viz. to Leave off Learning Mathematicks, this Dear Madam may att first seem an unreasonable thing, but I hope the Reasons which I am now going to give you will make you, according to your usual goodness, grant me this Request.

You Very well know, Dear Madam, that I have been an old Border, & therefore ought not to be slighted by Weston, which I have been very much. For This Morning I heard that Mr Weston was going out with some off the Gentlemen to teach them to measure Ground; upon this Report I took my hat and stood among the Rest off those who were going, when to my Great Surprise Mr Weston came down Stairs and bid me begon, for I only wanted to be Idle & told me I shou'd not go with him. This has netled me very much because the Boys he took out with him were no farther advanc'd in Mathematick's than I, As for his saying I only wanted to be Idle, I hope you will believe me when I tell you upon my Honour that the Chief and only end of my Desire to go out a measuring was to be instructed in that Art. Neither do I think I ever gave him half so much Reason to think me prone to Idleness as Barnet and Philips who went with him. If You will be so good then, Dear Madam, to grant me my earnest Request of Leaving off Mathematicks, I shall be exceedingly oblig'd to you.

You may Rember, Dear Aunt, that I have often told you that Mr Evans taught me Mathematicks in private, I shall still continue to Learn Mathematicks of Mr Evans who is more able to teach me than Weston. For I can asure you I have learnt more from Mr Evans than I ever did from Weston. I hope I have now given you Sufficient Reasons for my Desireing to Leave Learning Mathematicks from Mr Weston ; I therefore beg you'd be so good to me (Dear Madam) as to Grant my Desire. There is an old Saying one Story is good till another is told, but I can assure you on my Honour that what I have told you is true. I beg therefore that if you grant me my Request, that you will not be mov'd by Weston's fawning and funning, who cares no more for you nor I than what money he can make off us, else he wou'd not have us'd you in the manner he did when you came from Lady Lennards, to give you old heartychoaks for supper & to Lay you in Bed with frowsy Bet Rosam, to be devoured by Buggs.

The Quarter is now begining, therefore tis a very fit time to Leave off Mathematicks. I beg you'd Let me have a Letter from you as soon as possible, in which I hope to recieve Orders to tell Mr Weston that I Don't Learn Mathematicks any Longer off him, which will be an inexpressible pleasure to,

Dear Aunt,

Your most Dutifull Nephew,

T. Lennard Barrett.

P.S. I shall take Double pains in Latin and evrything else. I shall be so far from losing the Mathematicks I have already got that I don't doubt to make great improvements in them under Mr Evans' Care. Pray Don't tell Weston I Learn of Mr Evans.

*2. Private Schools, 1787*

*Chelmsford Chronicle,* July 6, 1787 (E.R.O.).

Boarding School for Young Ladies, Chipping-Ongar, Essex. Miss Binckes's takes this Opportunity of acquainting their friends and the public in general that their School will open again on the 23d of July, where they may be assured of the strictest attention being paid to every branch of the education of young Ladies committed to their care. Terms Sixteen Guineas a year. No Entrance required. Dancing and Writing by approved Masters.

*Chelmsford Chronicle,* Oct. 5, 1787 (E.R.O.).

Sutton-Hall Academy, near Hornchurch, Essex. Young Gentlemen are Boarded and Educated with the strictest attention to their morals and health. The English, Latin and French languages taught with the greatest propriety. Merchant accompts, drawing, geography, dancing and every branch of useful and ornamental learning. At twenty guineas a year.

### 3. *An Educational Reformer, 1807*

*Chelmsford Chronicle,* July 10, 1807.

Shenfield Academy, near Brentwood, Essex.

Mr Perry Begs leave to inform the Public, that his Academy will open again on the 20th instant. The very great improvements made in the above Seminary are existing proofs that a good plan of instruction, and unwearied attention on the part of the master (without the severity of corporal punishment) will render even the dullest youth a competent scholar, and must naturally conduct the boy of ability to the highest attainment in literature.

Mr P. from the liberal encouragement he has met with from his friends, as well as from promise of further recommendation, has been induced to take a larger house nearly on the same spot, which is a most healthy and pleasant situation.

The pupils have each an allotment of garden ground.

### 4. *Chelmsford Grammar School, 1848*

White, *Directory of Essex,* 1848, p. 317.

The School has room for 80 boys, and adjoining it is a playground of two acres, and also a large house, garden, etc, occupied free of rent, rates and taxes, by the master, who has a yearly salary of £220. According to the rules made by the governors in 1830, they should also employ an usher in holy orders, and allow him a yearly salary of £100, with the liberty of taking a curacy ; but the present assistant is paid by the master. The number of free scholars is limited to 40, twenty from Chelmsford and Moulsham, and twenty from the surrounding parishes, within the distance of six miles ; but there are now but few scholars, the present respected master, Rev. Jas. Hutchinson, being old and infirm. Many of the inhabitants of the town and neighbourhood would be glad to send their sons to this school, if the funds of the endowment were applied to the purposes of a general English Education ; and with this in view the governors, after the decease of the present master, ought to consult the Bishop of the Diocese, in conformity with the directions of the charter, and lay before his lordship the outline of a liberal plan, suited to the wants of the tradesmen and artificers of the town, as, indeed, they proposed to do in 1807. A large portion of the School income is exhausted by repairs, rates, tithes, and other incidental expences, and the payment of £20 to the treasurer.

### 5. *An Essex Undergraduate*

J. T. Ambrose writes from Cambridge to his parents at Mistley. Family Papers (D/DHw F6).

Dear Parents, St John's, Nov. 27, 1815.

As the term is drawing so very near its close, I think it time to inform you that I want a great deal of money for the payment of various bills not taken by the Tutor—as Cook's bill, which is for breakfast, dinner and supper all the term, £1 . 10 of which Jackson pays, the remainder will be about £8 or £10, but I cannot yet tell exactly. Then there is the Jyp's wages, amounting, I believe, to £2 . 2 . 0, and I am uncertain whether I pay the Bedmaker (the same sum) or Jackson ; then Fruiterer's bill and other minors, but I am happy to add no horse bill which generally swells an account. The washing, etc, I settle myself . . .

This place is terribly cold and damp, requires great fires day and night. Not near so much wine is drunk as formerly ; society consequently is more agreeable . . .

This is the first stage where a man feels his consequence in the world, and connexions here are everything. I am very pleasantly situated in that respect, having a very pleasant and at the same time a quiet society, men who reserve dashing propensities to be exhibited on a larger stage than Cambridge affords . . .

There is a man here, a famous mail-driver, foxhunter, etc, etc, who goes about college and into lectures in a green coat and red waistcoat, an established Buck whom I to my no small astonishment discovered to be an old friend of mine, by name Lippyatt, formerly of Felsted, but am happy he has not recognised me.

There is a fellow Commoner here, a very dashing man, whose father is about purchasing Mr Warren's. He has been remarkably civil to me, knowing we are to be neighbours. His name is Jarrett, a nephew of Berners. They are West Indians and I think you will find them rather purse proud, but this is only surmise.

I am your most affectionate, dutiful

J. T. Ambrose.

## *THE EDUCATION OF THE POOR*

### *1. A Charity School*

Morant, *History of Essex,* 1768, Vol. II, p. 6.

Chelmsford Charity Schools.

There are two Charity-schools in this town : One founded 17 August, 1713, for 50 boys ; the other, in April 1714, for 20 girls. The children are educated in the doctrine of the Church of England, in reading, writing, psalmody, and arithmetic. The girls are farther taught household-work to fit them for services ; they make up the linen, and knit the stockings for both schools ; and are taught to make their own gowns and petticoats. Both schools are clothed once a year ; the children are also frequently and publicly examined in the Church-catechism. And from both schools there have been many bound out to proper trades and employments. But of late, the trustees think it more for the good of society, to procure masters for them in husbandry, or to place them out in yearly services. The number of boys is at present reduced to 32. The school-house stands at the north-east corner of the Churchyard, in a lane leading to the Parsonage, and to Bishop's-Hall. And a house hath been lately purchased for the master to dwell in, whose salary is 30 pounds a year.

### *2. Charity School Finance*

Accounts of Chelmsford Charity School, 1796-7 (D/Q 8/3).

| | Receipts | | £ s. d. |
|---|---|---|---|
| | To cash remaining in hand brought forward | | 45 . 2 . 0¼ |
| July 2 | To subscriptions received for Midsummer | | 54 . 17 . 0 |
| Sept. 9 | To cash received of Mrs. Wallenger, four years' interest due 5th July being the dividend of the legacy of John Wallenger, Esq. | | 26 . 6 . 0 |
| 11 | To cash collected at the Sermon in the morning | 27 . 8 . 0¾ | |
| | and afternoon | 24 . 11 . 11 | 51 . 19 . 11¾ |
| | Mr. Willm. Stebbing, one year's interest on £80 due 10th Nov. | | 3 . 4 . 0 |
| | | | 181 . 9 . 0 |
| | | | 110 . 18 . 9½ |
| | Carried over | | 70 . 10 . 2½ |

| | Expenditure | £ s. d. |
|---|---|---|
| Oct. 17 | Mr. Tho. Stoneham for clothing the children | 38 . 9 . 1½ |
| | J. Franc's account for salary &c. to Michaelmas last | 9 . 13 . 0 |
| | Mr. Pirsson & Mr. Johns for breeches | 5 . 13 . 6 |
| | Mr. Towndrow for painting the schoolhouse | 2 . 15 . 0 |

| | | |
|---|---|---|
| Oct. 17 | Mrs. Cowland, Hen. Wiffin & Wm. Wicks for shoes | 5 . 11 . 7 |
| | Mr. John Pain, S. Saltmarsh & Ed. Scott for shoes | 5 . 7 . 6 |
| | Mr. Bentley for wine &c. for the Waltham singers | 13 . 0 |
| | Mr. Abell for 8 pr. buckles & Advertising the Sermon in the County Chronicle | 9 . 4 |
| | The children, for encouragement | 9 . 3 |
| | M. Franc, a present | 1 . 1 . 0 |
| | S. Jackson for hair-cutting | 3 . 0 |
| | R. Porter, Bailes, Halls, Tibbles &c. for distributing the hymns &c. | 13 . 0 |
| Feb. 18 | J. Franc's account for salary &c. to Christmas last | 15 . 17 . 0 |
| | Mr. Wm. Reed, half year to Christmas for teaching the children to sing | 2 . 2 . 0 |
| May 11 | J. Franc, one quarter's salary to last Lady Day | 9 . 11 . 0 |
| July 1 | Mr. Stanes, one year's insurance | 13 . 6 |
| 22 | J. Franc, one quarter's salary &c. to Midsummer last | 9 . 15 . 0 |
| | Mr. Wm. Reed, half year's to Midsummer last | 2 . 2 . 0 |
| | | 110 . 18 . 9½ |

### 3. *Essex Education Surveyed, 1807*

The following extracts are from reports by Essex clergymen. Archdeaconry Records, School Returns, 1807 (D/AEM 2).

There are in the parish of Great Baddow one Sunday school containing about thirty children and one day school containing fourteen children, both supported by voluntary benefactions . . . There is in the parish of Rainham one Sunday school, containing about thirty children, supported in the same manner. But besides the above eleemosynary schools there is in the parish of Great Baddow one free school for the education of twenty children of such parents as do not receive any parochial relief . . . and nine day schools (not supported by charity, though the parents be poor) containing about one hundred and ten children. In the parish of Rainham there are two day schools, not supported by charity, containing about thirty children of parents of the like description.

We have no Sunday schools but day schools in the parishes of South Benfleet and Thundersley, the former containing about 30 scholars, the latter about 20. The two parishes join in a House of Industry for the paupers, containing in both from 25 to 30 souls, but little or no reading or writing taught. I endeavoured to establish a Sunday school here and strongly urged the necessity of it to Dr Horsley when Bishop of Rochester (the Dean, Chapter of Westminster being then patrons of this Vicarage and impropriators of the great tithes) to no purpose. It is highly expedient that some good establishment should be set on foot speedily here to check the motley swarms of the disaffected, ignorant Dissenters and nondescript Vulgar as to religion.

[Abbess Roothing.] I wish it were in my power to say that we had a school of any description whatsoever for the education of our poor children. But we are too poor to set forward any such institution here, as we consist only of a few farmers, without any manufactory, and the greater part of our parishioners subsist by daily labour, whilst two or three men of rank in life carry off all the produce of their landed estates to a distant part of the country, not leaving a guinea behind them. Hopeless is the prospect that our children can spiritually differ from the wild life and colts.

[West Tilbury.] The only schools in my parish are of the following description, viz. One day school for male and female children, amounting to about 20, and supported at my own expense, wherein they are taught reading, and the girls plain work and knitting. There is another school in the village of the very same kind, kept by a poor woman who teaches reading and needlework. She has threepence per week for teaching to read and sixpence if they are taught to work. She receives scholars from other adjacent parishes, and the number of them in all is from 20 to 30. I have most earnestly wished to establish a Sunday School in the parish, but have hitherto found it impracticable from the difficulty of procuring a proper master and, what is worse, the extreme unwillingness of the common people to send their children to church regularly, as they are constantly enjoined, discourages any further attempt—as I am convinced it would be difficult to persuade them to submit to the necessary confinement at the school so much in the day as would be expedient for their instruction.

[Doddinghurst.] I have to inform you that the only school in my parish is one taught by a woman, who teaches about fifteen or twenty children to read. I established a Sunday school when I entered upon the curacy of the parish but it was, notwithstanding my utmost efforts, so badly attended after a few weeks that I was reluctantly obliged to discontinue it. Since that time it has been my earnest wish to set on foot a day school at my own expense, but a very limited income (having no preferment though I have now been 15 years in orders) has hitherto prevented me from putting so desirable a plan into execution. So thoroughly am I convinced of the utility of such establishments (I had almost said, of the absolute necessity of giving the poor a little education, as virtuous principles cannot in any other way be instilled into them) that in whatever parish it may be my lot to spend the rest of my life, the first wish of my heart shall be to establish a school for the education of the children of the poor.

In the parish of Chigwell there are two free schools, founded by Archbishop Harsnett in the reign of James 1st, one for the instruction of 12 boys belonging to Chigwell in classical learning and the other for teaching such boys of the parish as may be sent, writing, arithmetic and the principles of religion. The parishes of Woodford, Loughton and Lambourne are also entitled to send severally two boys to each of these schools. The Grammar School has not for many years had any scholars on the foundation and the master receives a considerable number of boarders into his house. The writing-master at present teaches only 12 boys of this parish and 6 from the three adjoining ones, but as the estate has been much advanced which supports the institution, it is now proposed to extend its advantages as far as possible. There is likewise a charity school here, in which 12 girls are clothed and instructed, supported by contribution, and also two Sunday schools in which about 60 children are taught to read and sing and are brought to church under proper care. Besides these, there is a school lately established by a congregation of Independents, wherein, as I understand, about 20 girls are clothed and educated.

[East Horndon.] The schools are as follows.
1. A girls' school supported by private individuals, containing 33 girls and little boys.
2. A boys' school kept by a Roman Catholic and supported by Lord Petre, containing 18 boys, 2 girls, 6 writing scholars at their own expense.
3. A girls' school kept by a Roman Catholic, containing 9 from Lady Petre, 20 from private individuals.
Of the two last one receives £20 and the other £9 per annum from Lord and Lady Petre, though I cannot learn that either of them is permanently endowed. They are neither of them confined to Roman Catholics and in the girls' school the church catechism is taught.

There is no public school of any kind in either of my parishes. The only one at present is in High Ongar and is supported by my wife and two other ladies whom she has induced to subscribe to it. It consists of about 20 girls, who are taught to read and work . . . The parish of Little Laver is very small and there is no regular school there, but I have occasionally sent some of their children for instruction to a neighbouring school.

In the parish of Purleigh there is a charity school, founded by a late Rector for the education of ten poor boys and ten poor girls, and as the present Rector has built a new school house at his own expense, it is his intention to add about four children more in lieu of any rent from the master. Besides this there is a reading and sewing day school, kept by an old lady who generally has about twenty scholars, chiefly of the lower orders.

[Laindon Hills.] There are no schools in my parish for the education of the poor.

### 4. *Teaching as a Last Resort, 1823*

Chelmsford Select Vestry Minutes, 1822-3 (D/P 94/8/4).

[Chelmsford.] At a meeting of the Select Vestry held the 28th day of April, 1823, . . . the Overseer was requested to hire some premises of Mr Chalk for one year at a rent of £5 and to assist William Walbier to the amount of £2 to relieve him from debt and enable him to set on foot a school for the support of his family.

### 5. *A Dame School, 1875*

The following extract is from a report by an H.M. Inspector of Schools.
*Halstead Times,* Aug. 14, 1875.

In one of these, in the town of Harwich, to which the Vicar conducted me, after climbing a stair more like a chimney, we found an old dame who had taught after this fashion for many years, and did not at all approve of this intrusion upon her premises, until, in the midst of her scolding, the Vicar informed her that I was a gentleman sent by the Queen to see what her school was like. Upon this she immediately altered her tone and received us most graciously, inquiring particularly after the health of her Majesty, and saying she would very much like to see her. Her one room was made to answer the threefold purpose of a bedroom, a schoolroom and a kitchen, in which ventilation was a thing unknown. Notwithstanding this becoming loyalty, I am still hard-hearted enough to condemn this system of Dame-schools.

### 6. *Sunday School Accounts, 1793*

It will be seen from the following extracts that Kelvedon Sunday School had given rise to a small day-school.
Minute Book of Kelvedon Sunday School, 1792-1833.

| | | | £ s. d. |
|---|---|---|---|
| Feb. | 6 | To Mr. Rivington, bookseller to the Society for promoting Christian Knowledge | 14 . 3 . 0 |
| Mar. | 2 | To Phoebe Edwards for a pair of shoes | 3 . 6 |
| | 25 | To John Bringis for teaching one quarter in the sunday school, for teaching children in the week day | 2 . 2 . 0 |
| May | 6 | Recd. subscriptions | 19 . 1 . 0 |
| Sep. | 3 | Recd. at the charity sermon for the sunday school | 12 . 14 . 6 |
| | 27 | Rewards for good behaviour | 8 . 8 |

| | | |
|---|---|---|
| Sep. 30 | To Jemima Blackwell for teaching the children one quarter | 10 . 6 |
| | Do. for cleaning the part of the church where the school is kept | 5 . 0 |
| Dec. 26 | Paid to John Bringis for teaching the sunday school one quarter | 1 . 1 . 0 |
| | To Do. for teaching 12 children one quarter to Christmas Day | 1 . 1 . 0 |
| | To rewards at Christmas | 8 . 0 |

## 7. *Rules of St. Edward's National Schools, Romford, 1854*

Sage Collection (E.R.O.).

1. Children of the age of 6 years, and upwards, or who are able to read words of one syllable, are admitted by application to the Committee, who meet at the Girls' Class Room, every Monday morning, at 9 o'clock. No child can be admitted at any other time or day. One of the Parents, or the Guardian *must* attend with the child to be admitted.

2. The School hours are from 9 to 12 in the morning, and from 2 to 4 in the afternoon. On Sundays the Children meet at half-past 9 in the morning, and at half-past 2 in the afternoon, and every Child is required to attend Divine Service at the Parish Church, morning and afternoon.

3. Every Child, not on the Foundation, must pay *Twopence* weekly, on every Monday morning. (In the case of two or more Children in the same family, a deduction from this payment is made).

4. The Instruction will consist of Scriptural knowledge and Religious Teaching; Reading, Writing, Arithmetic, History, Geography, Grammar, Book-keeping, and Singing. Children will also be instructed in other subjects as far as their ability, and the time of their stay at School will allow.

5. Every Boy and Girl, of the age of 13, or upwards, whose conduct has been praiseworthy, will on quitting the School, be presented with a Bible and Prayer Book.

6. Parents are required to send their Children neat and clean, with their hair combed, and properly cut, and their clothes mended.

7. No Child will be allowed to be absent from School without permission from the Master or Mistress. In case of illness, notice should immediately be sent to the School.

8. The Holidays are,—A month at Harvest-time; a fortnight at Christmas; a week at Easter; and two days at Whitsuntide.

9. Annual Examinations will take place, at which Rewards will be given to those Children who are the most deserving in their respective classes.

10. At the admission of any Child, the Parent will be presented with a Copy of these Rules, a strict observance of which must be required.

*8. Origins of a British School*

Kelvedon British School Minutes (E/MM 9/1).

At a meeting held July 3rd, 1845, in the Independent Chapel, Kelvedon, the Rev. S. Causby, Minister of the place, in the chair, the Rev. R. Ainslie, secretary of the Congregational Board of Education, and the Rev. T. W. Davids, secretary to the Essex Board of Education, being present as a deputation, it was determined to attempt the establishment of a day school and promises of support were given to the amount of £120, to be paid in equal annual instalments ranging over a space . . . of five years. A committee was formed of persons in connection with the Independent Church, who, desirous of making the school as popular and efficient as possible, determined upon adopting the principles of the British and Foreign School Society. Upon this ground, its free and unsectarian character, they sought the assistance . . . of some friends of education belonging to the Society of Friends, and a meeting for conference at the Friends' Meeting House was called, but proved a failure, and no course of action was decided upon.

The committee, not having funds at their disposal to enable them to build a school house, did not feel justified to borrow for that purpose and for some time could only meet and consult. Yet they adopted the principles upon which the school should be established, if established at all, and sought diligently to accomplish the great object.

*9. Education in Saffron Walden, 1848*

White, *Directory of Essex,* 1848, p. 642 foll.

The Free Grammar School, in Castle street, was endowed in 1525, by 'Dame Johane Bradbury', and her brother, the Rev. John Leche, who vested it in trust with the treasurer and chamberlains of the Guild of Holy Trinity, that the priest of that guild (appointed by the said Rev. J. Leche) should be appointed schoolmaster . . . The school was suspended from 1802 to 1815, when it was opened as a National School; but the small endowment having been improved by rebuilding the house in 1825 and purchasing the tithes of the school land in 1815, a master qualified to teach Latin and Greek was appointed a few years ago . . . The establishment is now conducted as a Grammar School by the Rev. A. E. Fowler, B.A., who receives 10s. entrance money and 10s.

per quarter from each of the 24 free scholars, of whom 16 are from Walden, 4 from Newport, and 2 each from each of the parishes of Little Chesterford and Widdington.

The Charity School, for educating and clothing 12 poor boys and 12 poor girls, was established in 1715 by subscription. Among the principal donations and bequests to this useful charity, we find £500 left by Thomas Penning in 1717 ; a yearly rent-charge of £5 out of Lumpitts and Limekiln Field ; £50 left by the Countess Dowager of Suffolk in 1721 . . . These estates were vested with new trustees in 1818 ; and the 24 children clothed and educated by the charity are instructed by the master and mistress of the National School, erected in 1845 in Castle street, where about 90 boys and 70 girls are educated. The British School, in East street, is a large building, erected in 1838 by W. G. Gibson, Esq., and family, and is now attended by 120 boys. The Girls' British School, in Gold street, is in connexion with the old School of Industry. In Abbey Lane is an Infant School, built by W. G. Gibson, Esq., and supported by dissenters ; and there is one in Little Church street, connected with the established church.

Academies (*take Boarders)

*Archer Catherine, Gold street ; Conway Elizabeth, Audley End ; British Schools, Wm. Jenkins and Margaret Jeff ; *Crisp, Matilda and Maria ; *Frye Thomas, Frye Emma ; *Grammar School, Rev. A. E. Fowler, B.A., Castle street ; Infant Schools, Annie Cohen and Harriet Overton ; Johnson Maria, High street ; *Jones Wm. Taylor, Grove House ; National Schools, Edw. Thos. Chambers and Emma Maple ; Pursey Wm., Pluckrett Sus. ; Sandon Miss A., Common end.

### *10. Obstacles to Education, 1839*

The Vicar of Coggeshall reports on the local National School.
London Diocesan Board of Education Parish Returns, 1839 (D/P 30/28/18).

The children of this parish are almost all engaged in various manufactories as soon as they are eight years old and it is difficult to persuade them to come to school even for part of a week . . . the master and mistress owing to want of funds to pay for better are very inefficient, and no actual registers have been kept . . . The parish is one of the poorest in the county and a considerable proportion of the more wealthy parishioners are dissenters.

### *11. Plea for Religion in Education*

The following extract is from a newspaper editorial.
*Essex Standard,* Sept. 14, 1838.

With all the advantages which Great Britain enjoys above all other nations, with the blessings of a high pitch of civilisation, the glory of her arms, her wealth, her industry, and the spread of education ; still is the country in a constant state of restlessness and dissatisfaction. The Schoolmaster is abroad to little purpose ; for his lessons seem to be principally of a political nature ; and instead of teaching men their duty towards God and their fellow men, the knowledge indiscriminately bestowed, in too many instances, makes the poor discontented with their station in life, without at the same time affording them the means to improve their condition. Education tends to create wants and desires, to which ignorance is a stranger—and

' When ignorance is bliss, 'tis folly to be wise '.

But let it not be supposed that we are the advocates of ignorance, and the enemies of education. We repudiate the supposition ; but we wish to see education united with scriptural instruction. Mere knowledge drove our first parents out of Paradise, and barren and stinted knowledge in the present day drives numbers of their children out of the paths of peace and happiness. To attempt to arrest the " march of knowledge " would be as useless as an effort to stem the swelling mountain torrent. Wise men will not waste their time and energy on so impracticable an object, but will address themselves to the more attainable one of directing the stream into proper channels—and the best adjunct in so beneficent a work is the Bible.

## *LATER PROGRESS IN EDUCATION*

### 1. *Educational Reformers, 1838*

Colchester Chartists criticise the inadequacy of educational provision. *Essex and Suffolk Times*, March 2, 1838 (C.B.L.).

That this meeting considers the education given to the working-classes of this empire of a kind by no means sufficient for their instruction, being for the most part confined to reading, writing and a little arithmetic. Whereas, at no greater expense, and at the same time, the children might be instructed in the elements of a more useful branch of knowledge, and thereby trained to more industrious, prudent and virtuous habits.

### 2. *The Influence of Her Majesty's Inspectors*

Matthew Arnold reported on Loughton British School in May, 1870. Log Book of Loughton British School (E/ML 51/1).

The present master, an old pupil teacher of mine, came here in July last. Both the attendance and the instruction have during the winter been greatly affected by scarlet fever, but the numbers are now considerable. The order is satisfactory. The cause of illness being removed, the weakness of the instruction, now far too great, must be remedied. The arithmetic is defective all through the school, and the spelling in the third and fourth standards. The answering in geography is good and this subject is taught in a way to interest the children. A competent person attends every afternoon to teach the girls needlework. The water is not yet laid on to the offices. The maps want renewing and they should be hung up in the schoolroom. My Lords will look for improvement as the condition of an unreduced grant another year (Article 52a).

### 3. *The Coming of Board Schools*

Under the 1870 Education Act some towns and villages set up School Boards with power to finance Board Schools from a public rate.

*Halstead Times*, July 20, 1872.

An adjourned meeting of parishioners was held in the vestry, Bocking, on Thursday morning, the Very Rev. the Dean in the chair, for the purpose of considering the education question. The following gentlemen were present, Messrs. S. Tabor, E. Holmes, H. J. Holmes, S. Courtauld, G. Courtauld, the Rev. McAll, Messrs. A. Young, J. Brown, J. Joyce, etc, etc. After a discussion of something like two hours' duration, the following resolution was adopted :—That in the opinion of this meeting the appointment of a School Board in this Parish would be very desirable (and chiefly as being the only means whereby a large number of children now growing up without education may be brought to School).

### 4. *Towards Universal Education*

From 1876 School Attendance Committees, appointed by Boards of Guardians, enforced general attendance and paid school fees in necessitous cases.

Romford Guardians, School Attendance Committee Minutes, March, 1880 (G/RM 80).

Barking Local Committee . . . At the meeting of the above Committee held on Tuesday evening last, a large number of cases of absentees were under consideration with the following results :— Payment of school fees recommended to [8 detailed recommendations]. In the following it is recommended that summonses be issued [11 cases]. The remaining cases were either left for further consideration or the parents promised compliance with the directions of the Committee.

5. *A School Attendance Committee at Work*

Halstead Guardians, Committee Minutes (G/HM 33).

[23rd November, 1877] *Appointment of School Attendance Officer*

A letter from the Local Government Board . . . was read, approving of the appointment of Mr Jacob Ralph for the period of twelve months at a salary of £40 per annum, subject however to the strict understanding that Mr Ralph will not continue his business of innkeeper after Ladyday next. On the motion of Mr Brewster, seconded by Mr Courtauld, the Clerk was instructed to write to the Local Committees, informing them of Mr Ralph's appointment and suggesting that, as he has received instructions to seek the assistance of the Committees in carrying out his duties, he should be requested to attend an early meeting of the Committee for each district.

[10th January, 1879] The Clerk reported that J— D—, H— B—, G— R— and H— P— of Halstead had been severally fined 1/-, costs 4/-, for non-compliance with the bye-laws; and that orders had been made at the Hedingham Bench for the attendance of the children of J— E— and M— D— of Sible Hedingham and W— B— of Great Yeldham; and that W— R—, Sible Hedingham, and W— S—, Sible Hedingham, had been severally fined 5/-, including costs, for disobedience of attendance orders.

A letter was read from Mr H. B. Rowan, H.M. Inspector of Schools, appointing Friday, February 7th, as the date of his proposed conference with the Committee with respect to the deficiency of school accommodation in the parishes of Sible Hedingham and Toppesfield.

[9th June, 1882] It was ordered that handbills be issued, warning parents not to withdraw their children from school for the purpose of pea-picking and that penalties would be enforced in all cases where the law is disobeyed.

[4th August, 1882] It was reported that the Halstead Bench . . . had fined A— H—, Halstead, 5/- and 20/- costs for illegally employing children in pea picking.

6. *Essex County Council Aids Technical Education*

An early function of County Councils was to administer a Government grant for technical education.
Essex County Council Minute Book (C/M 1).

July 7th, 1891.

Report of Technical Instruction Committee . . .

4. Your Committee have been in communication with various Urban and Sanitary Authorities and other Boards representing

all the parishes in the County and they have also obtained and considered Returns giving particulars of the Endowed Schools in the County.

5. Your Committee consider that the best means of spreading the benefit is by stimulating local interest and encouraging the formation of local Committees which shall undertake to carry out such schemes of Technical Instruction as are required in their respective districts.

6. Your Committee are glad to be able to report that this proposal is generally being taken up throughout the County. Local Committees have been formed and Schemes in different stages of development submitted on behalf of 134 parishes, chiefly in combination with centres conveniently situated. Further Committees are in course of formation. The Schemes in the Second Schedule to this Report have been approved by the Committee.

7. Such proposed Grants are calculated on the basis of 1d in the £ of the assessment to the County rate of the district concerned, and your Committee recommend that they be empowered to make grants on that basis to any of the following bodies submitting a detailed scheme of Technical Instruction satisfactory to your Committee, subject to such conditions as they shall prescribe, viz : (A) Urban Authorities whose district is assessed at £50,000 and upwards ; (B) Committees representing smaller towns in combination with adjoining rural parishes . . . (C) Similar Committees to the above, representing rural parishes which cannot conveniently come under B either singly or in combination with others.

8. In the case of B and C your Committee consider it desirable that instruction in subjects bearing on the theory and practice of Agriculture be included in the Scheme submitted, and that where practicable, every Scheme do make provision for extending an adequate share of its advantages to girls, by teaching Domestic Economy, including Cookery and other subjects suitable for them, and that in view of this object there be a proportion of women on the Local Committees.

Your Committee also recommend :

9. That as in most cases these classes will be held in the evenings, existing Schools or other buildings be utilised for the purposes of teaching, and that whilst leaving the fixing of fees to be charged in these Schools to Local Committees, it be recommended that they be sufficiently low to admit of all participating in the benefit of the instruction given.

# PROGRESS IN MEDICINE

In 1750 many Essex surgeons and apothecaries lacked economic security and social status. They sought them by pretentious advertisement of their skill and their secret remedies or by establishing Spas and sea-water baths. By the early nineteenth century, with the aid of such discoveries as inoculation and vaccination against smallpox, they had greatly increased public confidence in their capability. At the same time they were achieving greater unity within their profession. After 1800 this process continued, reinforced by improved medical training and increasing popular interest in medical services. By 1850 the Essex doctor was already a respected and substantial citizen.

*1. Prevalence of Smallpox*

*Ipswich Journal,* Jan. 6, 1749 (C.B.L.).

The Small-Pox is not in Dedham-Street and is only in Two Families at Prince's Green and no where else in the Town excepting the Pest-House (where only one or two have it).

[Signed by the Master of the Grammar School, two Churchwardens, two Overseers of the Poor and Apothecary.]

*Ipswich Journal,* Aug. 8, 1761.

Whereas it is confidently reported that some evil-minded People have set it forth in this County that the Small-Pox still rages in the Town of Romford to the great Detriment of the inhabitants there ; We whose Names are underwritten, do certify that the Small-Pox is intirely ceased in the said town of Romford.

[Signed by the Curate, three Churchwardens, three Overseers, two doctors and the Vestry Clerk.]

*2. Inoculation against Smallpox, 1766*

*Ipswich Journal,* May 31, 1766 (C.B.L.).

*INOCULATION*

Continued by Mr Wood at Danbury, Essex, with the greatest Care, Assiduity and Success, and on the most reasonable Terms ;

conscientiously considering the Circumstances of his Patients and the number of their Families, having at this time several very numerous ones under his Care, which he hath inoculated for very small Considerations so as not to injure them or their Children, but to prevent the fatal Consequences of their catching the Distemper in the Natural Way.

He thinks it quite necessary to inform the Public that he don't make use of any repelling Medicines in any Stage of the Distemper nor of any of the Gallimawfrey Compositions which a certain anonymous Author assumes the liberty of asserting in his notable Pamphlet of being the Method practised in the County of Essex; he dares venture to affirm likewise that even not one of the Gentlemen of the Faculty in the County of Essex or elsewhere make use of either the Powder, Pills, Mish-Mash, or Hotch-Potch Decoctions, prescribed by Doctor Catch-penny; they being very inconsistent with, and absurd to, the Rules of Practice, and of equal dangerous Consequence.

### 3. *Vaccination Welcomed, 1801*

The General Court of the Essex and Herts. Benevolent Medical Society passed the following resolution in 1801.
Essex and Herts. Benevolent Society Minutes (D/Z 15/1).

That the thanks of this court be given to Dr Jenner for his invaluable treatise on the Variola Vaccina, wherein he has clearly and satisfactorily demonstrated that the inoculated cow pox is a certain preventive of the small pox.

That as men of humanity, associated for the purposes of benevolence, we should be wanting to the character we assume, did we neglect the present opportunity of bearing our testimony to the value of this providential discovery, which, if generally practised we are of opinion, would effectually eradicate the small pox, one of the severest scourges of the human race.

That this court, in thus requesting Dr Jenner to accept their unanimous thanks for his inestimable publication, entertain no doubt but posterity will do honour to his memory and record his name amongst the real friends of man.

### 4. *Vaccination Campaign, 1815*

Coggeshall Vestry Minutes (D/P 36/11/11).

1815, Oct. 9th. It is this day ordered in Vestry that Mr Eagle and Messrs Godfrey be requested to use their best endeavours to vaccinate (free from charges to the parties) all the poor inhabitants . . .

1815, Nov. 13th. At a Vestry meeting . . . to receive the report of Messrs Godfrey and Eagle of the success of their endeavours to vaccinate the parishioners of this place, they report there appears a great disinclination to the cow pox, but, as we are convinced it is the mildest and a safe prevention to the small pox, we request the above gentlemen to use every endeavour to vaccinate . . .

### 5. *A Private Mental Hospital, 1780*

An Act of 1774 authorised Quarter Sessions to license private asylums and to appoint justices as visitors.
Quarter Sessions Order Book, Michaelmas 1780 (Q/SO 13).

Whereas application hath now been made to this Court by Thomas Baldwin of Waltham Holy Cross, gentleman, that this Court would be pleased to grant him a licence for keeping an house for the reception of lunatics, not exceeding ten, for one year from this day . . . We, being three of his Majesty's Justices of the Peace in general Quarter Sessions assembled, do hereby license the said Thomas Baldwin . . . provided always that, if [he] shall refuse James Barwicke and Edward Hillersdon, Esquires, two of his Majesty's Justices of the Peace and John Wilkinson, the physician now appointed by this Court to visit and inspect the said house, admittance into the said house in the day time on such their visitation, then this licence to be void.

### 6. *Colchester Dispensary Established, 1797*

*Ipswich Journal*, April 29, 1797 (C.B.L.).

We learn from Colchester that a Dispensary is now establishing in that town, for giving medical relief to the poor inhabitants, and is most liberally encouraged by Lord Muncaster and Robt. Thornton, Esq., members of Parliament for that Borough, Lady Grantham, Lady Lucas, etc, besides the benevolent inhabitants of the place. It is under the direction of Dr Loftus Woods, who was formerly Physician to the Surrey Dispensary in London, and will be ready to receive patients in the course of the next week.

### 7. *Medical Training, 1763*

*Ipswich Journal*, May 14, 1763 (C.B.L.).

Wivenhoe, May 10, 1763. The Practice of Inoculation is carried on, with the greatest Care, by Thomas Tunmer, who has now got a proper House for that Purpose. Wanted by the same an Apprentice after the Second of November next. N.B. He will have an Opportunity (if he turns out careful) of a pretty extensive Inspection among the Commonalty, a Thing greatly wanting to most Apprentices and what opulent Patients might not admit of. Reasonable Terms will be required.

### 8. *Professional Unity, 1786*

A benevolent society was founded at Chelmsford in 1786 to assist widows and orphans of medical men. A leading physician of the day greeted its foundation as follows.
Essex and Herts. Benevolent Medical Society Minutes (D/Z 15/1).

I have long wished to see such an institution effectually established. Every department of our profession is in general filled up with gentlemen of education, who are under a necessity of supporting a certain appearance of expence. They are exposed to numerous sources of infection and suffer premature death frequently thereby and the fair prospects of a family suddenly blasted and a painful reverse presented to persons well brought up, but thus cut off from future resources ! May this institution obviate the repetition of so dark a scene.

### 9. *A Medical Society, 1788*

*Ipswich Journal,* Jan. 26, 1788 (C.B.L.).

Colchester. This day se'nnight a respectable number of Physicians, Surgeons, and Apothecaries, of the counties of Essex and Suffolk held their first meeting at the Three Cups in this town and formed themselves into the Essex and Suffolk Medical Society . . . A capital library is to be established in the old Assembly Room.

### 10. *Medicine in the Early Nineteenth Century*

Dr. Dixon of Rivenhall recalls his apprenticeship in Wethersfield during the Napoleonic Wars.
*Essex Review,* Vols. 23, 24.

In the meantime the Doctor or Apothecary of the village, as well as for several parishes in the neighbourhood—Wiltsher, at Wethersfield—took it into his head that I might do for an apprentice. This was one day named to my father, and on the following Monday I commenced my career as a doctor. It was a queer start. To save apprenticeship fees, I was to live at home. My master was a farmer as well as doctor ; his residence was at the farm, a mile or so from the surgery, in the village where I had to take up my quarters during the day. I did not like my position at all, but consented to Hobson's choice, " that or none ". The routine of making mixtures and pills was an easy affair. I had two or three books to guide me so far, but he had otherwise no books in his library (as he called it) which were to a beginner of the slightest use. I could not find among the rubbish a single elementary work of any kind, and for a time the arrangement, so far as I was concerned, was a failure. I was nothing in fact but a shop-boy; I had no help from my master, who seemed to think that drawing teeth, bleeding and making mixtures and pills was all that was required of him as a teaching process. He had only one periodical publication, and that monthly, The Medical and Physical Journal, but this gave me an insight into the work of the medical profession. I had a craving for reading, and any book that came in my way I read . . .

The practice of Medicine was at that time a mysterious affair; I was constantly compounding medicines without anything like a clear conception of their use or application to the various disorders for which they were given. It seemed to me to be a hit-or-miss affair. My master had the care of four or five parishes as the doctor of the poor as well as of most of the well-to-do farmers and tradesmen. I had the former principally to attend to, and except in extreme cases of danger he gave but little attention to this part of his duty. I date the commencement of my professional life from this period—seventy years ago. Having to work alone, I formed opinions of my own, unaided by others. I was obliged to take this course, and I think that as far as the practice of medicine was in question I came to the conclusion that it was in a very unsatisfactory state, and was in fact, so far as it came under my notice, a system of quackery, not based upon the principles inculcated in the books which I then began to read for the first time. Chemistry as an elementary study especially seemed ignored. A celebrated M.D. was occasionally called in consultation in extreme cases; his prescriptions seemed to me to be a farrago of incompatabilities; powdered myrrh and spermaceti was his invariable mixture for consumptive patients; this was disgusting medicine, but it did no harm. He was also very fond of prescribing calomel, as were most doctors of that time. My master was a great bleeder; any person complaining of pain, whatever might be its character, was subjected to the lancet, no distinction between neuralgic or inflammatory disorder becoming part of the question as to its propriety. And so we blundered on, having the entire medical care of not less than 4000 people.

In the autumn of 1806, typhus fever broke out in a hamlet principally occupied by agricultural labourers in wretched damp cottages; forty persons young and old were at the same time down with it, and I was amongst them nearly all the day for the first ten or twelve days. Medicines of all kinds considered by my master as adapted to such cases I had to administer; there was but little nursing; everybody that could get away did. One or two died after being ill a fortnight, and at that time Sir Jas. Mclean, an M.D., of Sudbury, was called in to help us in our difficulties. He was the first man that I could understand, and I got a clearer insight into my work; but ten of the forty died, and the survivors recovered very slowly.

### *11. The Modern Doctor, 1823*

*Chelmsford Gazette,* June 27, 1823 (E.R.O.).

There are two classes of Village Doctors. Of the first is the old established practitioner, inhabiting, perhaps, the very house where his grand-father first drew teeth or breathed a vein; reckoning among his patients the lord of the manor or perchance the member for some rotten-borough, and looking down with contempt upon the new school of surgeons. And of the second class is the new practitioner, or the interloper—the spruce, knowing disciple of Ashley Cooper or Henry Clive, with perchance a concealed dash of recanting Lawrence, the taker of half-fees—just working into practice, with all the laurels of Guy's Hospital and the passage of the Dardanelles, which leads through Surgeons' Hall, still fresh in his memory—ridiculing the milk and water prescriptions of the sons of the old school and demonstrating on every occasion the astonishing efficacy of the Prussic Acid, the Crotan Oil or the Nitras Acid Bath.

Behold one of the last class making his entree into the village; imagine him to have beheld, out of the corners of his envious eyes, the old doctor driving off in his gig and calculating upon the visits, draughts, mixtures, and pills of the morning's ride—fancy with what importance he strides into the house of his first patient, a restless whig, or radical, " on change intent "—fancy with what modest sweetness he soothes his griefs and mitigates his sorrows by some Balsamic advice and pills of Opium—how he calls the very next day, at the most busy period, and how he details all the blunders of the old doctor's antiquated brains—and how rapidly his fame spreads.

Imagine farther how soon the old surgeon conceives a deadly antipathy against him—how he ridicules his puppyism, and imitates his strut—how he opens his eyes, with pretended astonishment, when he tells of his feats of gluttony, or of shooting, or hunting—how feelingly he foretells the poor young man's ruin—and how angry he gets when he hears of seceding patients.

Imagine all this, and the vision will in some degree resemble the daily scenes of more than one Essex village.

# THE USE OF LEISURE

Eighteenth-century Essex was sophisticated and gay. The great families enjoyed comfort, leisure and travel, with access to learning and the arts and with full opportunity for agricultural experiment or public service. Those less wealthy established their own centres of fashion and amusement where they might attend the Assembly or the theatre, drink Spa water or bathe in salt-water baths. Inns were busy places, where people from all classes drank heavily and watched cricket, cock-fighting and other spectacles arranged by the publican. The numerous fairs offered similar entertainment to townsman and villager alike. Sports were sometimes brutal, often the occasion for gambling. Meanwhile, though much squalor and vice remained around them, farmers, merchants and professional men could enjoy more amenities and refinements than before.

Several influences counteracted the prevalent self-indulgence. The moral discipline of Nonconformity sometimes encouraged serious thought and study. New local newspapers improved literacy and widened outlooks. Booksellers prospered in Essex towns. Humane magistrates used their power to ensure personal security, suppress brutality and diminish drunkenness. From 1800 Evangelicalism increased its influence among most Essex denominations and effectively reinforced the moral reformers. Manners and conduct thereafter improved, though there was perhaps less gaiety and some deterioration of taste.

In Victorian Essex many lived more happily and decently than their parents. Gas-works gave light for reading library books and edifying weekly newspapers published untaxed by an increasing number of Essex printers. Tradesmen and clerks frequented the so-called Mechanics' Institutes and attended tea-parties or sports organised by Temperance societies. Voluntary organisations were formed to cater for most cultural and athletic interests. Cricket clubs played more regularly and further afield, and from the Seventies Association football gained rapid popularity. Cycling, at first an expensive sport, commanded a column in the local press by the 1890's. Meanwhile bank holidays, railway extension in N.E. Essex and cheap excursions had brought the sea-side within occasional reach of all classes.

## *THE SOCIAL LIFE OF THE WEALTHY IN THE 18TH CENTURY*

*1. Life at Moulsham Hall, 1729-31*

The following are extracts from the accounts of Earl Fitzwalter of Moulsham Hall, near Chelmsford.

Mildmay Archives (D/DM A5).

|  |  |  |
|---|---|---|
| 1729 | | |
| Sept. 20 | Advanced to Mr Beard towards carrying on my building | 100. 0. 0 |
| 29 | To Symonds, one of the Maldon hoymen, in part of 50s. for bringing down 4,500 glazed tiles | 1.15. 0 |
| Oct. 4 | To Richard, Mr Greening's man, at 12s. per week, and 5 labourers in making my kitchen garden at 7s. per week each | 2. 7. 0 |
| 16 | To one of the carpenters who was hurt here in the building | 0.10. 6 |
| Nov. 28 | Pd. the dairy-maid one year's wages, due Midsummer last past | 4. 0. 0 |
| Dec. 3 | Pd. Stenton, the boy under the groom, yearly wages at £3 per annum in full to Xmas, 1728 | 0.19. 0 |
| 5 | Pd. Stanesby, one of my footmen, half a year's wages due Aug. 2nd last past | 3. 0. 0 |
| Dec. 7 | To Mr Ducane, writing master for Lady Caroline | 3.16. 0 |
| 1730 | | |
| May 22 | Brought with me in gold out of London | 133 guineas. |
| | Came to Moulsham Hall Friday, May 22nd, 1730, in order to settle my family here for the Summer | |
| | Spent at Romford | 0.10. 6 |
| | Gave the ringers at Ingatestone | 0.10. 6 |

| | | |
|---|---|---|
| | Spent at the Saracen's [Head] upon my neighbours who came to meet me, being the Minister and principal inhabitants of the town to the number of between 130 and 140 on horseback | 10. 4. 0 |
| June 1 | To the Countess Fitzwalter for housekeeping from Friday, May 22nd last past, to Saturday, the 30th of June, inclusive | 16. 8. 0 |
| June 6 | Gave to Mr Lucas for giving me the oath of Churchwarden | 0.10. 6 |
| July 3 | Pd. Wm. Banks, the Quaker, for locks and hinges | 2. 7. 6 |
| July 5 | To my Lady Harold's servants for bringing half a buck from New Hall | 0.10. 6 |
| 10 | Pd. Mr Mason in full for leaf gold for my Lady Fitzwalter | 1. 4. 3 |
| Aug. 24 | To my Lady Fitzwalter towards housekeeping, Count Dagenfeld and Lady Mary being here | 17.17. 9 |
| Sept. 19 and 21 | To Dr Shapeeste on my [Lady] Caroline Darcy's having the chicken pox | 2. 2. 0 |
| Oct. 30 | To Dr Coe for taking care of Dwinger, my house steward | 4. 4. 0 |
| Nov. 16 | Advanced to Mr Carpenter the statuary's 2 men, while they were here to set up the statues on Mr Carpenter's account | 1. 1. 0 |
| 1731 | | |
| April 16 | Advanced Mr Carpenter's man that came down to set up the lions over the grand piers | 0. 5. 0 |
| June 5 | To one Bolton for tuning and mending Lady Caroline's harpsichord here | 1. 1. 0 |
| June 26 | To Mr Amiconi, an Italian painter, for a picture of architecture and little figures over the S. East chimney below stairs in the principal apartment. N.B. There is also another of his drawing over the drawing room chimney-piece | 12.12. 0 |
| Aug. 21 | Pd. Humphreys of Chelmsford for a horse to London for eleven days | 0.16. 0 |
| Oct. 4 | Bought off and paid Mr Cottee, the farrier, for a black gelding, 6 years old, to follow my coach | 10. 0. 0 |

## 2. *Royal Visitor at Moulsham Hall, 1734*

The writer is Earl Fitzwalter of Moulsham Hall.
Mildmay Archives (D/DM A5).

Nov. 21st, 1734. The Princess Royal, having lain at Harwich 17 days for a wind for Holland, the King ordered her to wait no longer, but to come away directly for Dover, which she did and stopping at an inn at Chelmsford, as soon as we had advice of it, my Lady Fitzwalter took her coach and immediately went to her to invite her to Moulsham. She found her at dinner, and received her in the kindest and most obliging manner in the world and, leaving her people to dine, stepped into my wife's coach with her and came up hither and stayed there about an hour and a half and drank tea and coffee, but would have nothing else. I pressed her, as much as was proper, to stay and lie here, which she seemed very desirous to have done, but she said, as her route was fixed and the guards laid by the King's order, it was not in her power. She went that evening to Romford and lay at an inn there, next day went over London Bridge and lay at Dartford in her way to Dover, but did not go to St James' nor saw none of the Royal Family as she went through London. She stayed at Dover for a wind about a week and then went over in one of the King's yachts to Calais, where the Prince of Orange, her husband, met her; and after having recovered the fatigues of her voyage, being far gone with child, in five or six days they set out by land for Holland.

## 3. *Earl Fitzwalter's Summer Holiday, 1736*

The writer is Earl Fitzwalter of Moulsham Hall.
Mildmay Archives (D/DM A5).

1736

Wednesday, June 3rd. I set out from London with my wife and my Lord and Lady Ancram in order to go to Harrogate to drink the sulphur-waters. We stayed a few days at York and then went to Knaresborough and stayed there two months and went from thence every morning to drink the sulphur and chalybeate waters, which is an hour's driving from the town with six horses. At York the Earl of Holderness came to us, being gone into the North a few weeks before. Before we left Knaresborough, we went to Hornby Castle, a seat of my Lord Holderness, where I kept house for 4 days—expense £14 . 0 . 0. The 3rd of September I set out southward from Knaresborough and stopped at another house of my Lord Holderness at Aston, stayed there nine days and spent in house-keeping there £22 . 0 . 0. Then set out for Newark, and so on to Peterborough to make a visit to the Dean, and lay at the Deanery one night. From thence to Cambridge, so to Hockerill and arrived at Moulsham Hall on Friday, September 24th, with eleven saddle-horses, seven coach-horses and also a hired coach and six from London. We were in all 22 or 23 in number . . . £530 . 0 . 0.

| | | | |
|---|---|---|---|
| Oct. | 2 | Pd. three days' board wages due to nine livery servants, for beer in travelling and in full | 1 . 17 . 0 |
| | 12 | Pd. Ned Turner, my groom, his bill in full for turnpikes in coming from Knaresborough and for 6 purges for my horse's ear | 2 . 5 . 2 |
| | 14 | Mrs Dwinger a bill for board wages for a maid and herself for ten days when we went into the North, and coach and coming down to Moulsham Hall | 1 . 19 . 3 |

4. *Audley End Household Accounts, 1765*

A week's expenditure on food in a large household. This account is one of a series and is only slightly above the average.
Audley End Archives (D/DBy A18).

The Hon. Sir John Griffin, Dr. to Margaret Allen, housekeeper, for money disbursed as undermentioned.

| Pound Weight | Numbers | Weekly consumptions to Friday night October 4th, 1765 | | Price |
|---|---|---|---|---|
| 320 | | Beef being 22 stone, 12 lbs. at 3d per lb. | 4 . 0 . 0 | |
| 85 | | Veal at 4$\frac{1}{2}$d per lb. | 1 . 11 . 10$\frac{1}{2}$ | |
| | 2 | Calves' sweetbreads at 1s. each | 0 . 2 . 0 | |
| 19$\frac{1}{2}$ | | Pork at 4d per lb. | 0 . 6 . 6 | |
| | 4 | Calves' feet at 1$\frac{1}{2}$d each | 0 . 0 . 6 | |
| 66 | | Mutton at 3$\frac{1}{2}$d per lb. | 0 . 19 . 0 | |
| 54 | | Veal at 4$\frac{1}{2}$d per lb. | 1 . 0 . 3 | |
| 544$\frac{1}{2}$ | 6 | William Turner's butcher's bill | | 8 . 0 . 4 |
| 84 | | Flour being one bushel and an half at 9s. per bushel | 0 . 13 . 6 | |
| 247$\frac{1}{2}$ | 55 | Quartern bricks at 5$\frac{3}{4}$ each | 1 . 6 . 4$\frac{1}{4}$ | |
| | 3 | Strikes of bran | 0 . 1 . 9 | |
| | | To yeast | 0 . 0 . 6 | |
| 331$\frac{1}{2}$ | 58 | John Edwards' baker's bill | | 2 . 2 . 0 |

| Pound Weight | Numbers | Weekly consumptions to Friday night October 4th, 1765 | Price |
|---|---|---|---|
| | | [Brought forward] | 10 . 2 . 4 |
| 43 | | Butter paid for | 1 . 8 . 3 |
| | 168 | Eggs | 0 . 7 . 8 |
| | 24 | Lemons | 0 . 4 . 0 |
| | 17 | Fowls and chickens bought in this week | 0 . 14 . 2 |
| | | To cash paid for Salmon | 0 . 1 . 6 |
| | 8 | Rabbits | 0 . 4 . 10 |
| | 1 | Quart of split peas | 0 . 0 . 4 |
| | 2 | Geese | 0 . 5 . 0 |
| | | To cash paid yeast | 0 . 1 . 6 |
| 32 | | Being half a bushel of salt | 0 . 3 . 0 |
| 1 | | Sugar | 0 . 0 . 5 |
| | 12 | Herrings | 0 . 1 . 6 |
| | | To cash paid 3 quarts and an half of cream | 0 . 3 . 6 |
| 4 | | Lard | 0 . 1 . 8 |
| | 35 | Pigeons from Audley End dove house | |
| | 11 | Fowls and chickens, 7 fowls, four killed this week paid for in former account | |
| | 4 | Ducks killed this week, paid for in former account | |
| 50 | | One sheep killed this week | |
| | | Housekeeping expenses | 13 . 19 . 8 |
| | | Contingent bills this week | 2 . 5 . 8½ |
| | | Total | 16 . 5 . 4½ |
| Allowed K.G. | | Received October 4th, 1765, the above contents in full for one week's disbursements, £16 . 5 . 4½, by me Margaret Allen | |

5. *The Cost of Household Goods, 1820*

The following are extracts from a Cressing farmer's accounts. *Original spelling retained.*
Account book of Samuel Blyth (D/DBh A1).

| | | |
|---|---|---|
| Jan. | By 2 brewing tubs | 3 . 3 . 0 |
| | By a Larg Coper Boiler, wash Tub, 2 Pails and 2 Milk Pans | 2 . 0 . 0 |

| | | |
|---|---|---|
| Feb. | By 10 Knifs and 10 forks, 7 Meat Scures, & holdfarst | 16. 0 |
| | By 2 Table Clorths, 2 Rond Towels & 3 hand Towls | 10. 6 |
| March | By Six Pair Sheets | 2. 2. 0 |
| | By 3 Pair Pillow Cases, 4 Table clorths | 13. 0 |
| | By 9 towels & Knife Box & Linen Hutch | 18. 6 |
| | By Clothes Hutch & Chest Drawers | 1. 0. 0 |
| | Tin Bowl, Milkpail, Hogknife | 5. 0 |
| April | By a new Wash Tub | 10. 0 |

### 6. *The Amenities of a Country Estate*

Sale Catalogue of Coptfold Hall, Margaretting, 1828 (D/DMa B71).

Coptfold Hall is a most excellent and substantial built Mansion House, fit for the Residence of a family of Distinction, it was erected in 1755 and is most delightfully seated on a considerable and very pleasing Eminence, in a beautiful Park, containing One Hundred and Sixty Six Acres, very richly Ornamented with uncommonly Fine Stately Oak Timber, as is also the whole of the Estate, the greatest attention having been scrupulously observed for nearly a Century past in preserving the Growing Timber.

The Manor of Coptfold is extensive and affords every sufficient security for the uninterrupted Enjoyment of Field Sports; there are Court Barons held and the Country abounds with Game.

The Situation of this Property, whether as a Residence or as an Investment, must be highly esteemed, for as respects the former object it is in a most excellent and select Neighbourhood and in the Centre of the Fox Hunt and otherwise partakes of every facility for enjoying Field Sports, and in the other case the Quality of the Soil, its Proximity to excellent Markets and being contiguous to the Great Turnpike Road leading from London to Chelmsford are advantages too important to be overlooked. It is within Four Miles of Chelmsford and only about Twenty Five Miles from the Metropolis, yet as retired and possessing all the essentials of an Estate in a more remote County.

### 7. *Epitaph on an Essex Country Gentleman, 1788*

*Ipswich Journal*, April 12, 1788 (C.B.L.).

His morals were rather of the relaxed kind, but as his gratifications were always manly, and even benevolent, they may certainly be excused in these licencious times. His great wealth was acquired more by management than dishonour; and employed in promoting conviviality, and supporting indigence.

## *FARMERS' RELAXATIONS IN THE 18TH CENTURY*

### *1. A Farmer's Personal Expenditure, 1797-8*

The following are extracts from a wealthy Latchingdon farmer's accounts.
Parker Archives (D/DOp F7).

| 1797 | | |
|---|---|---|
| April 30 | Joseph Wiggins to prevent going to gaol | 1. 1. 0 |
| | Spice box and sugar cannister | 7. 0 |
| May 14 | Gave Freemasons' sermon | 1. 0 |
| June 5 | Expenses going bounds of parish | 4. 0 |
| 11 | Turnpikes to Rayleigh | 1. 0 |
| 21 | A bay horse for Mrs. Parker | 26. 5. 0 |
| July 6 | Coach to London | 5. 6 |
| | Play, John Wright and self | 10. 0 |
| | A pair of gold bracelets, Emma | 3. 13. 6 |
| | A toothpick case | 1. 16. 0 |
| | A square gold ring and case | 1. 8. 0 |
| | Repairing watch and gilding case | 16. 0 |
| | Stage home and breakfast | 7. 0 |
| July 16 | Races | 1. 5. 6 |
| 29 | Tiptree Fair | 1. 0 |
| | Men mending roads, Latchingdon | 1. 0 |
| 31 | Ringers | 2. 2. 0 |
| Aug. 16 | Quire gilt paper | 1. 2 |
| | Mending fan | 8 |
| 25 | 6 packs of cards | 10. 0 |
| Sept. 3 | Charity sermon, self and wife | 7. 3 |
| 9 | 6 letters | 1. 10½ |
| 25 | Largesse, Emma, Latchingdon | 1. 0 |
| 27 | Cake and orange flower water | 4. 0 |
| 29 | Crooks, for dogs' meat | 15. 0 |
| | Riding whip | 7. 6 |
| Oct. 5 | Two toys | 2. 0 |
| | Maldon Club | 1. 4. 6 |
| 13 | Black satin ribbon, Emma | 6. 9 |
| 16 | Brentwood Fair | 2. 6 |
| 18 | Blue Boar, Maldon | 5. 3 |
| 27 | Hunting | 1. 0 |
| | Boggis in garden | 1. 1. 10½ |
| Nov. 4 | Marrow 4d, 5 doz. of rose trees | 5. 4 |
| 11 | Mending snuffers | 6 |
| 24 | Large shirt buttons 6d, tartlets 15 | 1. 6 |
| | Charity | 6 |

|  | |  |  |
|---|---|---|---|
| Dec. | 1 | Ball, Mrs P. and Self | 15. 6 |
| | | Emma, hair cutting and dressing | 2. 6 |
| | 11 | Play, Emma and self | 12. 0 |
| | | Plated toast rack for present to Mrs Gepp | 10. 6 |
| | 13 | Hackney coaches | 5. 6 |
| | 19 | Walker, tuning pianoforte | 7. 6 |
| | 31 | Wright, Latchingdon, Xmas box | 1. 0 |
| | | Knife for Jack | 7 |
| | | Great-coat, Emma | 13. 0 |
| | | Wine and spirits | 34. 8. 0 |
| | | Beer | 21. 1. 2 |
| | | Wiffen, hairdresser, as per bill | 2. 19. 0 |
| 1798 | | | |
| Jan. | 1 | Shooting, Latchingdon | 2. 6 |
| | 16 | Bradwell Coursing Club | 14. 6 |
| | 18 | Maldon market | 4. 6 |
| Feb. | 24 | Cap, hunting | 1. 0 |
| Mar. | 24 | Dinner, Maldon | 6. 0 |
| April | 9 | Ball | 10. 6 |
| | | Parish meeting | 2. 0 |
| | 19 | Pomatum | 6 |
| | 25 | Rochford dinner | 10. 6 |
| May | 7 | Maldon Club | 12. 6 |
| June | 4 | Dinner, Black Boy, with Volunteers | 8. 0 |
| | 18 | Men going to Dunmow for troop | 5. 0 |
| July | 23 | Troop 6d, sundries 6d, races 6d | 1. 6 |
| | 25 | Crickitt for Danbury Venison Dinner | 5. 0 |
| Sept. | 19 | Dinner, Saracen's Head | 7. 0 |
| Oct. | 20 | Subscription for Nelson Fleet | 1. 1. 0 |
| Nov. | 5 | Troop Sergeant 5s., forfeits 2s. 6d | 7. 6 |
| | 8 | Tithe dinner, Latchingdon | 1. 9 |
| Dec. | 23 | Miller for troop jacket, waistcoat, etc. | 4. 5. 10 |
| | | Helmet and spurs | 1. 13. 6 |
| | | Biscuits for dogs, 5 cwt. | 1. 10. 0 |
| | | Mr Coverdale for subscription for Felsted School | 2. 2. 0 |
| | | Darby, hatter | 2. 1. 0 |
| | | Malt | 23. 2. 0 |
| | | Wine and spirits | 31. 9. 0 |
| | | Port, Dr. Brownlie | 15. 4. 6 |
| | | Port, Brown and Co. | 26. 7. 0 |

[Total expenditure for 1798] £476 . 12 . 7.

## 2. *Farmers' Social Club at Aveley, 1763.*

Farmers and their friends preferred moonlight nights for convivial gatherings, because the roads were safer then. *Original spelling retained.*

MS. Articles of Aveley Lunatick Club, 1763 (D/P 157/28/1).

Lunatick Clubb

Articles

1st It is hereby agreed that we whose names are under written do meet Monthly at The Sign of the Harrow in Aveley, there to Expend One Shilling, and be Subject to such Rules and Orders as are hereafter Express'd.

2ndly It is likewise agreed that the said meeting shall be on the First Monday after every full Moon in the Year.

3rd That some one Member of the said Body, be Chosen President or Chairmen for one whole year and no longer, unless Re'elected into the said Trust by a Majority of Voices.

4th That Every Member shall on his Admission pay Two Shillings and Sixpence, which shall goe towards the Publick fund for the use hereinafter mention'd,—And the Night of his Admission he shall be Exempt from any further payment.

5th That Every Member or Members after Signing his Name, shall on absenting himself or Themselves, forfeit the Sum of One Shilling, which forfeit or forfeitures, shall on the next night of their coming be deposited into the hands of the President or Chairman ; There to be kept untill there is a Sufficient fund for a Dinner, which Day is to be fixed by a Majority of Voices—The Two Shillings and Sixpence paid by a New Member to be apply'd to the same use as the forfeit Money.

6th That Every Member on his coming into the Clubb Room do pay Obeisance to the President or Chairman, and Imediately pay his Shilling & forfeit Money if any due ; If a New Member his Two Shillings and Sixpence.

7th That no Member do presume on any pretence Whatsoever to use ill Manners to a Brother Member, Such as saying, You Lye Sir ! or Swear or Curse on pain of being Mulch in the Sum of One Shilling, This to take effect during Clubb Hours only.

8th If any Member or Members do come into the said Clubb Room, Fuddled, Disguis'd in Liquor, or Vulgarly Speaking Drunk, him or them shall forfeit One Shilling . . .

## 3. *Farmers' Aspirations, 1807*

Arthur Young, *General View of Agriculture in Essex*, pp. 123-4.

The farmers, whose cultivation of land is considerably extensive, make a much more genteel and respectable appearance than heretofore. They give their children, both sons and daughters, a much more expensive education, the former sometimes, and the latter very generally, being sent to boarding-schools and costing, instead of 20/- or 30/- a year, as formerly, at some country day-school, from £30 to £50. The general modes of living, too, among the larger farmers at their own houses and the entertainment of their friends is greatly heightened. Their ordinary expenses at market for the sale of their corn and other productions of their farms are likewise greatly augmented. Fifty years ago their dinner at these places, together with the liquor they drank, seldom amounted to above a shilling or eighteen-pence; now it is commonly four, five, or six shillings. Part of this, indeed, arises from the advanced price of provisions, but principally from the superior quality of their drink. They having exchanged good strong beer for red port.

## *TOWN LIFE IN THE 18TH CENTURY*

### *1. The Attractions of Chelmsford, 1769*

*History of Essex by a Gentleman,* Vol. I, pp. 55 foll.

The town consists but of four streets, but is beautiful, regular, and well-built. The entrance to it from the metropolis is over an old stone bridge . . . No sooner is this passed over, than the attentive traveller is struck by the most agreeable surprise. A spacious ample street presents itself of a considerable length, in which are many handsome, good houses.

At the upper end, upon a little ascent, stands the shire-house, which, tho' no very magnificent building, has a pleasing appearance. Over this is seen the tower, spire, and chief part of the church, which venerable structure terminates this little elegant piece of perspective. Each street lies with an easy descent towards the center and is washed with a current of clear water. What contributes most to the peculiar cleanliness of this town is its being gravelled, and that with such skill and judgement as to form as it were a regular unjointed pavement.

The sign boards, which used formerly to project out so as to be a very glaring nuisance, are now entirely removed; and the inhabitants seem inspired with a laudable emulance in endeavouring to outvie each other in the neatness of their dwellings. The Chelmer and the Cann form here an angle, along which lie many pleasure gardens, etc. and some of them are agreeably laid out. On the banks of these rivers various temples and summerhouses are built, some of which are so pretty in their construction as to display an elegance of taste in the projectors. In an open space . . . adjoining to the shire-house stands a conduit . . .

Here are often public diversions, such as balls, concerts, etc. Two plates, value fifty pounds each, are given annually to be run for on Galleywood Common near this place; one of which is collected from the neighbouring nobility and gentry; and the other, called the town-plate, is subscribed for by the inhabitants.

## 2. *Some Disadvantages of Town Life, 1748-9*

Public nuisances, like those noted by the Maldon Jury in the following passages, were common in Essex towns in the Eighteenth Century. Maldon Borough Sessions Book (D/B 3/1/26).

April 18, 1748

The Leet Jury brought in their presentment as follows . . .

We present the Corporation for not repairing the bay below Cromwell House.

We present Mr Joseph Pattisson for laying dung in the highway in the back lane behind the Blue Boar garden.

We present the inhabitants of the parish of St Peter for a post lying or hanging across the road between Pound Mead and Pinchgut Hall.

We present Edward Hawker, Esq., for not cleansing his ditch leading from the town dung-hill to Pinchgut Hall.

We present the inhabitants of the parishes of Saint Mary and Saint Peter for not repairing Ram Alley Lane.

We present James Richardson for a sow and two pigs going in and about the highways without a follower.

October 2, 1749

The said Leet Jury brought in their presentment as follows . . .

We present the inhabitants of Saint Peter's parish for not cleaning and cleansing the gutter in Chequer Lane.

We present Mr Alderman Lawrence for a hole not being repaired, joining to Fullbridge.

We present Mr Joseph Pattisson for laying dung in the highway at the back of the Blue Boar.

We present Morris Frisby for letting his cows stand in the lane and damaging the footpath near his house in the lane behind the Blue Boar.

We present William Whetstone for a black gelding going in the highway without a follower . . .

We present William Willingale for a large heap of earth lying in the parish of Saint Mary in the highway there . . .

We present the parishioners of Saint Peter's parish for not

mending Butt Lane . . .

We present the inhabitants of Saint Peter's parish for not repairing a watercourse leading from Mr May's house into the cartrake.

### 3. *Colchester Amenities: a Foreigner's View, 1784*

Rochefoucauld, *A Frenchman in England,* Cambridge, 1933, pp. 161-2.

There are three things in Colchester to rouse the interest of a stranger. First, the castle is a square building of great antiquity . . . Secondly, there is an amusement hall, which is one of the most pitiable places I have ever seen. It holds only about 200 people, all seated on plain wooden benches. The back-scene of the theatre is an old wall, which, I imagine, can be made to represent either the palaces of the Caesars or the gardens of Semiramis or the beautiful squares of Rome or any other scene. The decorations are on a par with the rest and although we saw no actors there, we could form a good idea of what the performances must be like. Thirdly, there is an assembly room where dances are held. Public balls are held every fortnight. The hall is large and well lighted and is seventy-four feet by thirty-four.

## *18TH CENTURY AMUSEMENTS, GENTEEL AND VULGAR*

### 1. *Gossip from London*

A Londoner writes to his friend in Colchester.
Creffield Archives (D/DRc F17).

Xmas day, 1746.

Sir,

Last night between twelve and one arrived a barrel of oysters which I design to eat in a few hours and, as I doubt not they come from you, it becomes me to return my most hearty thanks and to wish both yourself and my good friend, Mrs Creffield, many happy Xmases and New Years and, as your Irish say, that you may live all the days of your life. I have no news to tell you but that the common talk is that his Majesty is got pretty well again and that the Duke has carried all his points in Holland, both which pray God send may be true. Lady V——, 'tis said, lives with Is—— Ch——. They were together at Epsom some time, but am told they are now in Epping forest. I think you folks who live in your country are extremely happy, if you know your own happiness, to be out of all our noise, stink and nonsense, and heartily lament that providence did not dispose my lot out of this cursed town. I should be very glad of a line from you and, if it were in my power to serve either you or Mrs Creffield, should esteem myself happy,

Who am, Sir,
Your most obliged, humble servant,
New Bond Street John Camfield

2. *Music, 1759 and 1763*

*Ipswich Journal*, Aug. 25, 1759 (Ipswich B.L.).

Colchester. Yesterday the Oratorio of the Messiah was performed before a very numerous and polite Audience in St Peter's Church. The Performance was extreamly elegant, and everything conducted without Accidents or the least Disorder.

*Ipswich Journal*, Oct. 15, 1763 (C.B.L.).

At Mr Arnold's New Music-Assembly-Room at Great Warley, near Brentwood in Essex, on Thursday the 27th of this Instant October, will be opened a fine new Organ, with a grand Morning-Concert of Musick, by some of the best Performers from London.

The Organ will be played by Mr Keene, Organist of St Mary's, Whitechapel.

Tickets to be had at Mr Arnold's at Great Warley aforesaid, a Quarter of a Guinea each, Stabling and Hay included.

The best of Tea, Coffee, Chocolate, Wine, etc, may be had at the Assembly-Room. To begin at Eleven o'Clock.

3. *Rural Relaxations, 1759*

*Ipswich Journal*, April 28, 1759 (C.B.L.).

This is to acquaint all Gentlemen and Ladies, That the Strawberry Gardens at Sible Hedingham in Essex, will be open'd on the First Day of May next, and due Attendance will be there given every Day, Sundays excepted, and be continued from that Time to the Michaelmas following; where Gentlemen and Ladies will be accommodated with Red and White Ports, as neat as imported, good made Wines at 6d to 8d a Pint, and meet with a hearty Welcome, from their humble Servant, John King.

N.B. Good stabling for Horses.

4. *Rural Theatre, 1777*

*Chelmsford Chronicle*, April 11, 1777.

At the Theatre in Castle-Hedingham, on Saturday April 12, will be presented a new Comedy called The Maid of the Oaks, with all the music, scenery, dresses, and decorations incidental to the piece, as performed thirty nights successively at the Theatre Royal, Drury Lane . . . To which will be added a Farce, call'd The Deuce is in Him . . . Boxes 3s. Pit 2s. Gallery 1s. To begin exactly at seven o'clock . . . On Monday Romeo and Juliet.

### 5. *Comedy, 1797*

Quarter Sessions Order Book, Midsummer 1797 (Q/SO 14).

WHEREAS application hath been made to this Court by Ralph Wewitzer Comedian of the Theatre Royal Drury Lane . . . [for] taking a Company of Comedians to South End in the Parish of Prittlewell pursuant to . . . "An Act to enable Justices of the Peace to Licence Theatrical Representations occasionally" . . . for Sixty Days . . . Now we . . . do hereby Licence Ralph Wewitzer . . .

### 6. *Country Dancing*

*Ipswich Journal,* Oct. 26, 1754 (C.B.L.).

Dedham, October 23, 1754

Our Peal of Eight Bells being now compleated ; Friday the First of November is fixed for Ringing them, when we believe they will be esteemed good Bells.

John Saunders, William Cross, Churchwardens.

N.B. In the Long Room at the Sun, in the Evening, will be Country Dancing ; proper Musick is provided.

### 7. *Dicing for Flowers*

*Ipswich Journal,* Oct. 22, 1763 (C.B.L.).

This is to inform all true Lovers and Coinosseurs of Tulips, That there is now a curious and valuable Collection of Bulbs ; consisting of the very best Bye-Bloomers, Bizarts, and other choice Flowers, all finely broke, lately imported from Holland ; also a Thousand of prime Ranunculas, Turkey and Persian ; all which will be Raffled for on Tuesday November the First, at Four o'Clock in the Afternoon, at the Sign of the Sun in Dedham, Essex, by thirty Gentlemen, each depositing the Sum of One Guinea : The highest of three Throws to be the Winner.

### 8. *Witham Spa, 1750*

*Ipswich Journal,* June 2, 1750 (C.B.L.).

Witham Spa in Essex. Notice is hereby given, That the Mineral Waters are now in their full Perfection, and that Attendance will be given there every Morning as usual. And that the Assemblies for the Year, 1750, at the Long Room by the Witham Spa, are appointed as followeth . . .

Any Person of a genteel Appearance (tho' no Subscriber) may be admitted to each Assembly, paying as usual 2s 6d.

*9. Wivenhoe for Sea Bathing, 1761*

*Ipswich Journal*, April 25, 1761 (C.B.L.).

WIVENHOE in Essex, April 21, 1761.

The Wivenhoe Sea Water Bath is continued by Tho. Tunmer, Surgeon and Apothecary, as usual. He letts and procures Lodgings, Board, etc, at a reasonable Rate ; and by him Dresses and a Guide, with proper Attendance, are provided.

Wivenhoe is admired for these Reasons ; being situated on the Banks of the Coln, about eight Miles from the open Sea, it is free from those noxious Exhalations that are consequent on a nearer Situation, while it enjoys all that can be reasonably expected from Sea-Water ; the Density of which, as proved by Evaporation, is little or nothing inferior to that in the open Sea. The Town is entirely free from all contagious Disorders, and the Country round hilly, healthful, and pleasant, abounding with Gentlemen's Seats.

*10. Southend, 1787*

*Chelmsford Chronicle*, Aug. 31, 1787 (E.R.O.).

We have much pleasure in informing the public, that South End is likely to become a place of fashionable resort and that there are a greater number of genteel families there this season than was ever known before.

*11. A Weekly Newspaper, its Purpose and its Readers, 1764*

*Chelmsford Chronicle*, Aug. 10, 1764 (E.R.O.).

THE CHELMSFORD CHRONICLE
OR
ESSEX WEEKLY ADVERTISER
FRIDAY, AUGUST 10, 1764 No. 1.

To be continued every Friday. This Number is intended as a Specimen, and given gratis.

To the PUBLIC.

It has often been thought surprising that the county of Essex, which is one of the most considerable in England, should be without a newspaper, the source of information and the channel of intelligence. The utility of such a periodical publication has been so well understood elsewhere that other counties, which have less occasion for one weekly paper, have two or three, whilst Essex has hitherto been under a necessity of receiving its whole intelligence from a paper printed in another county. The inconveniencies that must arise from hence are obvious, as every article of news peculiar to the county of Essex, and every advertisement of things lost, stolen, to be sold, to be lett, etc, must be first conveyed to a remote part, to be inserted in the paper there published. From hence delays must inevitably arise, which cannot, on many ocasions, fail of being productive of very ill consequences. Thus, for example, should a man lose a horse in the neighbourhood of Chelmsford, he would be obliged to apply to a printer in another county, in order to advertise a reward for finding him . . .

The paper now offered to the public will remove this inconvenience, and the gentlemen of Essex know where to apply for anything in the printing way. All manner of books, shop-bills, catalogues, etc, will be neatly and expeditiously executed by the printer of this Chronicle, which will not be confined to articles of intelligence only, for variety of useful, instructive, and entertaining matter shall be occasionally inserted in it, so that it will not be simply a newspaper but a repository of every kind of useful knowledge, and may not improperly be called THE FAMILY LIBRARY. As the proprietors of the Essex Chronicle have taken the utmost care to form such connections, and to open such sources of intelligence, as cannot fail of rendering it complete, they flatter themselves they shall meet with encouragement from all ranks in this county, as the work they now offer to the public is calculated as well for the nobility and gentry, as for the tradesman and farmer . . .

*12. The Pleasures of Village Fairs, 1762*

Quarter Sessions Order Book, April 20, 1762 (Q/SO 10).

At the General Quarter Session . . .

It being represented to this Court that many loose, idle and disorderly persons have for several years past used and accustomed themselves to assemble and meet together at several pretended fairs held in this County, not warranted by law, that is to say, Aveley fair, Bulphan fair, Corbetts Tye (in Upminster) fair, Corringham fair, Fobbing fair, Great Warley fair, Little Thurrock fair, West Thurrock fair, South Ockendon fair, Stanford-le-Hope fair, Stifford fair, West Tilbury fair, High Easter fair, Takeley fairs, Pleshey fair, Stanway fair, some of which fairs are continued for several days and great numbers of people stay there not only all days, but to very late hours in the night, and many unlawful games and plays, besides drinking and other debaucheries are encouraged and carried on under pretence of meeting at such fairs to the great increase of vice and immorality and to the debauching and ruin of servants, apprentices and other unwary people and many riots, tumults and other disorders are occasioned thereby.

For the preventing all such mischiefs and irregularities for the future, it is thought fit and ordered by this Court that the said fairs be henceforth absolutely suppressed . . .

*13. Tiptree Fair, 1787*

*Chelmsford Chronicle,* July 6, 1787 (E.R.O.).

Notice is hereby given that the Betting Day of the Fair will be on Wednesday, the 11th of July; the booths, etc, to be paid for when hired. Dinner on the Table at Two o'clock. By their humble servant, Joseph Auston.

Cricketing. Beckingham against Great Braxted. Wickets to be pitched at Eleven o'clock.

*14. Cheap Gin, 1764*

*Ipswich Journal,* Aug. 11, 1764 (C.B.L.).

A few Days ago, Gabriel Cole, a Bricklayer of Brentwood, drank 11 half Quarterns of Gin within an Hour, but attempting to drink a 12th expired.

*15. A Romford Public House, 1787*

*Chelmsford Chronicle,* April 20, 1787 (E.R.O.).

PUBLIC HOUSE TO BE SOLD

The Unexpired Term of Fourteen Years from Christmas last, of a PUBLIC HOUSE, present rent Twelve Guineas, land-tax deducted; the landlord to do the repairs. Paid to the brewer for beer delivered from September 14, 1785, to September 2, 1786, Two Hundred and Ten Pounds, which will appear by the brewer's books, exclusive of a large quantity of home-brewed, for which the house is noted—an eight hogshead cask of which is constantly emptied at Christmas in nine or ten days . . .

*16. Intemperance in 1800*

Dr. Dixon of Rivenhall (1787-1876) recalls, in his memoirs, the prevalence of spirit-drinking in his youth.
*Essex Review,* xxiv, pp. 7-8.

At the close of the last century, and in the beginning of this, the 19th, excessive drinking prevailed throughout all classes, not least amongst the aristocracy. It seemed to be a mark of distinction in favour of the man who could drink the largest quantity of wine without being quite drunk; many were put under the table and some carried to bed in a helpless condition. Farmers followed the example at their parish dinners—the chair commonly taken by the Parson—and at their private home parties. Their drink was usually Punch, made of brandy and rum. The artizans and labourers were content with beer, which was then what is called "home-brewed" . . .

Smuggling was then a business of an extensive kind. Buonaparte had shut us out of all dealings with continental powers, and smuggling was the only resort to keep up any intercourse with them in the way of trade. Our command on the seas was entire, and this facilitated the only means in our power to deal with our neighbours. Hollands, gin and brandy found their way thus to our Essex coast, and farmers and gentlemen gave their encouragement to the men employed in it. In fact we had no foreign trade but by smuggling and bribery. Many farmers near the coast were engaged in smuggling, and we were supplied in this way at our house, as well as our neighbours. It encouraged intemperance and drunkenness, and I well remember, when I was an apprentice, many cases of the kind in which medical aid could do nothing. I could give a list and names of many early deaths from this pernicious habit of spirit drinking, between the ages of forty and sixty. We had of course plenty of rum from our West Indian colonies, and with our home-made brandy the punch was made. We knew nothing of whiskey, which was the drink of Scotland and Ireland. In fact drunkenness prevailed to an awful extent in all classes. Beer drinking to excess was principally confined to the working classes, but its effects were far less injurious upon the constitution, and many of these topers lived to an old age.

## *18TH CENTURY SPORTS AND SPECTACLES*

### *1. A Traditional Village Playground, 1727*

Great Tey Charity Deeds (D/DBm T5B).

The close of land herein described is a common playing place and has been used as such time out of mind where the memory of man hath not been the contrary—and hath been always used on particular days of rejoicing for the making bonfires therein. The young people of Tey and the neighbouring parishes have been known to play at football and other games there constantly from time to time and particularly on every Trinity Monday, which is the time of the fair at Tey.

And we prove the [same] for upwards of 70 years, and the old witnesses who prove the same, when boys say they have heard their fathers say they did play there and make bonfires, and nowhere else in the said town. And in particular we have an arrow used in the shooting at butts in the said close or playing place above 60 years ago, which butts were standing in the memory of most of our witnesses . . .

2. *County Cricket, Essex v. Kent, 1761 and 1787*

*Ipswich Journal,* June 20, 1761 (C.B.L.).

A Match of Cricket will be play'd on the 27th of this Instant June, 1761, at the Crown at Billericay in Essex, by Eleven Men of Kent, and the best Eleven in Essex for a large Sum of Money. The Wickets to be pitched at One o'Clock.

*Chelmsford Chronicle,* July 20, 1787 (E.R.O.).

On Tuesday last the long depending match of Cricket, between Essex and Kent, was decided at Swanscombe, when the former gained a complete victory over their adversaries in that noble game, at only one innings, and had 44 notches to spare. This so exasperated the gentlemen of Kent, that they would not so much as drink with their competitors.

3. *Midsummer Football, 1787*

*Chelmsford Chronicle,* June 22, 1787 (E.R.O.).

On Monday, the 25th of June, 1787, there will be Eleven Pairs of Gloves, and Eleven Half Crowns, played for at Football; Bradwell and Tillingham against Dengie Hundred; and on the next day Eleven Pairs of valuable Gloves, to be played for at Cricket; Bradwell and Tillingham against Dengie Hundred; at the King's Head, Bradwell.

4. *Sailing Match, 1787*

*Chelmsford Chronicle,* Sept. 7, 1787 (E.R.O.).

A Silver Cup and Suit of St. George's Colours, given by the Members of the King's-Head Club, in Colchester, will be sailed for off Bradwell Chapel.

Regulations [include]

The distance of sailing, for the better prospect of the several shores, to be from a buoy to be stationed in the roads lying between Mersea Church and North Wick, on the Bradwell shore, down to (and double) another buoy below the Eagle Sand, round a third buoy off Mill-Stage, above Bradwell Creek, and to come in at the starting buoy in the middle.

5. *Writtle Races, 1787*

*Chelmsford Chronicle,* Oct. 12, 1787 (E.R.O.).

October meeting. On Thursday the 18th, 1787, will be run for, a

Subscription Purse, the value of which will be discovered by the winner, the best of three heats, by horses, mares, colts, or fillies, under the denomination of the Longeard species ; no one to start that ever won a king or queen's plate, and to run according to the king's plate articles, the stakes to go to the second best that wins a clear heat ; all disputes to be decided by the stewards ; and to start precisely at two o'clock, as much running is expected.

Clerk of the Course, Abram Grizzle.

Stewards, Rob. Rayney, Sen., Esq., Fidler Howard, Bart.

N.B. There will be a ball as usual.

### 6. *Boxing, 1788*

*Ipswich Journal,* July 19, 1788 (C.B.L.).

Wednesday se'nnight a pitched battle was fought at Tillingham, in this county, between R. King of Southminster, and Noah Church of Bradwell ; they met about 5 in the afternoon. The contest lasted about an hour and 5 minutes, during which time, it is supposed, more hard fighting was never known. Church being a strong powerful man, not less than 6 feet 2 inches high, and King only 5 feet 9 inches and a half, betts ran much in favour of him ; but King gained a complete victory over his antagonist, amidst a concourse of nearly 3000 spectators.

### 7. *Cock-throwing Suppressed, 1758*

Quarter Sessions Order Book, Epiphany, 1758 (Q/SO 10).

At the General Quarter Session . . .
This Court, taking into consideration the many riots, mischiefs and other disorders committed by persons following the cruel practice of throwing at cocks and being desirous to discountenance such barbarous customs in time to come, do hereby charge and command all Chief Constables and Petty Constables to use their utmost endeavours to suppress and prevent all such unlawful and disorderly meetings and practices and, if they shall find any persons throwing at cocks within any of their districts, that they do immediately take such persons into custody and carry them before a proper magistrate.

### 8. *Cock-fighting, 1787*

*Chelmsford Chronicle,* May 11, 1787 (E.R.O.).

Cocking.—This is to acquaint all Gentlemen Cockers, That there will be a Main of Cocks fought at the King's Arms, at Burnham, on the 21st of May, between the gentlemen of Dengie Hundred and the gentlemen of Rochford Hundred—To fight eleven battles for Two Guineas a battle, and Five the Main. Dinner at One o'Clock, by John King.

*9. Dancing Bears, 1753*

*Ipswich Journal,* May 12, 1753 (C.B.L.).

To be seen at the King's Arms in Harwich, the surprising Dancing Bears, Late arrived from Abroad, who by an infinite deal of Labour and Trouble are brought to foot it to a Violin, both in Comic Dances and Hornpipes, even beyond Imagination. The largest of them is eight Foot high, and dances to the Admiration of all Beholders. They have had the honour twice to perform before his Majesty King George, his Royal Highness the Prince of Wales, the Duke of Cumberland, and all the Royal Family, and upwards of 300 of the Nobility in London. They perform many other Particulars as expressed in the Bills ; and are separated by a Partition, that Gentlemen and Ladies may see their Performances without Fear.

*10. The Fire-eater, 1762*

*Ipswich Journal,* April 10, 1762 (C.B.L.).

Mr Powell, the celebrated Fire-Eater from London, will perform at the King's Arms, Colchester, in the Easter-Week, and no longer.

He intends to exhibit the following Articles :

1. He eats red-hot Coals out of the Fire as natural as Bread.
2. He licks with his naked Tongue red-hot Tobacco-Pipes flaming with Brimstone.
3. He takes a large bunch of Deal-Matches, lights them all together, and holds them in his Mouth till the flame is extinguish'd.
4. He takes a red-hot Heater out of the Fire, licks it with his naked Tongue several Times, and carries it round the Room between his Teeth.
5. He fills his Mouth with red hot Charcoal, and broils a Slice of Beef or Mutton upon his Tongue, and any Person may blow the Fire with a Pair of Bellows at the same Time.
6. He takes a Quantity of Rosin, Pitch, Bees-wax, Sealing-wax, Brimstone, Allum, and Lead, melts them over a Chaffing-dish of Coals, and eats the said Combustibles with a Spoon, as natural as a Porringer of Broth, (which he calls his Dish of Soup) to the great Surprise of the Spectators.

### *11. A Travelling Variety Concert, 1791*

Quarter Sessions Order Book, Midsummer, 1791 (Q/SO 15).

Samuel Cunningham, Isaac Cunningham and Eleanor Cunningham, having been committed to the House of Correction at Chelmsford by the Reverend Thomas Abdy Abdy, clerk, one of his Majesty's Justices of the Peace, to be there kept until this present session, they being convicted before the said Justice of publicly exhibiting in the town of Epping interludes of dancing, conversation pieces, tumbling and fiddling and, by means of a pretended lottery and other subtle craft, deceiving and imposing upon many unwary subjects of his Majesty, and being now brought before this Court, each and every of them . . . on examination of the circumstances of their case is . . . adjudged a rogue and vagabond and ordered to be continued in the said House of Correction for one week.

### *12. Mock Elections*

At Dovercourt the customary mock election, which followed the official chairing of the Harwich mayor, was the occasion for popular festivities.
*Colchester Gazette,* May 31, 1817 (C.B.L.).

The chairing took place before an immense concourse who had been attracted the two previous days by the amusing sports arranged principally by Mr Wyllie, of the Original White Horse ; and with which every person seemed highly gratified. A band played during the whole of the election. The principal amusements were—yawning for a watch-chain, smoaking for trowsers, running for shirts, gingling for hats, jumping in sacks for ditto, eating hot hasty-pudding, taking an orange out of a tub of water with the mouth, Jerusalem pony races, etc, etc. The evening concluded with a ball at the New White Horse Inn, which was elegantly lighted for the occasion, and at which were present the Mayor and Mayoress, the former of whom opened the ball with the accomplished Miss Rosey of Ramsey.

## *THE MOVEMENT FOR THE SUPPRESSION OF VICE*

### *1. Evangelical Influence, 1787*

Essex magistrates support the Royal Proclamation against Vice, issued at Wilberforce's suggestion.
*Chelmsford Chronicle,* July 27, 1787 (E.R.O.).

At a meeting of the Acting Magistrates of the County of Essex, holden at the Shire-Hall . . . It Was Resolved Unanimously,
1. That the acting Magistrates of this county will exert their utmost endeavours to inforce his Majesty's Royal Proclamation.

2. That it appears to this meeting that the neglect of the due observation of the Lord's Day and the depravity and dissipation of manners, which prevail so generally amongst the lower ranks of the people, have arisen principally from the great number of Alehouses and other public places of Entertainment; the scandalous and illegal behaviour of the persons who are licensed to keep such houses in suffering, and even encouraging drunkenness, gaming and every kind of debauchery, and from the neglect of the Constables in not making due presentments of these irregularities.

3. That it is therefore advisable to recommend to the justices of the peace that at their approaching sessions for licencing Alehouses they do on no account grant a Licence to any house which is not already licensed, except in the case where some other house in the same parish or place shall have been suppressed within the preceding twelve months, and also except such Alehouse shall really and evidently appear to be necessary for public utility and convenience.

4. That, as a check upon the keepers of the Alehouses already licenced, it be also recommended to the said justices that they do at least ten days previous to their next sessions for licencing Alehouses issue out their Precepts to the Constables within their divisions, directing them to give notice to the several keepers of public Alehouses that their licences will not be renewed, unless they shall bring with them fresh certificates under the hands of the Parson, Vicar, or Curate, and the major part of the Churchwardens and Overseers, or else of three or four reputable and substantial Householders . . . certifying the good behaviour of such Alehouse-keeper since the time when his or her last Licence was granted.

5. That it be also recommended to the Justices that at the same sessions for licencing Alehouses they give it in charge to the said Constables that they be particularly attentive to that part of their duty which respects the general conduct of the keepers of public Alehouses, and more especially that they take care to prevent any kind of tippling or disorders upon the Lord's Day, and that they fail not to make due presentments to the justices, at their Petty Sessions, of all persons whom they shall find offending in any of the particulars above mentioned.

6. It appearing to this meeting, that the neglect of the Petty Constables, may in several cases have arisen from the want of due attention of the Chief Constables to the discharge of their duty, RESOLVED, That the Clerk of the Peace be directed to write to

the Chief Constables representing to them that they are expected to be more vigilant in future in the execution of their office, and in particular in their attention to the conduct of the Petty Constables.

### 2. *Village Fair Suppressed*

*Chelmsford Chronicle,* June 8, 1787 (E.R.O.).

Pebmarsh, May 12, 1787.

We, the Minister, Churchwardens, and Principal Inhabitants of the said parish, taking into consideration the pernicious effects of fairs in country villages, do hereby give notice, That no booths or stalls will be suffered to stand before the King's-Head, or any other part of the said parish, upon the 25th of June next; and being fully determined to suppress this meeting called a fair, the constables of the said parish will attend, in order to prevent any number of persons assembling upon that day.

Signed by us, Randolph Ekins, Minister; John Chaplyn, Tho. Creffield, Churchwardens; John Thompson, John Pudney, George Carter, John Doe, Thomas Moore, John Collis, Principal Inhabitants.

### 3. *Essex Justices Ban Boxing Match, 1799*

Quarter Sessions Order Book, Midsummer, 1799 (Q/SO 17).

It is ordered by this Court that Thomas Berney Bramston, Esquire, Treasurer of the Western Division of this County, do pay to Eliab Harvey, Esquire, one of his Majesty's Justices of the Peace, the sum of five pounds and eight shillings to be by him . . . paid . . . to the several Constables . . . being the charges attending the preventing a riot at Fair Mead Bottom by order of the said Eliab Harvey, which riot was likely to be excited and to have happened, had not such means of prevention been adopted, by a meeting occasioned by an intended boxing match by prize fighters.

### 4. *Theatre in Disrepute, 1835*

*Colchester Gazette,* Aug. 1, 1835 (C.B.L.).

Chelmsford . . . In the provinces theatrical amusements are at a discount. Men are not now such fools as to expend their time and money in seeing men and women make fools of themselves. If the march of intellect has done nothing else, it has well nigh marched players out of the English counties . . . Few respectable people are ever found within the walls of country theatres. When any are there they avoid recognition—a fair criterion by which to estimate how much additional respectability they obtain within the walls of the playhouse.

### 5. *The Age of Sobriety, 1837*

*Colchester Gazette,* May 20, 1837.

Whitsuntide Village Fairs. We are gratified to learn that the Rev. John Bramston, Vicar of Great Baddow, has been endeavouring to prevent the holding of the annual fair in that parish. We are also informed that the Rector of Springfield . . . has used his influence for the same purpose in his own parish. In neither case has success resulted from these praiseworthy exertions, but we nevertheless trust that the above gentlemen, with their clerical brethren in other parts of the county, will persevere in their attempts to put down these annual scenes of iniquity. We do not object to village fairs because we are unwilling to see the middling and lower classes enjoying an hour of harmless mirth. Our wish is that they should possess a taste for more refined amusements. Jingling matches—jumping in sacks—grinning through collars—bobbing for oranges—and various other accompaniments of village fairs are remnants of bygone ages of political degradation and moral darkness, and ought to recede from view on the advance of superior enlightenment . . . Numerous other amusements of a more consistent nature are already devised. For the fair sex we might have archery societies, etc, and for males cricket clubs, fencing schools, and grounds for the practice of gymnastic exercises.

## *CIVILISING INFLUENCES IN THE 19TH CENTURY*

### 1. *Foundation of Chelmsford Mechanics' Institute, 1833*

*Essex Mercury,* Jan. 15, 1833 (E.R.O.).

Chelmsford Literary Society. A society, under this title, but, in effect, upon the principles of a Mechanics' Institute, has recently been established at Chelmsford under the superintendence and patronage of Mr F. Marriage, a member of the Society of Friends, and other influential gentlemen. The avowed objects of the institution are the diffusion of scientific and useful knowledge among the mechanical class, the formation of a permanent library of select books, the establishment of a reading room, and the delivery of lectures upon literary and scientific subjects. Hitherto the projectors of this society have been very successful; between 70 and 80 young men, most of them journeymen mechanics, have entered their names as members, many volumes of standard works have been presented to the library, and one or two scientific gentlemen have promised to deliver lectures as soon as the necessary arrangements for that purpose have been made.

### 2. *Cheaper Books*

The following extract is from an address to the Witham Literary Institute by its chairman.
*Essex Standard,* Oct. 27, 1848 (C.B.L.).

We live in a period possessing singular advantages for education. Books are everywhere to be obtained at a cheap rate, and no man need now despair of success. How different fifty years since. How superior our advantages to those who lived then. The chairman then alluded to the scarcity of his books in his younger days, which was felt so much by him and others, that it led them to the formation of a Book Club as long back as the year 1807, which was the first Book Club established, he believed, in North Essex. But now they lived amongst books, and had only to shut their eyes and stretch forth their hands to the shelf, to be put upon learning made easy.

### 3. *Progress at Earls Colne, 1861*

*Essex Standard,* Oct. 9, 1861 (C.B.L.).

This pleasing spot in the Colne vale is rapidly improving under the spirit of progress evoked by the presence of the iron road. It can boast of a commodious room on the Terrace, answering the two-fold purpose of a village Hall and Mechanics' Institute. The old meeting-house has given place to an elegant chapel ; and now the parishioners . . . are bestirring themselves to secure the illumination of their residences by means of gas.

### 4. *The Facilities of a Village Literary Institute, 1878*

Printed Book of Rules, 1878 (T/P 68/18).

STANSTED LITERARY INSTITUTION, established 1849

President :— William Fuller Maitland, Esq., M.P.

Vice-Presidents :— Rev. T. G. Luard ; Rev. D. Davies.

Daily Papers taken at the Reading Room :—Times, Telegraph, Standard, Daily News.

Weekly Papers :—Chelmsford Chronicle, Herts and Essex Observer, Illustrated London News, Punch, Fun.

Magazines :—Cornhill, Leisure Hour, All The Year Round, Good Works, Chamber's Journal.

Draughts and Chessmen in the room . . .

Lady Subscribers may have free access to the Library and Papers.

Subscriptions :—

| | £ s. d. |
|---|---|
| Honorary Members | 1. 1.0 |
| Ordinary Members | 0.10.0 |
| Ditto | 0. 6.0 |

The Postmaster or Postmistress for the time being act as Librarian, from 9 a.m. to 8 p.m.

### 5. *The Temperance Movement in Kelvedon*

William Crowe, *Kelvedon as it is at Present* (*c.*1867, MS. in private hands).

About the year 1837 a few thoughtful men determined to try to bring about a better state of things. Temperance became a prominent question among them . . . Mr Harding, a member of the Society of Friends then an inhabitant of Kelvedon, our friend Mr Seabrook and one or two others . . . used to meet at a private house to chat the matter over. This in time led to public meetings, one of the first of which was held in the National School Room, after that in some maltings lent for the purpose, and they used to borrow the stools from the Friends' Meeting House. They had candle shades made by the late Samuel Humphrey to hang on the walls of these places. We can see by this the difficulties they had to contend with. In our day we have only to wish for a room and we find it ready for our use ; they had great difficulty in getting one . . . besides which they were exposed to all kinds of petty annoyances, rough bands outside and often times very noisy audiences inside . . .

Notwithstanding all opposition, which perhaps made them the more persevering, our friends formed a regular pledged society in the year 1843 . . . Out of this movement sprang a Mutual improvement Society which flourished for some time . . .

The Band of Hope was started in May, 1862 . . . A house to house visitation was arranged and carried out by a committee. On the first visit a copy of the parents' certificate containing the pledge was left at each house with verbal explanations and a week later another call was made to ascertain how many would agree to join. The result was that 21 signatures were obtained in Inworth, 14 in Feering and 74 in Kelvedon, total 109. The first meeting was held in the Friends' Meeting House on March 6th, 1862.

On September 2nd, 1862, the first Band of Hope Festival was held. A procession was formed at the Public Hall and marched through the street . . . Tea was held in the Public Hall and Mr Varenne presided at the meeting afterwards. In October, 1863, the Band of Hope Library was started . . .

Until 1867 no provision was made for obtaining refreshments other than at public houses, but during that year as a result of the increased temperance work a coffee room was opened, conducted by Mr W. Scott, which has been largely patronised by non-abstainers as well as temperance men. We can now boast of a handsome Temperance Hotel which had the audacity to plant itself opposite to what was formerly one of the most successful public and posting houses.

### 6. *Dress in Early Victorian Times*

An Earls Colne resident recalls the fashions of his youth.
*Halstead Times*, Feb. 21, 1903.

It is interesting to recall some of the dress which confronted us as we trooped out of church. The " gentry " wore swallow tail coats, similar to those now worn as evening dress. They also had high collars, reminding one of the caricatures of the late Mr Gladstone. The schoolmaster was thus attired. Several old ladies of the 'Almshouse' type wore long scarlet cloaks ; perhaps they do so now. Boys sported white duck trousers as a Sunday costume in summer. In winter they had long buskins of rough leather, reaching to the thighs, and fastened by a strap to a button at the waist. Many of the labourers wore their best smocks, nicely gathered into quaint ornamentation about the bust, their costume being completed by their best wideawake hats. A few old fogies, a grade above labourers, were gorgeously arrayed in plush waistcoats of dazzling colours, fastened with bright buttons. Solomon in all his glory was not arrayed like one of these.

## *SPORTS AND HOLIDAYS IN THE 19TH CENTURY*

### 1. *Cricket in the Making, 1825*

Rules of Chelmsford Cricket Club, 1825 (Chelmsford B.L.).

4. That each member, on his admission, shall pay the sum of ten shillings and sixpence, as his subscription for the season ; and no member to be permitted to play until such subscription be paid . . .
6. That the Club do meet for the purpose of playing every Monday and Thursday evenings at five o'clock. The names to be called over at a quarter past five, and those absent to be subject to a fine of sixpence . . .
8. That all disputes relative to the game, which may occur on the playground between members, be decided by a majority of those present, who may adjudge a fine, or expulsion from the Society.
9. The bowlers for each party (or such other persons as they shall choose among themselves) shall direct the play . . .
17. That every member do appear on the ground for playing, in a dress consisting of a straw hat, white jacket bound with purple, white or nankeen trowsers, shoes, and white stockings, or be subject to a fine of sixpence . . .

20. That all disputes relative to the laws of the game be decided by the rules of the Mary-le-bone Club . . .

*2. Lobs versus Overarm Bowling, 1849*

*Essex Standard,* Sept. 28, 1849 (C.B.L.).

Cricket. On Tuesday last a match was played upon the Chelmsford ground to test the comparative excellence of the old-fashioned slow bowling and the more modern method of round-arm swift throwing. There was some excellent play on both sides, and it proved one of the best contested matches of the season, the fast bowlers winning by 4 runs, and thus giving a numerical advantage to the modernized style ; but the excess was so small that it formed no exact criterion by which to judge of the superiority of either practice.

*3. Association Football, 1874*

*Halstead Times,* Oct. 31, 1874.

Earls Colne. Football. This exhilerating and popular game has just been started at Earls Colne, and there is every prospect of a first rate club being established.

*4. The 'Penny Farthing', 1877*

*Halstead Times,* June 23, 1877.

Braintree. Bicycle Race. The members of the Braintree Bicycle Club had a race a few evenings since, the course being from the Bay Tree Farm to the County Court Office, in the Coggeshall Rd., a distance of about two miles. There were ten starters who were handicapped according to the diameter of the wheels of their machines . . . As soon as the start was effected, a good race was maintained between Beard, Davies and the brothers Crittall as far as Mr Henry Hobbs' ; at that point, however, the two latter moved far ahead of their competitors and raced each other almost neck and neck to the finish, the younger of the two, F. H. Crittall, and captain of the club, just succeeding in winning. The race was witnessed by a large number of spectators.

*5. 'Emancipation', 1895*

*Halstead Times,* April 20, 1895.

The number of cyclists who passed through Halstead during the holidays was unusually large, the great proportion of them being from London. A lady and gentleman on a tandem were observed on Monday, the lady who occupied the rear seat being attired in a large coat of fashionable cut and the most daring of 'rationals', while gaiters and a pair of eyeglasses completed her costume.

### 6. *Walton in 1839*

*Essex Mercury,* July 2, 1839 (C.B.L.).

The inhabitants of this delightful and much frequented Watering-Place are much occupied in making preparation for the reception of visitors. The terrace and Lodging Houses present a scene of busy activity, numerous workmen being employed in painting, colouring, and otherwise decorating the interior and exterior of the houses. The old weatherbeaten sailors, who have passed the bleak, cold nights of winter in endeavouring to earn a miserable pittance by fishing, now convert their little barks into pleasure boats, while their wives attend to the donkeys, polish their harness and re-paint the chaises for the accommodation of invalids and aged visitors. It is astonishing what has been done in Walton in the last few years, in the erection of splendid houses, reading rooms, a jetty, etc. Its superior beach and salubrious air have caused it to become the most frequented Watering Place on the South Eastern Coast. Coaches, vans, etc, ply to it daily from Colchester, and the Ipswich Steam Packets call on their passage to and from London.

### 7. *The Rise of Southend, 1863*

*Gazetteer of Essex,* 1863, pp. 392-3.

Southend in Prittlewell parish is a handsome town and fashionable bathing place, delightfully situated at the terminus of the London, Tilbury and Southend Railway, near the mouth of the Thames . . . which is here about five miles broad. The town stands picturesquely on the side and crown of a woody eminence rising boldly from the sands, opposite Sheerness, and is distant . . . 42 miles E. of London, to which steam vessels ply daily from the wooden Pier, which here projects about 1¼ miles into the estuary and was constructed under the powers of acts of parliament passed in 1830 and 1835. Southend first began to attract visitors as a watering place about the close of last century, but continued nearly stationary for a considerable time owing to the failure of the original proprietors of the principal buildings, which were sold by auction in 1800 to James Heygate and Thos. Hope, Esqrs. In 1804 it was visited by Queen Caroline and Princess Charlotte and by several families of distinction ; and since then several spacious hotels and many large and handsome lodging houses, etc, have been erected, so that it and its immediate suburbs now contain about 2000 settled residents and have often as many visitors, Southend being a favourite resort of the inhabitants of London.

Since the opening of the railway in 1856 the town has much increased and in summer it is often crowded by numerous pleasure parties from the metropolis, who leave their pent-up offices, shops and dwellings for a day's excursion by rails or steam-packets to Southend . . .

Many handsome houses have been built here during the last 15 years, especially on the Marine Terrace, Grove Terrace, the Marine Parade and in Cliff Town. There are most agreeable walks in front of the Terraces and also along the beach upon the extensive and firm beds of smooth sand left by the tide. The air is dry and healthy, and the water, notwithstanding its mixture with the Thames, is clear and sufficiently salt. The bathing machines, baths, etc, are clean and commodious, and the neighbouring country affords many delightful walks and drives and is highly cultivated and plentifully wooded. Gas works were established here in 1855 and Water Works in 1860.

### 8. *Clacton, 1875*

*Halstead Times,* June 19, 1875.

Clacton-on-Sea. Extensive Improvements. Extensive improvements have been made in this watering-place since last year . . . Handsome residences have sprung up in all directions, and the town, as viewed from the pier, now presents a general outline of the plan originally laid down by the promoters of the undertaking. Those who remember what the place was a few years ago would hardly recognise it now. The cliffs to the north of the pier are now surmounted by clusters of neatly designed houses, flanked by the Royal Hotel . . . The pier, which is 500 feet long, will be lengthened another 500 feet at the end of the season.

# ESSEX AND NATIONAL POLITICS

In 1750 the county of Essex and the boroughs of Harwich, Colchester and Maldon each returned two Members to Parliament. The county electorate comprised some thousands of freeholders, whose choice lay usually between candidates from the great landed families. At Harwich the few electors were mostly Crown employees or pensioners and faithfully supported the Government's nominees. At Colchester and Maldon, where low qualifications permitted wider enfranchisement, the four candidates appealed for support to the political principles of the electors, while reinforcing their appeal with lavish expenditure on bribery and entertainment.

Reform movements awakened popular interest in politics. The cause of John Wilkes and the attempt to obtain more Parliamentary seats for county constituencies gained much support in Essex. The French Revolution raised hopes of a new democratic age, though it also occasioned the 'anti-Jacobinism' which, as the Revolution proceeded and War began, overwhelmed the reformers. After 1815 support for Reform rapidly increased. The middle classes, augmented in wealth and number, felt entitled also to political privileges, while many workingmen saw in political enfranchisement their best prospect of social betterment. Both these groups supported the Reform Bill during the vigorous struggle of 1830-32. The Reform Act of 1832 enfranchised the middle classes of the boroughs and, like Corn Law Repeal in 1846, was seen as a middle class triumph. There followed the rise of the Liberal Party with its programme of free trade, equality for Nonconformists and cautious electoral reform. The Conservatives, rallied by Peel and Disraeli, quickly regained ground and in Essex remained the stronger party throughout the century. With further enfranchisements in 1867 and 1884 the nature of electioneering changed. Both parties built strong constituency organisations and gave prominence in their programmes to social reform. At the same time the women's suffrage societies engaged in decorous publicity and received lukewarm recognition from members of both parties.

Towards the end of the century Labour was becoming an independent force in politics. In Essex the working-class movement was comparatively weak. It had originated in the sporadic local societies formed in the eighteenth century by weavers and other skilled trades. It had been influenced by Robert Owen and Cobbett, and during the years of Chartism between 1838 and 1850 it had won the allegiance of most urban workers. After 1860 individual Chartists, disappointed at Parliament's refusal of adult suffrage, formed co-operative societies and branches of the new national craft unions in several Essex towns. From about 1890 many new Trade Union branches were formed, including some among 'unskilled' workers, and the co-operative societies expanded rapidly. Encouraged by their success and urged on by the new Socialist groups, some working-class leaders contested local elections and advocated the creation of a Labour party independent of the two existing parties.

## *PARLIAMENTARY POLITICS BEFORE 1832*

### 1. *How to Win Elections, 1761*

The enrolment of additional freemen on the eve of the poll by the dominant party in the Corporation is recorded as having taken place both at Colchester and at Maldon.
*Ipswich Journal,* Jan. 31, 1761 (C.B.L.).

Maldon, January 24. On Thursday, the 22d Inst., this Town was much alarm'd by the Bailiffs, Aldermen, and Common Council being convened at Nine o'Clock at Night, to make a large Body of honorary Freemen to support the Election of two Candidates who had met with no favourable Reception in their Canvass; and at Midnight a Resolution was taken to make Two hundred and Seventy Freemen.

### 2. *A Borough Electorate, 1826*

Many men, who lived elsewhere than at Maldon, acquired the freedom of that town by gift, purchase, inheritance or marriage to a freeman's daughter. In the 1826 election 2527 electors lived in 'Maldon and the Country' and 586 in London. The candidates were Winn, Lennard and Dick.
*Poll for the Borough of Maldon,* 1826 (E.R.O.).

| | W | L | D |
|---|---|---|---|
| Lacey, Joseph, stone mason, Southend | — | | — |
| Lagden, Richard, farmer, Kelvedon Hatch | — | | |
| Lake, William, grocer, Maldon | | — | |
| Lake, John, wheelwright, Barking | | — | |
| Lake, John, jun., cordwainer, Barking | | — | |
| Lake, Richard, wheelwright, Barking | | — | |
| Lamb, Thomas, mariner, Burnham | — | | — |
| Lamb, John, blacksmith, Burnham | — | | — |
| Lambert, Thomas, labourer, Steeple | | | — |
| Lambeth, John, mariner, Colchester | — | | — |
| Lamprell, A. J., bath proprietor, Brighton | — | | |
| Lamprell, Daniel, game-keeper, Margaretting | — | | — |
| Lamprell, John, miller, Springfield | — | | — |
| Lamprell, Richard, builder, Great Dunmow | — | | — |
| Lamprell, William, surveyor, Great Dunmow | — | | — |
| Lane, Joseph, mariner, Colchester | | — | — |
| Lankaster, H. B., ironmonger, Newport, I. of Wt. | | — | |

### 3. *Harwich Electorate before Reform*

A critical Assistant Commissioner reports on Harwich politics. *Commission on Municipal Corporation,* 1835, Part IV, pp. 2276-7.

The Corporation of this Borough has long ceased to be identified with the "Tenants, Residents and Inhabitants" who are incorporated by its charters. The inhabitants are not admitted to the freedom; the majority of the freemen are not residents; and neither freemen nor inhabitants have any voice in the election of municipal officers, or in the management of corporate affairs.

The constitution supplies no check against the abuse of municipal power. The mayor is elected by the capital burgesses out of the aldermen, the aldermen by the capital burgesses, and the capital burgesses by themselves. These are the elements of the council, which is invested with all the powers and privileges of the corporation, without being subject to disturbance from any external control. They appoint the local magistrates, who tax the borough, and they have the unlimited management of the town revenues.

This select body was also entrusted, by the charters, with the choice of "two discreet and honest men, to be burgesses of Parliament for the same borough", who were to continue "at the cost and charges of the mayor and burgesses", so long as the Parliament was held. It is this exclusive electoral privilege which has given to the corporation its present character.

The honesty and discretion they sought was found for many

years among the members of the Government ; and, in return, the Government found among the members of the select body, qualifications for many public appointments. This reciprocity of confidence or dependence, which connected the borough with the Government, was only destroyed when the Reform Bill had proposed to transfer the right of voting from the council to the inhabitants.

Whether the election and attendance in Parliament was at the costs and charges of the Corporation or of the public, may be collected from a recapitulation of the various offices and pensions conferred upon the electors.

Among the resident members of the Council are the collector of Customs ; the comptroller of Customs ; the former agent of Government packets, now a Government pensioner ; two commanders of packets, also Government pensioners ; and a third, whose command descended to his son, now on the redundant list ; besides surgeons attached to the Ordnance and Victualling Departments of the port.

Among the non-resident members are the Barrack-master of Sheerness ; the Collector of Customs at Wisbeach ; landing-waiters in the Customs of London and Barbadoes ; and a clerk in the Stamp-office of London. All these are either aldermen or capital burgesses of the borough of Harwich.

But the number of public appointments heaped upon this Municipal Council is not more remarkable than the transformations which the members have undergone on entering upon their new functions. A linen-draper became a landing-waiter in the Customs ; a ropemaker was changed either into a Barrack master or a clerk in the Stamp-office ; and a surgeon was elected to be clerk of the cheques and storekeeper of the Navy.

These offices, however, numerous as they are, with the accompanying pensions, are not the only links by which the loyalty of the council has been rewarded and strengthened, if not secured, to the ministers by whom the offices were conferred. Not only themselves, but their sons, brothers, nephews and cousins were secured for the service of the State . . .

Twelve sons, besides brothers and other relations, are engaged in the public service and the members of the council, with their families, who are at the cost and charges of the public, are receiving from the public purse a sum exceeding £7000 a year, as a compensation for the services they have rendered or are still rendering to the State.

## 4. *An Election Agent Presents his Account*

The following were the expenses of C. C. Western, Whig candidate for the county in 1826.

Western Archives (D/DWe A1).

### Essex Election Account, 1826

| | £ s. d. |
|---|---|
| Fearnley, Saracen's Head and waiters | 249 . 18 . 0 |
| Albra, Bell | 108 . 7 . 7 |
| Wade, White Hart, Moulsham | 83 . 10 . 0 |
| Tavener, King's Head | 76 . 3 . 0 |
| Webb, Half Moon | 20 . 0 . 0 |
| Reed, Cross Keys | 17 . 7 . 0 |
| Baines, Lion and Lamb | 18 . 17 . 0 |
| Cobbin, Nelson's Head | 7 . 14 . 0 |
| Count, for committee room and ribbons | 45 . 16 . 0 |
| Count, for servants | 1 . 1 . 0 |
| Johns, for ribbon and for injury sustained by Wm. Whips, one of the bearers | 10 . 0 . 0 |
| Braintree band | 22 . 14 . 6 |
| Mr Pattisson, sundry bills at Witham | 26 . 15 . 0 |
| Mr Baker, Do. Rochford Hundred | 61 . 16 . 3 |
| Thos. Count, jun., bill as committee clerk and for his attendance | 12 . 0 . 0 |
| Wm. Botsford, attendance as clerk and expenses to and from London and at Chelmsford | 7 . 10 . 0 |
| Wm. Fuller, as clerk and expenses | 3 . 3 . 0 |
| Hamberger for flags | 10 . 18 . 0 |
| Sundry bills at Witham paid by Mr Fuller | 25 . 7 . 9 |
| Marsden, stationer | 1 . 11 . 7 |
| Josselyn for chair, etc. | 21 . 12 . 0 |
| Paid the bearers | 7 . 7 . 0 |
| Paid moiety at hustings, Sheriff's clerk of County Court, etc. | 29 . 9 . 6 |
| Paid sundries as per account, journeys and chaise hire and advertisements, postage, etc. | 42 . 13 . 6 |
| For my own trouble and attendance from 28th May to 3rd July relating to this election and examining, settling and paying the accounts, etc., and for clerk's attendance and assisting therein | 63 . 0 . 0 |
| | 974 . 11 . 8 |

### 5. *Comforts for Electors*

*Colchester Gazette,* Jan. 1, Jan. 15, 1820 (C.B.L.).

Yesterday se'nnight, D. W. Harvey, Esq., M.P. for this borough, distributed 500 bushels of coals amongst the resident Free Burgesses.

J. B. Wildman, Esq., M.P. for this borough, has given upwards of 700 bushels of coals to the free burgesses.

## *REFORM MOVEMENTS*

### 1. *Support for John Wilkes, 1769*

Essex freeholders passed the following resolution of protest against the refusal by the House of Commons to allow John Wilkes to take his seat.

*Chelmsford Chronicle,* Dec. 22, 1769.

We your Majesty's dutiful and loyal subjects, the freeholders of the county of Essex, animated with the most unfeigned zeal and affection for your majesty's person and family and the principles of liberty, which, in consequence of the glorious revolution, called in your royal ancestors to the government of these realms, beg leave to approach your majesty and in the most humble manner to complain of a measure planned and supported by your majesty's ministers.

The assent of every branch of the legislature is necessary for the establishment of every new law, and the majority of legal electors have the right to chuse any man their representative in parliament, who is not disqualified by the law of the land.

In defiance of these constitutional principles, we have seen with the utmost concern, an officer of your Majesty's army declared the representative of the county of Middlesex, by a resolution of one branch of the legislature only, although a very great and confessed majority of legal freeholders voted in favour of another candidate, not disqualified by the law of the land.

At the same time that we admit the jurisdiction of the house of commons in all cases where it becomes necessary to determine on which side a majority of legal votes has been given, we cannot allow that they can create a disability by a vote of theirs unknown to the law.

Permit us, therefore, royal sire, to request your majesty to restore the confidence of your people in the justice of parliament by an immediate DISSOLUTION of the present and by sending us to a new choice of representatives.

## 2. *The Early Reform Movement, 1780*

Discontent with the burdens of the American War gave occasion for the passing of the following resolution by an influential meeting at Chelmsford.
Coller, *People's History of Essex*, Chelmsford, 1861, pp. 170-1.

That this nation has been engaged for several years in a most expensive and unfortunate War; that many of our valuable colonies, having actually declared themselves independent, have formed a strict confederacy with France and Spain, the dangerous and inveterate enemies of Great Britain; that the consequence of those combined misfortunes has been a large addition to the national debt, a heavy accumulation of taxes, a rapid decline of the trade and manufactures and land-rents of the kingdom. Alarmed at the diminished resources and growing burthens of this country and convinced that rigid frugality is now indispensably necessary in every department of the state, your petitioners observe with grief that, notwithstanding the calamitous and impoverished condition of the nation, much public money has been improvidently squandered and that many individuals enjoy sinecure places, efficient places with exorbitant emoluments and pensions unmerited by public service, to a large and still increasing amount, whence the crown has acquired a great and unconstitutional influence, which, if not checked, may soon prove fatal to the liberties of the country.

## 3. *Fox's Advice to Essex Reformers*

Charles James Fox, the Whig leader, writes to Sir Robert Smyth, a prominent Essex Reformer.
Smyth Archives (D/DFg Z1).

Sir,

As businesses of the greatest importance have sometimes turned upon points apparently trifling, I will take the liberty of troubling you with a few lines upon a subject which I could not well touch upon in my public letter.

When I read your letter to the Westminster Committee I observed some persons to be a little startled at the word "Delegates". I mark the word, because it was clear afterwards that it was the word and not the thing that alarmed them; for when somebody talked of the committee sending agents, I perceived that many of the same persons seemed to be inclined to a measure which they had before seemed to dislike. I am so very anxious for some meeting such as you hint at, that I should be very much vexed indeed to lose the thing for the sake of a word and therefore, if I may take the liberty to advise, I could rather wish that (without giving any reason for it) you would drop the word "Delegates" and avoid every word that has been used in the commotions in America as much as possible. A meeting of "Agents" or "Deputies" may be considered as a very innocent measure, when a Congress of "Delegates" would alarm the whole Kingdom. I hope you will excuse the liberty I have taken in giving you these hints and trust to your good sense for perceiving that this letter is of a confidential nature.

I am, Sir, your most obedient, humble servant,

St James' Street, C. J. Fox.
February 11, 1780.

Mr Burke makes his motion today and it is thought Lord North will accede to the leave for bringing in the Bills ; if so, the most strict attention to the Committees upon these bills will become necessary, as well as from you gentlemen of the Committees out of Parliament as from us who attend them.

P.S. Leave is given to bring in Burke's bill without opposition.

### 4. *Tom Paine's Works Sold at Colchester, 1793*

*Ipswich Journal*, Jan. 19, 1793.

Three bills of indictment were preferred before the grand jury, who found the same, against Richard Patmore, baize-maker of this town, for vending and distributing Paine's second part of the Rights of Man, etc., and other seditious publications. Bail is given for his appearance at our next Quarter Sessions, himself in £600, and six sureties of £100 each.

### 5. *Political Reformers Condemned, 1793*

Great Dunmow Overseers' Accounts (D/P 11/12/1).

At a meeting of the inhabitants of the Hundred of Dunmow holden at the Saracen's Head in Great Dunmow.

Whereas certain publications, at once inconsistent with the fundamental principles of English Government, subversive of civil subordination, destructive of social happiness and, by their fallacious plausibility, strongly tending to excite sedition, have been dispersed . . . and an opinion generally prevails that associations have been formed and correspondences entered into, calculated to introduce confusion and anarchy,

We think it our duty to declare our zealous attachment to the British Constitution, our full conviction of the advantages derived from it to persons of all ranks and all denominations and our firm conviction that, as it has attained its present degree of perfection by successive improvements through a long series of ages, so it is fully competent to make such further improvements as from time to time may be found expedient.

And we do therefore resolve that we will oppose . . . all attempts to subvert, injure or disparage it, and use our best endeavour to bring to justice all such persons as shall utter treasonable words, post up or distribute inflammatory handbills or adopt any such means to raise commotions, excite disloyalty to the King or disaffection to the Government.

And it is recommended to the officers of the several parishes and hamlets within the Hundred of Dunmow to transcribe the said resolutions and to request a signature of approbation of them from all such principal inhabitants, that may not have attended this meeting, that such signatures and [those] now obtained be entered . . . within the parish book . . . and that they be brought for the inspection of the Magistrates at their next meeting.

### 6. *Protest against Peterloo*

The following extracts are from the draft of a speech to be made by T. B. Lennard, a leading Essex Whig, at a county meeting of protest against the 'Peterloo Massacre' of 1819.
Barrett Lennard Archives (D/DL O44/3).

Gentlemen, this is by no means an occasion on which it is necessary to discuss or express opinions on political principles. Upon this occasion, no matter whether we are Whigs or Tories, reformers or no reformers, here we are met, I hope to assert our right to discuss grievances, to express our horror and indignation at unnecessary bloodshed, to sympathise with the unhappy victims of wanton cruelty and to vindicate our own character, to make it manifest that we are not approvers of the crime which has been committed—and this we may do whatever may be the political differences among us on other occasions. And surely it is now incumbent upon all to come forward. The friends of reform should always be ready to assert their country's rights and to them I need not address myself ; but if there are amongst us any enemies of all reform, let them now shew that they are not enemies to law, to common justice and humanity. If there are amongst us any magistrates desirous to assert the character and respectability, the integrity and impartiality for which English magistrates have so often been distinguished, let them now shew that there is nothing in common between them and the magistrates who have been so unfortunately conspicuous in the late abominable transactions. If there be amongst us the members of any corps of yeomanry enrolled for the defence or the honor of the Country, let them now shew that they are not ready to be executioners, that they have not hearts to approve the perpetration of a massacre . . .

Other persons have politely warned me not to promote revolution, and the answer which I give to the warning [is] that I stand here to use my best endeavours to oppose revolution. I need not repeat that, if the proceedings at Manchester are sanctioned, the constitution is subverted and a revolution already effected, not indeed by an insurrection of the people but by their disgraceful submission to an act of lawless and tyrannical power. Let us, I say, prevent a revolution or a civil war by raising our voices before it be too late and no appeal be left but to the sword. It is near 40 years since Mr Fox declared that, if it was understood that a set of men were to be let loose on the constitutional meetings of the people, all who went to such meetings ought to go armed. He said well, because the danger of a conflict is less than the mischief which would happen from there being no meetings ; but who can reflect on such a state of things without horror and alarm, who does not see that, if both sides were to persevere, civil war and revolution must be the result. Gentlemen, I call upon all the friends of peace and constitutional order to come forward now whilst our voices may avail to check this sanguinary disposition of the ministry, before the nation is driven to extremity and nothing but violence can command attention. I call upon the enemies of revolution, and I hope we are all such, to come forward now and insist upon the removal of ministers who have shewn that they are resolved to proceed in a course which must make a revolution inevitable.

## 7. *Queen Caroline's Funeral Procession, 1821*

Reformers championed Queen Caroline's cause against George IV and made her funeral procession from London to Harwich the occasion for a demonstration.
Press cuttings (C.B.L.).

When it left Chelmsford, the greater part of the population went along with it, the gentry all dressed in decent mourning and the labouring classes either in black or in their best holiday clothes. On their return, deep sorrow was visibly imprinted on the faces of them all. The same symptoms of grief were also discernible in the inhabitants of Springfield ; in that neighbourhood the hedges appeared to be teeming with human beings, and it was evident from the spectacle then exhibited that it was not merely the visitors on the exact line of road that had come to mourn at her Majesty's untimely fate, but also those from a considerable distance . . . At the pleasant little villages of Boreham and Hatfield there was the same prevalence of good, kind, genuine English feeling as had been witnessed all along the road. The populous township of Witham, however, in its exhibition of mournful attachment to her Majesty, rivalled, if it did not surpass, any township there has yet been occasion to mention. From the highest to the lowest persons in the town, all were in mourning, and it could not have been more general had every family in the place lost a near and dear relation . . . The housetops were crowded with numbers of well-dressed females, most of them in tears ; the male inhabitants appeared to be all engaged in preceding the Procession on horseback to Colchester. Indeed, the cavalcade of horsemen at this place [Kelvedon] is immense and, as it is mostly formed of substantial farmers, assumes a very imposing appearance.

### 8. *The County Election of 1831*

Chelmsford Petty Sessions Minutes (P/CM 13).

26th April, 1831. The approaching election and Horticultural Show in the Shire Hall absorbed the attention of the morning.

29th April, 1831. Six householders resident in Chelmsford attended with a requisition . . . for the appointment of Special Constables during the ensuing election, which was complied with by the Bench, who issued their precepts for seventy persons to be sworn in.

13th May, 1831. T. S. Carritt v. John Brown, John Thomas, William Shearing, for hawking and selling printed papers in the town of Chelmsford and were convicted as pedlars and petty chapmen, but the real truth is they were engaged by partizans of one of the election candidates to sing a scurrilous ballad about the blue one. Mr. Derbyshire, the law agent of Mr. Wellesley, made application on their behalf and the convicting magistrate was disposed to listen to him, but in the interim Mr. Payne of Maldon, as one of the Committee of Mr. Western, having thrown out an intimation of moving the Court of King's Bench for a writ of Habeas Corpus, he was sent for to explain, when it turned out he had fallen into common error that the men were committed for ballad singing. The defendants were then heard upon their own petition and, solemnly promising not to repeat the offence, were discharged.

### 9. *Fervour for Reform, 1832*

*Essex Mercury*, May 22, 1832 (E.R.O.).

Harwich. It is not a little interesting to a by-stander here to observe the countenances of all parties among the inhabitants who have, as well as expect to have, a vote for the return of the representatives of the borough under the reform Bill. The leading articles of the London papers are seized on their arrival with all possible eagerness, and the inference drawn by the reader is immediately exhibited in his countenance as on a dial-plate. Groups collect and ask, " What's the news this morning ? " " Anything fresh by the mail ? ", " Will Herries and Dawson offer themselves ? ", " We must have members attached to the existing Government ", and a hundred such expressions daily arise.

### *10. Reform Beneficial to the Manufacturers*

An Essex landowner analyses the effects of the Reform Bill.
*Essex Standard,* June 17, 1831.

Now, since I have been in this room, I have made a calculation of the change contemplated, and which will show the altered situation in which the agricultural interest will stand. 168 members are to be abstracted from the number of the house ; of these 110 were in the class of country gentlemen—men like himself, mixed up with the landed interest and belonging to that class. We may add 42 to the manufacturing interest who *are* to be elected, which will give a total majority against the soil of 152. Take from this the 56 new members that are to be, and the final result will leave agriculture in a decided minority of 96.

### *11. Support for Reform*

The following is the draft of a resolution to be submitted by T. Barrett Lennard to a county meeting, called to protest against the rejection of the Reform Bill by the House of Lords.
Barrett Lennard Archives (D/DL O44/1).

[Your petitioners] beg leave humbly to represent to your Lordships that it was with feelings of the most poignant regret they received the information in the last Session of Parliament of your Lordships having rejected the Reform Bill, sent up from the House of Commons, without even allowing it to go into a Committee. They do indeed deeply deplore this decision of your Lordships, defeating as it did for the time his Majesty's patriotic and beneficent intentions, and so cruelly dashed the cup of hope from the lips of an anxious and highly excited people, so astonished and disappointed them that your Petitioners were seriously apprehensive of consequences dangerous, if not fatal, to the dearest interests of the Country.

Your Petitioners do now most earnestly entreat your Lordships to reconsider this vital question. The People do conceive that, by the Constitution and the Laws, they may claim as a right to be freely and fully represented and with equal confidence they think themselves authorised in saying that Nomination Boroughs are in effect an egregious outrage both upon the Law and Constitution of these Realms.

Your Petitioners have heard with infinite surprise that the existence of these Nomination Boroughs, and the possession of some by your Lordships, have been recently and openly avowed within the walls of your Right Honourable House and, more extraordinary still, have been represented to be essential to the preservation of the British Constitution.

## *POLITICS, 1832—1867*

### 1. *Maldon Elections, 1832-47*

*Suffolk Chronicle,* Dec. 30, 1848 (C.B.L.).

From 1832 to 1847 every election in the town of Maldon has seen a contest. All have been in character the same—all corrupt from first to last. In '32 the contest was only comparatively pure. In '35 the cost was much increased. In '37 the place was quite corrupt. In '41 'twas very much so. In '47 nothing could be worse . . . A month before the election they commenced their active canvass. In the midst of it the tap, as usual, was let loose. It always had been before, and why not therefore now ? " Supper parties " became fashionable ; at several of these the candidates attended. Wine, punch, brandy, anything you pleased, was the order of the day. The punch was mixed in mighty bowls, the brandy-grog in tubs. No small measures satisfied the folks of Maldon . . . For full three weeks one shocking scene of drunkenness prevailed in Maldon and its adjacent hamlets. One man died from the effects of drink. Another was run over by a waggon, as he went home drunk at night, and killed. Verdict " Accidental death " . . .

### 2. *The Case for the Secret Ballot*

A Colchester candidate recalls the victimisation of his supporters.
*Essex Standard,* April 19, 1861 (C.B.L.).

After the contest had closed, when men's passions ought to have subsided, when those who had been opposed to each other should have shaken hands at the end of the strife, as they had done before it began, and let bygones be bygones, it was told to him—and he could never repeat the fact without emotion—that the morning after the poll-book was published, the farmers of the neighbourhood came into the town and, going among the small tradesmen of the borough with that poll-book in their hands said to one and another ' No, you voted for Wingrove Cooke ; we shall never darken your door again '.

### 3. *An Argument against Universal Suffrage*

*Essex Telegraph,* Aug. 20, 1859 (C.B.L.).

May we not all learn a lesson from the Builders' Strike, the work of a confederacy against capital ? The men, too, engaged in these combinations which have brought one important branch of business to a standstill in the metropolis, are soon to be invested with electoral power. The inevitable tendency of public opinion is in the direction of strengthening democracy. What sort of democracy is it to be ? That country, whose proletaire order —the class that has no property but is solely dependent upon masters and wages—outnumbers all the rest, cannot fail to be in constant danger of disorder, if the issues of government are placed in their hands.

### 4. *Support for the Second Reform Bill, 1866*

Stansted Mountfitchet Political Papers (T/P 68/38).

*REFORM*

*A PUBLIC MEETING*
*WILL BE HELD AT THE*
*AGRICULTURAL HALL, SAFFRON WALDEN,*
*ON MONDAY EVENING, 9TH APRIL, 1866,*
*TO CONSIDER THE GOVERNMENT MEASURES FOR*
*LOWERING the FRANCHISE.*
*THE REV. ALEXANDER GOALEN, M.A.,*
of New Inn Hall, Oxford, and Lecturer in Natural Science at St Mary's Hall, will Address the Meeting, which will be open for Discussion.

### 5. *The Anti-Corn Law League*

A leading Colchester Free Trader recalls his part in the agitation against the Corn Laws.
*James Hurnard, A Memoir,* n.d., pp. 131-4 (C.B.L.).

Second Month 7th, 1842—Went to London to attend the great Anti-Corn Law Conference as a deputy from the Colchester Association. The meetings lasted five days. The principal speakers were O'Connell, George Thompson, Joseph Hume, Cobden . . . I feel assured, from the spirit which was exhibited, that the Corn Laws will soon be swept away . . .

The Corn Laws . . . which prevented the importation of foreign grain except when home-grown corn reached a famine price, filled me with disgust. These laws were plainly designed by a landlord-Parliament to raise the rent of land by diminishing the supply of food to the people.

Fourth Month, 21st. We have received four bales of Anti-Corn

Law packets, which I am to distribute to the electors of this town, I find the League have done me the honour to print my sonnet among the selected contents of their packets, in company with passages from Byron, Cowper, Eliot and others.
Seventh Month, 1843. The day of the great Anti-Corn Law meeting at Colchester. Cobden obtained a complete victory over Sir John Tyrell and his party. We had Cobden, Villiers, Diogenes, R. R. Moore, Harbottle, and several others to dinner and, after the meeting, to tea with us. They were all in the highest spirits at the result.
Twelfth Month 5th, 1845. Last night I read in the Times newspaper the joyful tidings that the Peel-Wellington Government has, at length, resolved to bring forward a measure for the total and immediate repeal of the Corn Laws at the commencement of the next session. The power of the League and the terror of approaching famine, with all its concomitant evils, have combined to overthrow this oppressive law, in spite of the most powerful aristocracy in the world. Those who have laboured in the great work, who have endured insult, contempt, ridicule, and oppression for its sake have a right to exult at the victory, which will bring comfort and plenty to tens of thousands of firesides in Great Britain, and will be a blessing to Europe and America and every other country on the face of the globe.
Fifth Month 16th, 1846. Last night the Bill for the repeal of the Corn Laws was read the third time in the House of Commons and passed by a majority of ninety-eight.
Sixth Month, 26th. This day the Bill for the abolition of the Corn Laws received the Queen's assent. Free Trade for ever !

### 6. *The Protectionists Counter-Attack, 1846*

A Protectionist newspaper notes the Free Traders' opposition to legislation protecting women and children in factories.

*Essex Standard,* May 15, 1846 (C.B.L.).

We can hardly tell what free trade means, judging from the conduct of its advocates in the House of Commons. That body has very recently been charging the country gentlemen of England with wishing to domineer over their dependents and to keep the country upon short commons. Who, we should like to know, are more amenable to these censures than the free-trade manufacturers themselves ? They grind down their workpeople to the lowest pittance and insist upon their privilege to do this without restraint.

The Factory Bill, now before the House of Commons, is likely to receive a severe mutilation if it goes into committee, of which there seems great doubt. The probability is that the measure will never get beyond the second reading. The country, we feel persuaded, will much regret the loss of this bill. The League people oppose it because they like to do what 'they will with their own'—a principle they have always abused when adopted by others. They have no notion that their jurisdiction should be interfered with by a rude Act of Parliament. They want an unreserved right over the persons they employ. This was the argument expressed by those League members who spoke on the debate on Wednesday. These men have a great notion of dignity, and none are so ready to enforce its worship in their own person. The bill before Parliament they fear will have the effect of curtailing this influence, by making the factory operative less a tool in the business upon which he is employed. They oppose its merciful provisions upon the plea that they cannot therefore successfully compete with the foreigner. They always said so. The bill in 1815 was a frightful experiment according to their predictions. We know that its results have been eminently successful.

### 7. *In Defence of the Corn Laws, 1839*

Lord Western, an Essex Whig and a leading Protectionist, gave the following advice to Essex farmers.

*Essex Standard*, Feb. 8, 1839 (C.B.L.).

I am inclined to think that the best plan will be to send up a petition from every parish in the country, with signatures of names and residence; and their trades and profession should be given, as I trust we shall have nearly as many tradesmen in proportion as agriculturalists, aye, and labourers too, for they most of them know that *foreign corn is in effect foreign labour introduced amongst them*; that *AWAY* goes employment at home, and *DOWN* comes wages; that they generally go down faster than the corn markets. The fraud practised on the working classes by the great capitalists and political economists is the grossest and most egregious of any that ever was palmed upon them. I am astonished that they do not see that low wages is their object—is it not avowed? How can any operative feel any certainty that a fall in the price of flour shall be so much more rapid than the declension of the rate of wages—for such it must be to benefit them. Do they not see that the agricultural labourers will, by distress, themselves flock into the great towns? It is true that comparatively few can turn their hands to manufactures—but some can, and their children can, and in numbers sufficient to reduce the demand for labour. It is the very thing the mill-owners would like; it really does astonish me that they, the working classes, should be the dupes of imposition so audacious, and to the degree of making them an absolute cat's paw, with danger of more seriously burning their fingers than in taking chestnuts out of the fire. They are actually stirring up the working classes to riot in favour of foreign corn, to which many a victim may suffer, but the instigators will take care not to be of the number.

## *THE EMERGENCE OF THE POLITICAL PARTIES*

### 1. *Conservative Philosophy, 1838*

*Essex Standard,* Oct. 5, 1838.

The men of Essex are not apathetic in politics, but possess as strong a feeling for the nation's prosperity and the nation's glory as is professed by the most violent of demagogues; but they adopt a more rational and intelligible mode of promoting these two great objects. They neither possess the puling, maudling cant of the *soi disant* modern philosophers, nor do they display the ferocity of the trading sedition-mongers; but they obey the laws, and, while they maintain their own rights with all the steadiness of true Englishmen, they do not wish to infringe on the rights of others. Loyalty to the throne is their characteristic, and it is no idle theory that can induce them to abandon the *conservation* of the fundamental principle on which the monarchy is founded. They are sensible that in all human institutions there must be blemishes, and are willing to support all useful reform; but they look cautiously to the qualification of those who offer to repair and beautify that which time may have, in some degree, injured or defaced. Many an ancient painting of inestimable value has been destroyed by the bungling hands to which its restoration has been intrusted.

### 2. *The Conservative Case, 1865*

A Conservative candidate at Harwich states his policy.
*Essex Standard,* May 12, 1865 (C.B.L.).

In stating to you my political opinions I will begin by saying that I am a Conservative. I am for preserving intact the glorious institutions of our country, for I think it behoves us to hand down to our successors those institutions free and uninjured. At the same time I do not mean to say that I am not for removing abuses; on the contrary, I shall be prepared to support all such measures as may render those institutions more useful and satisfactory to the existing circumstances of the country; and living as we do in an age of great and rapid progress, I think we should be at all times ready to support such judicious measures as may be from time to time brought before us for increasing the general prosperity and happiness of the people. But while I would support progress under wise and safe guidance, I am strongly opposed to all sweeping and dangerous innovations . . . I am strongly in favour of maintaining our Army and Navy, for I firmly believe that by so doing the maintenance of peace is much more likely to be preserved, and real and judicious economy effected. Nor can I lose sight of that most glorious force, the British Volunteers. Our Volunteer force, numbering now upwards of 150,000 men, all in a high state of discipline and ready at any moment for active service, is a force of which any country might be proud. Indeed in all probability it is the envy of all the nations in Europe . . . I am in favour of removing all restrictions upon trade and commerce—I mean all restrictions that bear unduly upon trade and commerce—and I should, if you do me the honour of returning me, be prepared to support all measures to remove or modify those inequalities which press unfairly upon precarious incomes—for I think that some alteration of the incidence of taxation might be made with great advantage to very many persons. In accordance with the enlightened age in which we live, I am of opinion that every man ought to receive a fair education and I shall have much pleasure in assisting to carry that into effect. As to Church-Rates, I shall give my adhesion to any well-considered measure that would settle this long-vexed question.

### 3. *Towards Tariff Reform, 1893*

Lord Petre's estate agent, F. J. Coverdale, urges a moderate tariff to protect wheat from American competition.

Petre Archives (D/DP E17).

In my opinion there is but one remedy that will in any way preserve the Agricultural interest from collapse, namely that the British farmer should be put upon an equal footing with his foreign competitor, and that the burdens on land should be considerably reduced.

I do not insinuate that anything like a return to protection in its former state is either practicable or desirable, but I submit that to allow a great industry to die out cannot be sound policy, and that, when its staple commodity cannot be profitably produced, then such a tariff should be imposed as would raise say for instance wheat to a price not exceeding 40/- per quarter, or at all events to put a duty upon the manufactured article, i.e. flour. At times it is almost impossible for farmers to procure what they require in the way of offal, i.e. bran pollard, middling, etc., and that means not only the loss of this product but the fact that a large percentage of the mills and their occupants have gone to the wall . . . A 5/- duty ought not to increase the price of the loaf more than one halfpenny ; if found to do so, then I submit that it would be the duty of the Government to protect the poor man and, as in France for instance, regulate the price of the loaf.

### 4. *The Conservative Case, 1892*

This extract is from the address of the Conservative candidate for Saffron Walden at the 1892 election.
Stansted Mountfitchet Political Papers (T/P 68/38).

I am in favour of the Government which has managed our affairs well and wisely during the last six years. With God's blessing it has

*KEPT PEACE WITH OTHER NATIONS.*

It has *KEPT BREAD CHEAP.*

It has *LOWERED THE TAXES ON TEA AND TOBACCO.*

It has *TAKEN OFF THE SCHOOL PENCE.*

It has helped the people to get

*ALLOTMENTS AND SMALL HOLDINGS.*

It has made a law for

*BETTER HOUSES FOR THE POOR.*

It has made

*IRELAND QUIET AND PROSPEROUS.*

It has set up the County Councils and has formed a Board of Agriculture.

It has given large relief to the local rates out of the Imperial Taxes. Trade and Commerce have improved. The deposits in the Savings Banks have risen. The number of Cattle and Horses in the Country has increased. The next thing to do is to set up *DISTRICT COUNCILS* and to *REFORM THE POOR LAW,* and to form a plan of *OLD AGE PENSIONS,* so that Aged Persons may live in comfort in their own homes without going to the Union Workhouse. This plan, however, must not interfere with the noble work of Friendly Societies and Benefit Clubs.

### 5. *Liberal Progress in Rural Essex*

*Essex Telegraph,* April 18, 1891 (C.B.L.).

He remembered when the Tory magnates used to boast that there was not a Liberal or Dissenter in [Tolleshunt] D'Arcy, and he believed it was then true, and the first men who began to say they were Dissenters or Liberals were boycotted. The Tories dared not boycott them now. He believed they had more Liberals in D'Arcy than they had Tories. In former days it was not safe for

Liberals at the time of an election to go about the village. Their premises were tarred, and all sorts of things were done, but they dare not do it now.

### 6. *The Liberal Case, 1892*

The following extract is from the address of the Liberal candidate for Saffron Walden Division at the 1892 election.

Stansted Mountfitchet Political Papers (T/P 68/38).

To the Working Classes I appeal with confidence. They form the great majority of my constituents and their interest has always had my warmest support. The excessive migration of the younger inhabitants of the villages to the towns is a lamentable fact, injurious alike to country and urban life. How to maintain labour on the land, as well prosperous as plentiful, is without doubt an urgent problem which must be considered by every statesman who does not neglect his duty to the rural districts. The solution of the difficulty, in my opinion, lies in using every effort, legislative or otherwise, to render village life more attractive and more remunerative to the working classes. The agricultural labourer has never yet had the same opportunity of rising in life as his fellow workman in the cities, and it too often happens that an honest, thrifty, and industrious man has nothing better to look forward to in his old age than the workhouse.

I strongly advocate a reform of the Poor Law. A clear distinction should be drawn between the deserving and the undeserving poor, and I would heartily support any just and equitable scheme whereby the aged poor should be enabled to end their days in their native villages rather than be driven forth to die in the Workhouse.

I am a staunch Free Trader and will never consent to legislation which will in any way endanger the Cheap Food of the People.

I am in favour of a complete measure of Land Reform, making land as easy to be purchased and transferred as any other commodity; of compulsory powers to acquire good and convenient land for Allotments and Small Holdings; and of the creation of Village Councils, which shall enable the working classes to exercise a just influence, and take a fair share, in those matters of Village life which vitally affect their comfort and prosperity.

### 7. *Labour Enters Politics*

A Liberal paper deplores independent Labour candidatures.

*Essex Telegraph*, Sept. 26, 1891 (C.B.L.).

Mr Keir-Hardie poses as a Labour candidate and seeks to split up the democratic vote in North West Ham. Mr Keir-Hardie is not a Tory, but he is doing Tory work nevertheless. The interests of Labour and Liberalism are identical, and any attempt to draw a line between them can only result in damaging both, especially the former. Labour leaders can only hurt their own cause by splitting up the Radical Party into groups and sections and by so doing play directly into Tory hands.

## *WOMEN'S SUFFRAGE MOVEMENTS*

### 1. *The Status of Women, 1777*

*Chelmsford Chronicle,* July 18, 1777.

Monday last Jonathan Heard, gardener at Witham, sold his wife and child, a fowl and eleven pigs, for six guineas to a bricklayer of the same place. He this day made a demand of them and received them with open arms amidst a prodigious concourse of people. The knowing ones think the bricklayer has a very hard bargain.

### 2. *Women in the Reform Movement*

Essex women of the middle classes were stirred by the idealism of the Reform movement of 1830-32.

*Essex Mercury,* May 3, 1831 (E.R.O.).

Mr Waylen, Secretary to the Coggeshall Reform Committee, informs us that the ladies of Coggeshall, participating in the general enthusiasm and emulating the noble spirit of their sex in Poland, have determined that the honour of sending Reformers as representatives of Essex shall not rest with men alone ; and, in accordance with such determination, they have, almost without exception, contributed to the funds of the Committee.

### 3. *Female Politicians Deplored, 1838*

An Essex editor deplores the interest taken by women in the Chartist movement.

*Essex Standard,* Dec. 21, 1838 (C.B.L.).

A Female Radical Association has been formed at Hull ; and 'the Ladies' gave a dinner there to Mr Vincent the other day. One Mrs Kay was in the chair. In order to make the affair 'stink in the nostrils' of all decent people as much as possible, the Chairwoman held forth upon the influence which woman had in society and their right to use it for political purposes. She called upon every mother to educate her children in thorough Radical principles, and upon the maids to *marry none but Radicals.*

Women may influence great possess
But on certain conditions ;
And one of them is—they must ne'er
Set up for politicians.

Mothers, for Radicals who train
Their babes—not for the Lord—
May live to reap, in rebel sons,
Their bitter just reward.

Those maids, too, must expect to meet
The fate they well deserve,
Who all their smiles for Radicals,
And them alone, reserve.

Not but you're welcome, luckless girls—
Quite welcome those to pet ;
For who a Radical would wed
That could another get.

### 4. *The Victorian Suffrage Movement*

*Halstead Times,* March 14, 1874.

*WOMEN'S SUFFRAGE.*—On Thursday evening a meeting was held at the Chelmsford Institute, under the auspices of the National Society for Women's Suffrage, when addresses were delivered by Miss M. Beedy and Miss H. Downing and other advocates of the removal of the electoral disabilities of women.

## *WORKING-CLASS MOVEMENTS*

### 1. *Braintree Weavers on Strike, 1758*

*Ipswich Journal,* Dec. 2, 1758 (C.B.L.).

From the Weavers' Camp at Bocking and Braintree. Whereas the Clothiers of Bocking and Braintree have added to the Length and Stoutness of their Bays, without any additional Wages ; and of late (thro' the Deadness of Trade) have stinted us a Fortnight, three Weeks, and a Month in a Bay, and a considerable Number were unemployed, by means whereof they had Reason to believe that many of us were under the greatest Circumstances of Distress ; and then to add to our Calamity, they made a Demand of our Waste, without offering any Allowance for the same ; (and by Degrees, did we tamely submit, we should be brought under a Yoke which would have some Affinity to that of the Egyptian Bondage). Tho' we would not presume to deny, but that afterwards through the Instigation of the Right Hon. Robert Nugent,

Esq. they offered us 3d. per Bay in Lieu thereof. The Waste is a small Perquisite hath been granted us for several hundred Years past, which we are able to prove by our antient Books of Record, which have been no less than 14 or 15 Times ratified and confirmed at the General Quarter Sessions. We solemnly declare that our refusal to carry home the Waste for our Master's Inspection, is not with any Intention to wrong or defraud them; but there be many Inconveniencies which will unavoidably attend it, (some of which have been laid before the said Hon. Rob. Nugent) and we should gladly mention them here if they did not exceed the Bounds of a Common Advertisement. Upon the Waste being demanded, the Weavers made a general stand on the 7th of this Instant, and 5 or 600 continue out of Employ; but have behaved in so regular and decent a Manner, that no Disturbance hath been made. We have neither acted in Defiance to the Legislative Power, nor in Opposition to our Masters, any further than to support our antient Custom. We, in Submission to our Masters, have (in a Petition presented to the said Robert Nugent) offered everything that is honest, just and equitable, in hopes to accommodate the Affair, which they have refused to accept; nevertheless, we will not pretend to determine who are the Oppressors and the Oppressed, but shall leave that to every judicious, impartial, and unprejudiced Person to judge.

2. *An Early Co-operative Society, 1758*

*Ipswich Journal,* Sept. 30, 1758 (C.B.L.).

Whereas we have been certainly informed that Flour is much dearer in the Country than at London, and that Millers often make as much of their coarsest sort here, poor and hungry as it is, as of their finest there; which is as if an ingrossing brewer should sell his small Beer at the price of Strong. We hereby propose to our poor Brethren that a publick Meeting of Weavers and others be held at the White Hart in Braintree on Saturday the 21st of October, at Six in the Evening, to consider of a proper Method, and to raise a publick Purse to get Flour, or Meal, from London, by which we shall make great Savings for our Families.

Timothy Manlove Zachary Freeman

3. *An Early Trade Union, 1785*

*Chelmsford Chronicle,* Sept. 30, 1785.

To Shoemakers in General

Whereas by an Act of the 5th of Eliz. it is enacted (amongst other matters therein contained) that, " It shall not be lawful for any person or persons to follow the trade of a Shoemaker, except he shall have been brought up therein *seven years* at least as an apprentice ; nor to employ any person therein who shall not have been such apprentice as aforesaid, upon pain of forfeiture for every default, Forty Shillings for Every Month : and also, that every person that shall have three apprentices, shall keep one journeyman; and for every apprentice above that number, one other journeyman, upon pain for every default therein of forfeiting Ten Pounds : and further, that all indentures, covenants, and bargains for the taking and keeping of any apprentice, contrary thereto, shall be void ; and that every person taking an apprentice contrary to the true meaning thereof shall forfeit for every apprentice so by him taken the sum of Ten Pounds."

And whereas many persons do follow the said trade who have not served a legal apprenticeship, nor wrought at the same *seven* years, (which has been held to be *equal* to *serving an apprenticeship ;*) and others have taken apprentices for a less term than seven years, or have had more than three at one time without employing the proportionate number of journeymen required by law, to the impoverishment of the craft, and by which means many hundreds of workmen, who have served a legal apprenticeship to the business, are destitute of employment to the great distress of themselves and their families.

We the Cordwainers of Saffron-Walden and places adjacent, through the example of our brothers in London, Chelmsford, and many other towns in England, for the prevention of all such illegal practices, united in one Friendly Society, with the approbation of the tradesmen in general, solicit the company of every person that has a right to follow the trade, *masters or journeymen,* at Mr Thomas Erswell's at Cross-Keys Inn, on Tuesday the 18th of October, at six o'clock in the evening. Here the company of every legal cordwainer will be looked upon as a favour, as the United Society of Cordwainers have no object in view but the general good of the trade, they call upon every man that hath a right to work at the trade to stand forth and assist in such a lawful undertaking. By Order of the Select Committee

John Smith, President John Baron, Secretary

### 4. *Opposition to Trade Unionism, 1834*

Robert Owen's Grand National Union established branches in Colchester in 1834.
*Essex Standard,* May 24, 1834.

Trades Unions. We are sorry to learn, from good authority, that the emissaries of these unconstitutional associations have been at work among the mechanics of this town, who have established provincial branches here to co-operate with the Parent Societies in London, the sole object of which is to organise an odious tyranny by the workmen over their masters and their customers, the public. We rejoice, however, to find that it is in contemplation very shortly to call a meeting of the inhabitants to counteract these illegal combinations, when it will be proposed to pass a determined resolution not to employ any tradesman who allows a Unionist to work for him.

### 5. *Opposition to Chartism*

When in 1838 the Chelmsford Chartists advertised a public meeting, the local Magistrates considered banning it under a recent law restricting meetings held by night.

Chelmsford Petty Sessions Minutes (P/CM 18).

7th Dec., 1838. Working Classes. A meeting of these persons having been fixed for Monday *evening,* 10th Dec., by placard to be held in the Market Place at Chelmsford, the attention of the Bench was called as to the legality of the proceeding, when it was finally determined that the Clerk should enclose one of the printed placards, with a letter which was approved of by the Bench, to the Secretary of State, Lord John Russell, for his advice on the subject; giving at the same time directions to the Clerk of the Peace not to allow the parties the use of the Court or the Corn Market, their meeting not being held in the day time.

### 6. *Rural Chartism*

The rise of Chartism in S.W. Essex was attributed by its opponents to the instigation of the five 'Tolpuddle Martyrs' who had been settled on farms in that area by public subscription after their pardon.

*Essex Standard,* Dec. 20, 1839, quoting *Morning Post* (C.B.L.).

The new settlers at Greenstead and High Laver had not been long established amongst the hitherto quiet and well-conducted population of these parishes before they began to agitate, and to agitate in a manner and with a degree of success which showed but too plainly that their mission of mischief had not been entrusted to unpractised or unskilful hands. Chartist newspapers were quickly seen in active circulation. The beer-shops in which they were to be found became more frequented and more noisy than heretofore. A Chartist Association was formed at Greenstead and, by the combined or alternate influence of persuasion and of terror, nearly the whole of the agricultural labourers in that and the adjoining parishes were induced to join it. A weekly subscription was exacted from each of them, and they were told that, when their fund amounted to a certain sum, it would be increased by the committee in London. Frequent meetings were held, the time selected for this purpose being generally on a Sunday morning during the hours of divine service. The meetings became progressively more and more numerous. At first the farmhouse occupied by the new settlers was large enough to contain them, but ere long the farmyard was found insufficient, and the assemblies were held in an adjoining field. Delegates attended the meetings from Waltham Abbey, Epping, Harlow, Hatfield Broad Oak, etc, etc. Delegates and orators from London, sometimes to the number of forty, were also occasionally present. The project of a general rising of the Chartists on or about the 12th of August was discussed and entertained. The effect of these proceedings was to diffuse a general sense of insecurity throughout that part of the country and so far to disturb the habitual relations between the farmers and labourers that the former thought it necessary to adopt a system of hiring for the last harvest different from their previous practice and to engage their labourers on such terms that, in case of desertion from their work, they might be liable to summary punishment.

### 7. *Consumers' Co-operation*

John Castle records how he and some former Chartists decided in 1861 to found the Colchester Co-operative Society.

*Colchester Wheatsheaf*, May 1936, quoting the MS. Diary of John Castle.

I had read a good deal about politics and co-operation. I had visited a weavers' club, which had done good but through bad trade had broken up. I felt tired of taking part in politics or in anything else on behalf of the working people. They did not seem to appreciate what anyone might do for their good, they did not seem to like to see one of their own class advance themselves in the social scale.

A friend named Dand used often to call and see me. He was a man who desired to see workingmen raise themselves in the social scale. He often discussed co-operation with me and urged me to call a meeting of the working-class people on the subject, but I would not. At last he prevailed upon me to say that I would attend a meeting if he called one. He accordingly called a meeting of about twelve respectable men at Thompson's coffee room, Short Wyre St. This was at the beginning of 1861 . . . We discussed the desirability of a co-operative society in Colchester and decided that it was quite necessary that something should be done to elevate the people.

### 8. *Victorian Trade Unionism*

The secretary of the Colchester branch of the Amalgamated Society of Carpenters and Joiners describes the benefits enjoyed by its members. *Colchester Mercury,* March 29, 1879 (C.B.L.).

Each member subscribed 1s. per week and for that he received 10s. per week when out of employment and 12s. per week when sick; and during the time such relief was paid, the weekly subscription was not called for, a feature, he believed, novel in Benefit Societies. Any member meeting with an accident, which permanently incapacitated him from following his trade as a carpenter and joiner, received £100; and for partial disablement, a sum of £50 was paid. The subscription also covered insurance of tools; and on the occasion of the fire at Mr Dobson's premises at Colchester, some men who were members had their tools replaced at a cost of £50. Any person after being a member 18 years was entitled to a superannuation allowance of 7s. per week, and after 25 years membership to 8s. per week for life . . . On the death of a member his widow or relatives received £12, and should a member lose his wife he received £5 . . .

With regard to the Colchester Branch of this Society, at the end of 1877 they had a balance of £233 . 15s. . 1½d. For out of work benefit they had paid during the year £3 . 10s. That was a light amount, but fortunately the depression which had raged throughout the country had not extended to Colchester, and the enterprise of Colchester business men had kept the building trade active. Their total expenditure for 1878 was £28 . 17s. . 8½d., including £14 . 2s. paid for sick benefit. Their income for the year was £110 . 11s. . 11d., so they had a balance left of £82. Although there were something like 200 carpenters and joiners in the town, this Branch only numbered from 45 to 50 members.

### 9. *The Objects of Colchester Trades Council, 1891*

*Essex Telegraph,* Sept. 5, 1891 (C.B.L.).

The establishment of a more intimate connection and friendly relationship between all branches of the operative classes, so as to secure their sympathy and united support on all questions affecting or which are likely to affect, their interest, whether in a local or a national sense; to foster and strengthen all existing trade and labour organisations; to organise the skilled and unskilled workers of both sexes amongst whom no Society at present exists; to secure labour representation on all public bodies and the Imperial Parliament; to use every endeavour (when appealed to) to bring any dispute that may arise, either amongst the several trades and labour organisations comprising the Council or between the employers and employed of the same, to an amicable and satisfactory settlement.

### *10. The Origins of the Labour Party*

A Colchester Trade Unionist advocates Labour representation in Parliament.

*Essex Telegraph*, March 7, 1891 (C.B.L.).

Mr Stanton was in favour of the legal eight hours if they could get it, but since the passing of the Reform Act giving voting power to working men, he wanted to know what workingmen had done with that power to better their condition? They could count upon their fingers those Members of Parliament who represented labour, and that was after having had the vote for 24 years. They should look politically at this question, for if working men thought that the men they now sent to Parliament would pass an eight hours bill that would be useful to them, they made a great mistake.

# INDEX

This is an index of persons, places and subjects. Only persons well-known in local and national history are indexed, but all Essex parishes to which reference is made in the text are included. Subjects are fully cross-referenced as in other Essex Record Office publications.


Acts of Parliament : 29-30, 64, 181. *See also* Reform Acts
Adult education : 178. *See also* Books ; Libraries ; Literary Institutes ; Mechanics' Institutes
Agriculture : 15-16, 25-36, 37, 51, 80, 133, 144, 151, 194, 200-2 ; cloth industry provides market, 3 ; dairy-farming increases, 35, 36; depression, 24, 28-9, 32-6, 37 ; improvements, 25-7, 31-2 ; machinery, 31-2, 48 ; poultry-farming, 35 ; rents, 25, 28, 31, 33, 36 ; smallholders' difficulties, 26 ; tithe, 31, 34. *See also* Commons; Corn Laws; Farm labourers; Farmers; Gardens; Harvest; Hops; Open fields ; Seedgrowing
Ague : 108
Aldham : 43-4, 57 ; Ford Street, 44
Allotments : 44, 127, 201, 202
America : 19, 24 ; War of Independence, 189
Amusements : 70, 86, 151-182 ; farmmers' amusements, 31, 158-61. *See also* Assembly rooms ; Dancing ; Dancing bears ; Drunkenness ; Fairs ; Gambling ; Holidays ; Music ; Sports ; Theatre
Anti-Corn Law League : 196-9
Apothecaries : 111, 145, 148, 166
Apprenticeship : 5, 12, 71, 72, 104, 107, 110, 111, 119, 133, 147-8, 167 ; regulations broken, 4, 205-6
Arch, Joseph : 49
Archery : 169, 176
Archives, storage of : 73
Ardleigh : 18 ; incendiarism, 49
Arnold, Matthew : 141-2
Assembly rooms and balls : 148, 151, 162, 163, 164, 165-6
Audley End : 42, 140, 155-6
Australia : 20-1
Aveley : 53, 87 ; fair suppressed, 167-8 ; 'Lunatick Club', 160

Baddow : 56
Baddow, Great : 45, 62, 176 ; education, 134 ; family allowances, 116
Baddow, Little : 29
Ballingdon : 91, 95
Ballot, Secret : 195
Balls. *See* Assembly rooms
Band of Hope : 178
Bardfields : 45, 46, 59
Barking : 63, 117, 142, 185. *See also* Ilford
Basildon : 28
Bays and says. *See* Cloth
Beer : 38, 39, 40, 44, 45, 48, 54, 70, 72, 88, 96, 111, 112, 114, 125, 155, 159, 161, 168-9, 205
Belchamps : 27
Belchamp Walter : 95
Benfleet, South : 134
Bentley, Great : 41 ; pauper funeral, 112 ; pesthouse set up, 112
Bicycles : 152, 180
Billericay: 28, 93; cricket match, 170
Bobbingworth : 58
Bocking : 1, 2, 4, 6, 7, 45, 110, 142, 204 ; Poor Law expenditure, 117
Books : 149, 151, 167, 176-7 ; Club, 177 ; farmers reading more, 27. *See also* Libraries
Boreham : 117, 192 ; Poor Law expenditure, 117
Borley : 27, 95
Boroughs. *See* Municipal Corporations
Boundaries : 73, 76, 158
Bow Street Runners : 92
Boxing : 171, 175
Boxted : 71
Bradfield : 28
Bradwell-juxta-Mare : 159 ; boxer, 171 ; football in 1787, 170 ; sailing match, 170
Braintree : 1, 2, 6, 11, 16, 17, 25, 35, 50, 59, 125, 187 ; bicycle club, 180 ; economic occupations, 16 ; Local Government, 97, 118-19 ; Poor Law, 114, 117, 118-19 ; transport, 63, 65 ; working-class movements, 127, 204-5
Bramston family : 30, 69, 93, 176
Braxted, Great : 120-1 ; cricket team, 168
Braxted, Little : 120

Braybrooke family : 44-5, 92-3. *See also* Audley End
Brentwood : 87, 164, 168 ; fair, 158
Breweries : 1, 2
Brickworks : 1, 2, 14
Bridges : 54, 56, 66, 69-70, 74, 161
Bright, John : 32
Bromley, Great : 49
Bulmer : 27, 45, 95 ; Poor Law expenditure, 117
Bulphan : fair suppressed, 167-8
Bumpstead, Steeple : 19-20
Bumpsteads : 59
Burial : 73, 112
Burnham : 39, 98, 185 ; coach to London, 63 ; cock-fighting, 171-2 ; sheep-stealing, 90
Burstead, Little : 28

Canada : 2, 20
Canals and navigations : 63-5 ; Chelmer Navigation, 64-5
Cement, Roman : 16-17
Charity : 37, 45, 77, 113, 125, 158 ; allocation of commons to poor, 29. *See also* Schools
Chartism : 98, 103, 141, 184, 203, 207-8 ; opposition to New Poor Law, 127
Chelmsford : 9, 15, 33, 35, 55, 59, 61, 63, 69, 70, 76-8, 90, 100, 111, 120, 125, 148, 152-4, 157, 161, 167, 175, 187, 189, 192, 193, 204 ; Chartism, 207; Chelmer Navigation, 64 ; coach to London, 61, 63 ; cricket club, 179-80 ; economic occupations in 1831, 15 ; education, 130-1, 133-4, 137; Local Government, 93, 96-7, 118 ; Mechanics' Institute founded, 176 ; Poor Law, 115, 117, 118 ; population, 19 ; trade union, 206; water-supply, 161; workhouse, 37-9, 114-15, 118
Chesterford, Little : 140
Chigwell : 136
Children : 74; employment, 7, 9, 12, 29, 37, 39, 110, 140
Chingford : economic occupations in 1831, 16
Cholera : 67, 95, 96
Church of England : 133. *See also* Churches ; Churchwardens ; Clergy; Schools, National ; Rates
Churches : 77, 87, 94, 138, 161, 165
Churchwardens : 20, 66, 72, 76, 77, 95-6, 103, 105, 107, 110, 111, 112, 113, 145, 165, 174, 175 ; accounts, 87-8 ; Earl Fitzwalter serves, 153 ; Poor Law activities, 104
Clacton, Great : economic occupations in 1831, 15 ; rise of Clacton-on-Sea, 182
Clacton, Little : 79, 107
Clavering : 45, 46 ; family allowances, 117
Clergy : 76, 78, 94, 118, 120, 124-5, 131, 134-7, 142, 153, 168, 174, 175-6
Clerk of the Peace : 68
Cloth, woollen : 1-9, 190 ; combing, carding, 5, 14 ; fullers' company, 4; rowing mill, 4-5. *See also* Spinning ; Weavers
Clothiers : 1, 6, 7, 190 ; Dutch baymakers, 2, 3, 6 ; opposition to French treaty, 2
Clubs : 152, 158-60, 170, 176, 177, 179, 180
Coaches, coaching : 42, 52, 55, 57, 59, 61-3, 90, 153-5, 158, 159, 181 ; Machine Fly, 61 ; stage-coaches on Essex road, 63 ; steam coach, 62
Coal : 38, 52, 63-4
Cobbett, William : 184
Cobden, Richard : 8, 32, 196-7
Cockfighting : 151, 171-2
Cock-throwing : 171
Coggeshall, Great : 1, 2, 8-10, 11, 20, 45, 51, 54, 72, 120-1, 140, 203 ; coach to London, 63 ; free vaccination, 146-7 ; Poor Law, 109, 117, 120 ; preparations against invasion, 80-6 ; road in disrepair, 55 ; Vestry calls in Scotland Yard, 92 ; Volunteers, 82, 86 ; wages, 119-20
Coggeshall, Little : 120-1
Colchester : 1, 2, 5-6, 7, 8, 15, 22, 25, 55, 88, 92, 93, 123, 148, 163-4, 185, 193, 196-7 ; amusements, 163, 165, 172 ; coaches, 62, 63, 90, 181 ; dispensary established, 147 ; economic conditions, 12, 15, 209 ; food riots in 1772, 68 ; housing, 100 ; Lighting Commission, 75-6 ; politics, 183, 188, 190, 195 ; Poor Law administration, 106, 109-10 ; water supply, 99-100; working-class movements, 127, 141, 206-10
Colchester (All Saints) : 86-7, 106
Colchester (St. Giles) : 106, 117
Colchester (St. Leonard) : 72
Colchester (St. Nicholas) : 7
Colchester (St. Peter) : 164
Colchester (St. Runwald) : 103
Colne, Earls : 25, 54, 56, 110 ; dress, 179; football club, 180; Mechanics' Institute, 177; straw-plaiting, 17-18; workhouse built, 113-14

Colne Engaine : 41, 104-5 ; parish committee, 117 ; workhouse master, 113-14
Commons : 24, 29-30, 162
Communications. *See* Bridges ; Canals ; Footpaths ; Railways ; Roads
Conservatives : 183, 199-201. *See also* Tories
Constables : chief, 72, 89, 92, 171, 174-5; petty. 66-7, 72, 73, 87, 89-93, 96, 103, 171, 174-5 ; special, 48, 118, 193. *See also* Bow Street Runners ; Police
Co-operative Societies : 51, 184, 205, 208-9
Copford : 119
Corn Laws : 32, 183, 196-9
Corringham : fair suppressed, 167-8
County Councils : 67, 100, 143-4, 201
Coursing : 159
Courtauld family : 11, 142, 143
Cressing : 156-7
Cricket : 151-2, 168, 170, 176, 179-80 ; overarm bowling introduced, 180
Crime : 44-5, 90-3 ; penal code, 91, 120. *See also* Highwaymen, Incendiarism ; Poaching ; Smuggling
Crimean War : 46
Crockery : 7, 38, 41
Crompton and Co. : 18

Dagenham : 91 ; economic occupations in 1831, 16
Danbury : 145-6, 159
Dancing : 8, 70-1, 130, 131, 159, 165, 171, 173. *See also* Assembly rooms
Dancing bears : 172
Dedham : 2, 145 ; amusements, 165
Defoe, Daniel : 2, 25, 109-10
Dispensaries : 147
District Boards : 67
Docks and harbours : 16-17, 22, 65
Doctors : 112. *See also* Medicine
Doddinghurst : 135
Domestic service : 15-16, 42, 110, 133, 152, 155
Dovercourt : 173
Drama. *See* Theatre
Dress : 38, 45, 49, 106, 108, 110, 133-4, 158-9, 179 ; for cricket, 179 ; for cycling, 180 ; extravagance of silk workers, 9 ; of farm labourers, 32, 37, 179 ; of farmers, 31
Drunkenness : 40, 43, 70, 91, 92-3, 151, 160, 168-9, 174, 195
Dudley, Rev. H. B. : 47-8, 60
Dunmow, Great : 121, 185, 190 ; fire brigade, 78 ; opposition to toll-gates, 59

Easter, High : fair suppressed, 167-8
Education : 128-144, 200, 201 ; administration, 131-2, 138, 142-4 ; for farmers' children, 27, 128, 161 ; 'half-timers', 12 ; inadequacy in 1838, 141 ; Inspectors, 129, 141-2 ; school routine in 1854, 138. *See also* Adult education ; Schools
Elections : 183-8, 193, 195, 201-2. *See also* Ballot, Secret ; Franchise
Electricity : 100 ; telegraph, 65 ; telephone, 18
Emigration : 98, 119 ; emigrant's experiences, 20-1 ; parish encourages, 19
Enclosures : 23, 24, 29-30
Engineering : 2
Epping : 58, 173, 208 ; economic occupations, 14 ; family allowances, 117
Epping Forest : 22-3, 163

Fairs : 118, 151, 158, 167-8, 169, 176
Fairstead : 120, 121
Farm labourers : 15-16, 37-51, 168-9, 198, 202 ; allotments, 44-5 ; boarding-in rare, 42-3 ; distress during Crimean War, 46-7 ; dress, 37, 179 ; effect of New Poor Law, 123, 124, 126-7 ; food, 37, 45, 46 ; Friendly Society, 43-4 ; health, 149-50; housing, 46, 149; migration, 37 ; petition against New Poor Law, 126 ; smallholdings sought, 51 ; strikes, 47-8 ; support for Chartism, 207-8 ; trade unions, 37, 48-51 ; wages, 37, 39, 46, 119-20. *See also* Agriculture ; Allotments ; Arch, Joseph ; Gleaning ; Harvest ; Incendiarism; 'Speenhamland' system
Farmers : 15-16, 24, 60-1, 77, 90, 103, 128, 135, 148, 151, 156-7, 193, 195 ; amusements, 31, 158-61, 168-9 ; education, 27, 128, 161 ; enterprise shown, 25-8 ; failures in depression, 33, 34 ; paternalism to labourers, 42-3 ; Scottish, 24, 33, 34, 35-6 ; smallholders, 26, 51 ; smuggling, 169; wages accounts, 39; widening outlook, 25-8, 31, 32, 160-1. *See also* Agriculture ; Farm labourers
Farmhouses : 33, 34
Faulkbourne : 120, 121
Feering : 120-1, 178

Felsted : 30, 59 ; school, 132, 159
Finchingfield : 59, 91
Fingringhoe : 12, 89
Fire brigade : 78
Fishing industry : 1, 12, 38, 181
Fobbing : fair suppressed, 167-8
Food : 37-9, 45, 85, 110, 111, 114, 125, 155-6, 158-9 ; sale of, 70, 71, 72 ; subsidies, 115 ; voluntary rationing, 86 ; workhouse diet, 114. *See also* Beer ; Prices ; Tea
Football : 152, 169, 170, 180
Footpaths : 74, 76-7
Fox, Charles James : 189-90, 192
Foxearth : 95
France : 2, 189. *See also* French Revolution ; Napoleonic War
Franchise : 67, 183-4, 185 ; plural voting in Local Government, 97. *See also* Reform movements ; Women, suffrage
Free Trade : 24, 32, 183, 196-7, 200, 202 ; silk industry, 11
French Revolution : 183
Friendly Societies : 43-4, 146, 148, 201 ; trade union benefits, 209
Frinton : 79 ; population, 19
Fryerning : workhouse inmates, 114
Funeral expenses : 112
Furniture : 41, 157 ; in weaver's home, 7

Gambling : 73, 151, 165, 168, 171
Games. *See* Sports
Gaols : 73, 74, 91. *See also* Houses of Correction
Gardens, gardening : 131, 152, 158, 161, 164, 165, 193
Gas : 67, 151, 177, 182
Gestingthorpe : 27, 79, 95
Gladstone, Mr : 179
Gleaning : 37
Gosfield : 6, 57
Greenstead-juxta-Ongar : 207
Guardians, Boards of : 59, 67, 98, 100, 101, 102, 120-2, 125, 142

Halstead : 1, 2, 11, 17, 56, 57, 125, 143, 180 ; House of Correction, 69 ; opposition to Board of Health, 98 ; workhouse, 113
Ham, East : 107
Ham, West : 91, 202-3 ; growth of industry, 22 ; population, 19. *See also* Stratford
Harlow : 58, 88, 208
Harvest : 37, 40, 138, 208 ; wages, 39-40
Harwich : 12, 68, 79, 137, 154, 173, 192 ; Corporation, 74-5, 100, 185-6 ; dancing bears, 172 ; economic conditions, 12, 16-17 ; electricity, 100 ; politics, 183, 185-6, 193, 199 ; tradesmen resent hawkers, 74
Hatfield Broad Oak : 208
Hatfield Peverel : 91, 120-1, 192 ; Poor Law expenditure, 117
Health : 141, 147, 169 ; in prisons, 69 ; sick benefit, 43-4. *See also* Ague ; Cholera; Health, Boards of; Medicine ; Poor Law ; Sanitation ; Smallpox ; Typhus ; Water supply
Health, Boards of : 67, 95-8 ; constitution of, 97
Hedingham, Castle : 45, 46, 95, 114; Poor Law procedure, 104, 119; theatre, 164-5; volunteer cavalry, 79
Hedingham, Sible : 46, 57, 79, 143 ; Poor Law expenditure, 117 ; Strawberry Gardens, 164
Hedinghams : 2, 27, 39
Henny, Great : 119
Heybridge : 65, 92
Highway Boards : 67
Highwaymen : 90, 91 ; 'Gallows Corner', Romford, 30, 90
Highways. *See* Roads
Holidays : 22-3, 152-5, 181-2. *See also* Spas
Holland, Great : 79
Holland, Little : 107
Hops : 28, 38
Hornchurch : 30, 131 ; Board of Health, 95-6
Horndon, East : 34, 136
Horse racing : 158-9, 162, 170-1
Hotels : 178-9, 182. *See also* Inns
Household accounts : 155
Household utensils : 7, 38, 41, 156-7, 158
Houses of Correction : 48, 69, 87, 173. *See also* Gaols
Housing : 15-16, 33, 34, 46, 71, 97, 99, 100, 106-7, 201 ; in Chelmsford in 1831, 96
Hunting : 31, 132, 150, 157, 158-9

Ilford : 63, 90, 91. *See also* Barking
Improvement Commissions : 67, 75-7
Incendiarism : 24, 37, 49
Industry : 1-23. *See also* Courtauld family ; Fishing ; Railways ; Ships ; Silk ; Weavers
Ingatestone : 55, 90, 152
Inns, beerhouses : 39, 44, 56, 70-3, 76, 79, 88, 90, 95, 96, 120, 121, 151, 153, 154, 158-60, 162, 165, 170-5,

179, 187, 205-7 ; details of Romford inn, 168. *See also* Hotels
Invasion preparations : 80-6
Inworth : 120-1, 178

Jenner, Dr : 146
Justices of the Peace : 47-8, 54-6, 60, 62, 66-72, 73, 74, 76, 79, 87, 89, 90, 95, 96, 99, 102, 107, 109, 123-5, 151, 171, 173-4, 191, 207 ; apprenticeship, 111 ; Lunatic asylums, 147 ; Poor Law, 72, 102, 103, 105, 115-16, 117 ; riot, 68, 175 ; roads, 54, 55 ; Sabbath observance, 71-2. *See also* Quarter Sessions

Keir-Hardie, James : 202-3
Kelvedon [Easterford] : 2, 25, 45, 51, 120, 193 ; education, 137-8, 139 ; opposition to emigration, 119 ; perambulation of boundaries, 76 ; Temperance movement, 178-9. *See also* Western family
Kelvedon Hatch : 185

Labour Party : Keir Hardie's candidature, 202-3 ; origins, 184, 202-3, 209-10
Lamarsh : 113
Lambourne : 52, 136; roadmaking, 88
Landowning classes : 24, 25, 93, 135, 151-7, 183, 194, 196 ; agricultural depression, 32-4 ; Audley End servants, 42 ; paternalism, 43-5. *See also* Bramston family ; Braybrooke family ; Justices of the Peace ; Lennard family ; Majendie family ; Mansions ; Mildmay family ; Quarter Sessions ; Western family
Langdon Hills : 137
Langenhoe : 92
Latchingdon : 39, 60, 158, 159
Laver, High : 207
Laver, Little : 136
Lawford : 45, 70 ; Poor Law expenditure, 117
Leighs : 126
Lennard family : 53, 129-30, 191, 194-5
Lexden : 58
Liberals : 183, 201-3
Libraries : 148, 176-7, 178. *See also* Books
Liston : 95
Literary Institutes : 177
Littlebury : 44, 91
Local Government : 66-101 ; officials, 66, 69, 70, 73, 87, 95, 98, 99, 121. *See also* Boundaries ; Bridges ; Burial; Churchwardens; Constables; County Council ; District Boards ; Fire brigade ; Guardians ; Health, Boards of ; Highway Boards ; Improvement Commissions ; Justices of the Peace ; Lunatic asylums ; Municipal Corporations; Overseers; Parish ; Parish Councils ; Police ; Poor Law; Quarter Sessions; Rates; Rural Sanitary Authorities ; School Attendance Committees ; Schools, Boards ; Street lighting ; Surveyors ; Vestry
London's influence on Essex : 1, 2, 15-16, 22-3, 24, 28, 157, 180, 181-2 ; dairy-farming encouraged, 35 ; Harwich sends fish, 12 ; Londoners purchase estates, 25 ; migration to London, 22 ; poultry-farming encouraged, 35. *See also* Bow Street Runners
Lord Lieutenant : 68
Loughton : 136, 141 ; in 1861, 22-3
Lunatic asylums : 147

Machine-breaking : 4-5, 37
McAdam, John : 59
Majendie family : 27, 28-9, 56, 79, 119
Maldon : 25, 33, 35, 62, 73, 74, 98, 109, 122, 125, 158-9, 162-3, 193 ; coach to London, 61, 63 ; deepening of Blackwater, 65 ; Mayors, 73 ; opposition to Chelmer Navigation, 64-5 ; politics, 183-5, 195 ; railway, 65 ; Sergeants at mace, 73 ; shipping, 152 ; town dunghill, 73
Maltings : 14, 178
Manningtree : 25 ; overcrowding, 46
Manor : 24, 29, 150, 157
Mansions : 152-7 ; parkland, 157. *See also* Audley End
Maplestead, Great : 79 ; Poor Law expenditure, 117
Maplestead, Little : 79; population, 19
Margaretting : 185
Mechanics' Institutes : 151, 176
Mechi, Alderman J. : 60
Medicine and medical services : 108, 111-12, 145-50, 153 ; Benevolent Medical Society, 146, 148 ; doctor's bill in 1777, 112 ; Medical Society founded, 148 ; medical training, 147-50. *See also* Apothecaries ; Friendly Societies ; Health ; Lunatic Asylums ; Pesthouses ; Physicians ; Sea-water baths ; Spas ; Surgeons
Mersea, East : 89 ; economic occupations in 1831, 15
Mersea, West : 170

Messing : 120
Migration : 37, 50
Mildmay family : 152-5
Mills : 1, 2, 57, 85 ; tide-mill, 70
Mistley : 79, 132
Morant, Rev. Philip : 3
Moreton : 86
Mundon : 74, 111
Municipal Corporations : 66-7, 73-6, 99-100, 162-3, 184, 185-6 ; Borough property, 73, 74-5 ; Colchester corporation inactive, 6
Music : 71, 87, 153, 159, 162, 164, 173 ; weavers' concert, 8
Mutual Improvement Society : 178

Napoleonic war : 24, 37, 79, 80-6, 88, 102, 115, 118, 148, 169, 183 ; barracks, 73 ; invasion precautions, 80-6
Navigations. *See* Canals
Navy recruitment : 68
Newport : 69, 140
Newspapers : 151, 166-7, 177, 193, 194, 207
Nonconformists : 67, 93-4, 128, 134, 136, 139, 140, 151, 177, 183, 201. *See also* Quakers ; Roman Catholics
North Weald Bassett : 58
Norton Mandeville : 58

Ockendon, South : 49 ; fair suppressed, 167-8
Ongar : 35
Ongar, Chipping : 58, 130
Ongar, High : 58, 136
Open fields : 24
Overseers of the Poor : 20, 37, 41, 66, 72, 77, 95-6, 99, 102-19, 124, 137, 145, 174 ; accounts, 37-8, 105, 108 ; election of, 103 ; rota of service, 103
Owen, Robert : 184, 206

Paglesham : 40, 91
Paine, Tom : 190
Parish : 73, 74, 76-95. *See also* Churchwardens ; Constables ; Overseers ; Poor Law ; Rates ; Surveyors ; Vestry ; Workhouse
Parish Councils : 37, 67, 202
Parliament. *See* Acts of Parliament ; Elections ; Politics
Pebmarsh : fair suppressed, 175
Peldon : 92
Penal code. *See* Crime ; Prisons
Pesthouses : 112, 145
'Peterloo Massacre' : 191-2
Petre family : 31, 33, 136, 200
Petty Sessions : 59, 79, 90, 174, 193, 207
Physicians : 147-50
Pleshey : fair suppressed, 167-8
Poaching : 23, 93
Police : 50, 73, 89-93, 123 ; county, 18, 67, 92-3, 100-1 ; voluntary night watchmen, 92. *See also* Bow Street Runners ; Constables
Politics : 50-1, 183-210 ; growing urban influence, 22 ; corruption in, 183-6, 189, 194-5. *See also* Chartism ; Cobden ; Conservatives ; Elections ; Franchise ; Free Trade ; Liberals ; Reform Acts ; Reform movements ; Tories ; Whigs ; Women ; Working-class movements
Poor Law : 37, 66-7, 102-27
New Poor Law : 37, 67, 102-3, 119-27, 201-2 ; Relieving officers, 121 ; subsidised emigration, 20
Old Poor Law : 37-8, 67, 72, 87, 88, 102-19 ; apprenticing, 110, 111 ; care of disabled, 55 ; clothing, 38, 106, 108 ; employment of poor, 9, 37, 105, 110, 137 ; expenditure, 117, 118 ; food subsidies, 115 ; foster-parents, 109-10 ; fuel provided, 108, 111, 117 ; funerals, 108, 112 ; health services, 102, 111-12 ; nursing, 112 ; old persons assisted, 102, 108, 109, 114, 115, 118 ; orphans, care of, 102, 108, 109-10, 114, 118 ; pauper inventories, 7, 41 ; rent paid, 108, 118 ; School of Industry, 134 ; Settlement, 88, 106-7, 108 ; sick allowances, 106 ; subsidised emigration, 19, 119 ; widows assisted, 102, 107, 108, 109
*See also* Guardians ; Select Vestry ; 'Speenhamland' system ; Workhouse
Population : 1, 2, 15-16, 19, 22. *See also* Emigration ; Migration
Postal services : 59, 68, 177, 186
Prices : 7, 11, 22, 24, 37-9, 41, 46, 115, 155-9, 161, 164, 165, 198, 200-1, 205
Prisons. *See* Gaols
Prittlewell : economic occupations in 1831, 16. *See also* Southend
Purleigh : 136-7

Quakers : 83, 139, 153, 176, 178
Quarter Sessions : 4, 48, 66-72, 74, 89, 95, 100-1, 108, 123, 147, 190, 205; cock-throwing suppressed, 171; county police, 92 ; fairs suppressed, 167-8 ; Friendly Societies, 43-4 ; licensing, 70-1, 165 ; preserving the

peace, 68; prisons, 69; 'quarterage', 108; roads, 52, 54-5; shire-hall, 161-2; surveyor employed, 69, 70; wage-fixing, 5-6
Quendon: population, 19

Railways: 22-3, 34, 63, 65, 152, 181-2; effect upon villages, 177
Rainham: 63, 134
Ramsey: 69, 79, 173
Rates: 28, 77, 99, 106; church, 67, 93-4, 200; county, 100, 108; highway, 52-3; poor, 9, 24, 98, 100, 102, 104-5, 108, 113, 116, 118, 119, 120
Rayleigh: 158; population, 19
Recreation. *See* Amusements
Reform Acts: 37, 67, 102, 183, 186, 193-5, 196
Reform movements: 120, 183-4, 188-95, 203; opposition to, 190-1; 'Peterloo Massacre' condemned 191; support for Wilkes, 183, 188. *See also* Chartism; Women
Religion: 49, 136, 140, 151. *See also* Church of England; Nonconformists; Sabbath observance
Rivenhall: 120-1, 148, 168
Rivers: 52, 63-4, 65
Roads: 30, 52-63, 66-7, 77, 88, 158, 160, 161-3; administration, 52-61, 66-7, 88, 95; Colchester Paving Commission, 76; compulsory labour, 52-3, 66-7; restriction of traffic, 56. *See also* Coaches; Surveyors; Transport; Turnpike Trusts
Rochford: 33, 45, 125, 159; workhouse inmates, 114
Roman Catholics: 136
Romford: 30, 61, 125, 152, 154, 168; Church rate opposed, 94; economic occupations in 1831, 16; education, 138; smallpox, 145
Roothing, Abbess: 135
Roothing, High: economic occupations in 1831, 15
Roothings: 33, 59
Roxwell: 30
Rural District Councils: 67
Rural Sanitary Authorities: 67, 98

Sabbath observance: 71-2, 78, 138
Saffron Walden. *See* Walden, Saffron
Sailors: 20-1, 68, 181; apprenticeship, 12
Sampford, Great: 53
Sanitation: 73, 95-9, 162-3
School Attendance Committees: 142, 143
Schools: 74, 110, 128-44; Boarding, 128, 129-30, 131, 140, 161; Boards, 128, 142; British, 128, 139, 140, 141-2; Charity, 77, 128, 133-6, 140; Dame, 135, 137; Grammar, 96, 128-9, 131-2, 136, 139-40, 145, 159; National, 128, 138-40, 178; Private, 128-31, 140; Sunday, 128, 134-8; Technical, 129, 143-4
School teachers: 77, 129-31, 133, 134, 136, 137, 139, 140, 179; writing-master, 152
Sea-water baths, bathing: 151, 166, 181-2
Seedgrowing: 24, 51
Select Vestry: 78, 96, 118-19, 122, 137
Shelley: 58
Shenfield: 59, 63, 91, 131
Ships, shipping: 1, 12, 16-17, 20-2, 63-4, 152, 181
Shoemakers, bootmakers: 2, 14, 71, 127, 185; trade union, 205-6
Silk: 1, 9-12, 14, 105
Smallpox: 78, 111, 112, 145-7; inoculation, 145-7; vaccination, 78, 145-7; pesthouses, 112, 145
Smuggling: 1, 12-14, 89, 169; seizures, 13; types of vessels used, 13
Snuff: 125
Southend: 15, 165, 166, 181-2, 185. *See also* Prittlewell
Southminster: 27, 91, 171
Spas: 151, 154, 165
'Speenhamland' system: 37, 45, 102, 115-17, 119-20, 124
Spinning: 1, 3, 5, 8, 9, 37, 41, 105; earnings, 7
Spirituous liquors: 31, 39, 89, 112, 159, 161, 168-9, 195
Sports: 30, 157. *See also* Bicycles; Boxing; Cockfighting; Cock-throwing; Coursing; Cricket; Football; Gambling; Horse racing; Hunting; Yachting
Springfield: 18, 90, 176, 185, 192
Stanford-le-Hope: fair suppressed, 167-8
Stansted Mountfitchet: 45, 91, 112; Literary Institute, 177; Poor Law, 105, 108, 117, 119; workhouse inmates, 114
Stanway: fair suppressed, 167-8; population, 19
Stapleford Abbots: 29
Steam power: 32, 62, 181
Stebbing: 45, 59
Steeple: 47
Stifford: fair suppressed, 167-8
Stisted: 104, 119

Stondon Massey : 103
Stratford : 63, 90
Straw-plaiting : 1, 17-18
Street lighting : 75-7
Strikes : 47-8, 196, 204-5
Surgeons : 44, 106, 145, 148, 150, 186 ; bath-proprietor, 166
Surveyors of the highways : 52-4, 60, 66-7, 86-7, 95, 103 ; called to account, 88
'Swing' riots : 10, 48

Tailors, tailoring : 1, 2, 12, 18, 127
Takeley : fair suppressed, 167-8
Tariffs : 1, 2, 200. *See also* Corn Laws
Tea : 45, 46, 114, 154, 164 ; weaver's teapots, 7
Telephone : 18
Temperance : 151, 178-9
Terling : 27, 120, 126
Tey, Great : 169
Thaxted : 45, 59, 106 ; smallpox treatment, 111 ; Vestry allocates pews, 77
Theatre : 151, 158-9, 163-5, 175
Theydon Garnon : 106-7 ; election of parish officers, 103
Thorpe-le-Soken : 45, 79 ; family allowances, 116
Thundersley : 134
Thurrock, Little and West : fair suppressed, 167-8
Tilbury, West : 135; fair suppressed, 167-8
Tillingham : 31, 99 ; boxing match, 171 ; football team, 170
Tiptree : 51, 60 ; fair, 158, 168
Tithe : 94, 134 ; dinner, 159
Tobacco : 31, 38, 125
Tollesbury : 99
Tolleshunt D'Arcy : 71, 99, 201
Tolleshunt Major (Beckingham) : 99, 168
Tollgates : 56, 57, 63, 87, 157, 158 ; evasion, 57, 58 ; list of charges, 57 ; opposition to, 59. *See also* Turnpike Trusts
'Tolpuddle Martyrs' : 207
Toppesfield : 143 ; fined for poor roads, 54
Tories : 124-5, 191, 201. *See also* Conservatives
Totham, Great : 48, 99
Town Clerks : 73
Trade. *See* Fairs ; Free Trade ; Industry
Trade Unions : 129, 184, 206-7, 209-10 ; carpenters', 209 ; shoemakers', 205 ; 'Tolpuddle Martyrs' in Essex, 207 ; weavers' combinations, 6, 184, 204. *See also* Farm labourers ; Strikes
Trades : 14, 15-16, 72, 88, 106, 111, 113, 185, 209. *See also* Apprenticeship ; Farm labourers ; Sailors ; Shoemakers ; Spinning ; Tailors ; Weavers
Transport : 1, 14, 52-65 ; increasing traffic, 52 ; regulation of vehicles, 56, 57. *See also* Bicycles ; Canals ; Coaches; Docks; Railways; Roads; Ships ; Turnpike Trusts
Turnpike Trusts : 52, 55-8, 60, 67 ; accounts, 56-7 ; borrowing money, 58 ; farming of tolls, 58. *See also* Tollgates
Typhus : 97, 149

Ugley : economic occupations in 1831, 15
Ulting : 109, 120
Unemployment : 3, 10-12, 37, 62, 204
Universities : 132
Upminster : Constables' accounts, 87 ; Corbetts Tye fair suppressed, 167-8
Urban District Councils : 67

Vaccination. *See* Smallpox
Vagrants : 90, 96
Vange : 28
Vestry, parish : 28, 37, 66, 76-7, 86, 87, 89, 92, 93-4, 95, 113, 119, 159 ; allocates pews, 77 ; committee system, 28, 66, 102, 117, 119 ; election of officers, 52, 103; fire brigade, 78; free vaccination, 146-7 ; home defence, 80-6 ; paid officers, 66, 87, 95, 102, 113-14, 118-19, 122, 145 ; recruiting for armed forces, 79 ; supervision of expenditure, 104, 106, 119 ; voluntary food rationing, 86. *See also* Churchwardens ; Constables ; Overseers ; Poor Law ; Rates ; Select Vestry ; Surveyors ; Workhouse
Volunteer corps : 79, 159, 200

Wages : 21, 48, 116, 124, 152, 153, 155, 198 ; cloth industry, 5, 6, 7 ; domestic service, 42 ; London's higher wages, 22 ; straw-plaiting, 18 ; tailoring, 18. *See also* Farm labourers
Walden, Saffron : 9, 44-5, 50, 65 ; economic occupations in 1831, 16 ;

education, 139-40; Reform meeting, 196; trade unions, 205-6. *See also* Audley End
Waltham Holy Cross: 25, 71, 91, 208; lunatic asylum, 147; sheep-stealing, 91
Waltham, Great: 45, 126; family allowances, 116
Waltham, Little: 119, 126; family allowances, 116
Walthams: 134
Walthamstow: 24
Walton: rise as resort, 181
Wanstead: 91
Warley, Great: 164; fair suppressed, 167-8
Water supply: 67, 96, 98-9, 161, 182
Weavers: 1, 7, 184, 204-5; Co-operative Society, 205; procession, 8; wages, 5, 6, 7; silk weavers, 10, 11, 208
Weights and measures: 66
Western family: 25, 57, 187, 193, 198
Wethersfield: 46, 49, 59; parish doctor, 148-50; charity school, 77
Whigs: 124, 191, 198
Wicken Bonhunt: 46
Wickham Bishops: 41, 45, 48, 120, 121; apprenticing of poor child, 111; family allowances, 116; Poor Law expenditure, 117
Widdington: 140; subsidises emigrants, 20
Widford: 55, 90
Wigborough, Great: 89
Wilkes, John: 183, 188
Witham: 25, 46, 99, 119, 120, 121, 122, 187, 193, 203; Defoe's description, 25; Literary Institute, 177; Poor Law, 114, 116; railway, 65; sanitation, 97; Spa, 165
Wivenhoe: 147-8; Churchwardens' accounts, 87-8; sea-water baths, 166; smuggling, 89
Women: 144, 177, 180, 203-4; education, 130; employment, 29, 37, 42, 69, 152; politics, 203-4; suffrage, 184, 203-4. *See also* Domestic service; School-teachers; Spinning; Straw-plaiting; Tailors
Woodford: 58, 107, 136
Workhouse, parish: 7, 41, 47, 95, 96, 102, 105, 106, 113-15, 120; accounts, 37-8; ages of inmates, 114; diet, 114; strong beer allowed, 115
Workhouse, Union: 120-7, 201-2; Christmas Day, 125-6; diet, 121, 125-6; separation of married couples, 121-2, 123, 127; unruly inmate, 123
Working-class movements. *See* Chartism; Co-operative Societies; Farm labourers; Labour Party; Trade Unions
Writtle: 58, 91; Green, 30; racing, 170-1

Yachting: 170
Yeldham, Great: 57, 79, 143